Inside the Fed

Inside the Fed

Monetary Policy and Its Management, Martin through Greenspan to Bernanke

Revised Edition

Stephen H. Axilrod

The MIT Press
Cambridge, Massachusetts
London, England

For information about special quantity discounts, please email <special_sales@ mitpress.mit.edu>.

This book was set in Sabon by Graphic Composition, Inc. Printed and bound in the United States of America.

Library of Congress Cataloging-in-Publication Data

Axilrod, S. H.
Inside the Fed : monetary policy and its management, Martin through Greenspan to Bernanke / Stephen H. Axilrod. — Rev. ed.
    p.   cm.
Includes bibliographical references and index.
ISBN 978-0-262-01562-2 (hardcover : alk. paper)
1. Monetary policy—United States. 2. Board of Governors of the Federal Reserve System (U.S.). 3. Banks and banking, Central—United States.
4. Federal Reserve banks. I. Title.
HG501.A95   2011
339.5'30973—dc22
                                                          2010036045

10 9 8 7 6 5 4 3 2 1

Contents

Preface

Both the initial edition of this book, published in the spring of 2009, and this revised edition are ultimately the outgrowth of an effort first begun mainly to make my family (in particular its second and third generations) and a few friends aware of the highlights of a long professional career in central banking and in other, often closely related areas of private and public finance. That effort turned into a long essay on diverse topics, but the essay did include a large section about the Federal Reserve System that focused mainly on the Arthur Burns and Paul Volcker years there. Because of my position at the time, I was an active participant in monetary history as money-supply disputes raged and the battle against the great inflation, as it is now often called, was being waged. I thought of that section as a rather belated response to a much earlier suggestion from the late Milton Friedman, and also in more recent times from Ben Friedman, that I write up my view of events in those years.

The part on the Fed became the core of the original edition of this book. In the end, considerably expanded, it encompassed a period of more than half a century from William Martin's days as chairman through Alan Greenspan's tenure and after, into the first two years of Bernanke's term through the early spring of 2008.

As it turned out, that book unfortunately could cover no more than the early stages of a credit crisis that eventually became deeply threatening not only to the nation's financial stability but also to the economy and social order as a whole. It became as, or indeed more, dangerous to the nation's well-being than the great inflation. Having morphed into a great credit crisis, it occasioned many questions in markets, the halls of Congress, and the general public—not to mention in my own mind—about whether the Fed as an institution had used the full range of its monetary and also regulatory powers as well as it could or should have to minimize and to contain the potential for disruption in underlying market trends and practices of the time.

This revised edition has been enlarged to take fully into account the Fed's dramatic, and in many ways mind-bending, experiences in the great credit crisis of 2007–2009. It extends the evaluation of the Bernanke years with a new, separate chapter that covers all of his first term and the early part of his second. It assesses the wide range of Fed's unusual and innovative actions, and also inactions, during the crisis and the beginnings of its aftermath. It includes, as well, substantial changes in the final two chapters, which evaluate the Fed's image and offer concluding remarks. Alterations and conforming changes have also been made in other sections of the original book.

Important to the process of preparing the original edition were very valuable comments and insights from Bob Solow; his communications also provided a sense of appreciation that was quite reassuring. Dave Lindsey—a good friend and in earlier times a highly valued colleague at the Board of Governors of the Federal Reserve System who retired as deputy director of its Division of Monetary Affairs in the latter part of Greenspan's tenure—generously read with considerable care two full drafts of the initial version. The three anonymous reviewers of the original edition for the MIT Press provided useful comments, one of which was lengthy and provided much food for thought. In addition, John Covell, senior editor at the Press, was instrumental in encouraging me forward. Of course, I am responsible for all interpretations and any remaining errors of fact.

Finally, recognizing that this project started as part of a broader essay for my family, I dedicate the book to six marvelous grandchildren (in order of appearance, Ben, Mike, Lindsey, Matthew, Eric, and Clio), three great kids (Pete, Emily, and Rich), and, above all, my wife, Kathy, a real artist (readers of the book will understand the reference) and a loving, cohesive force for us all.

Introduction

My professional life as an economist was of surprising interest, something I never expected and did not quite realize was happening. It turned into a career that brought me—in the process of policy support, implementation, and advice—into contact with the top central bankers of this country, complemented as time went on by experiences with key players in the international central-banking community and in private financial markets.

As a young man, I thought, for a complex variety of reasons, that the best career in the world would be to teach at a lovely, small, private college. Indeed, in the early 1950s when adulthood was at hand for me, such idyllic places of escape still seemed practically possible. Nonetheless, but not so oddly enough, I would never seriously make an effort to get to the ivory tower. A more worldly ambition lurked, though many years passed before I even began to recognize what was going on inside myself.

In the event, I drifted into something of an in-between career—neither sheltered within the quiet, picturesque spaces of academe (as unrealistically viewed by the young me) nor exposed to the gut-wrenching competitiveness of the marketplace. I came to be something like a public economist, engaged in work that combined the intellectual challenges and insights of professional and academic economic research with the need for practical understanding of turbulent, uncertain market processes—a market participant at a safe remove, so to speak.

The formative and longest part of my professional experience as a public economist, from mid-1952 through mid-1986, was at our nation's central bank, the Federal Reserve System, otherwise known as "the Fed." I spent the whole period in Washington, D.C., at the Fed's headquarters, the Board of Governors of the Federal Reserve System, and, as it happened, came into increasingly close contact with the various chairmen of the time.[1]

This period spanned the chairmanships of William McChesney Martin, Arthur Burns, William Miller (whose tenure was brief), and Paul Volcker. I worked at the sides of the last three as the top staff person for monetary policy during the turbulent times of intensifying inflation in the 1970s, followed by the paradigmatic shift to a determined anti-inflationary policy under Volcker at the end of the decade. As a young economist in attendance at meetings of the Federal Open Market Committee (FOMC) starting in the early 1960s, I viewed Bill Martin in action. But before that I had played tennis against him in regular noon doubles matches that form one of my most pleasurable memories of those early days.

After mid-1986, when I accepted a position in private markets, my perspective on public policy shifted radically from that of a key participant in the monetary policy process to that of a very interested observer. For a little less than a decade (from 1986 to 1994), I served as vice chairman of Nikko Securities International, the U.S. subsidiary, headquartered in New York City, of Nikko Securities, with worldwide headquarters in Tokyo, then a major Japanese and striving international firm. As a final professional act, I have spent a number of years consulting on occasion with foreign monetary authorities in developing and transitional countries on the implementation and organization of monetary policy and related market issues, as well as with market participants in the United States about current policy developments and market impacts.

The prominence and skills from my experiences at the Fed apparently came to define me in the eyes of the market and the public world (occasionally to my mild annoyance) and were no doubt crucial to those interesting outside opportunities that opened for me relatively late in my life. When the Japanese equivalent of the *Wall Street Journal* asked me to write a monthly column for them, they did not place a photo of me, the author, in the small circular identifying space beside the column, as was customary with them, but instead inserted a photo of the Fed's headquarters building in Washington.

Thus, although I saw the Fed as managed by Alan Greenspan and subsequently by Ben Bernanke only from the outside, not directly from the inside, a small part of me lingered there like a ghost from time past. In any event, for a long time the market and foreign monetary authorities seemed to have some sense that I was imbued with all of the arcane knowledge that comprised the central bank's ethos—that I was in a spiritual sense still there. To a degree, of course, I was, and I have never really ceased watching the institution with an insider's often partial and perhaps all too understanding eyes.

In assessing Greenspan's role, I have more specifically drawn on memories and impressions derived from a number of direct contacts during and just prior to his tenure, as well as from close observation of events and statements—a more inferential perspective than from the inside out, but one well tempered by experience. During his time, and more particularly in the Bernanke years as the great credit crisis gathered momentum, the Fed became transformed into a much more complex place, something like how your birth family might come to appear to you once you lead your own life but do not fail to keep a wary eye on the family's doings.

All in all, the ensuing chapters reconstruct, as an organized collection of memories, how this particular economist saw, interacted with, and came to understand policy leadership and formulation at the Fed over almost six decades, roughly from the mid–twentieth century into the early twenty-first. Memories of the Fed, its chairmen, and other places and events over such a long span tend to present themselves almost as much in a synchronous way as they do in a more conventional diachronic time frame. It is not because the memories are confused. Rather, experience begins to seem more compressed and interactive as time goes on. (Appendix A tabulates in chronological order the tenure of chairmen discussed in this book and the overlapping dates of the presidents of the United States responsible for their appointments and under whom they served. Appendix B charts the behavior during the chairmen's time in office of the two key economic objectives for the Fed and also of key indicators for the stance of monetary policy.)

As everyone's Aunt Sally has said, "No matter how long you have lived, it seems like no more than a minute." In such condensed time, influences and interconnections, reverberating forward and backward, become more apparent. In that spirit, although the main chapters of this book focus chronologically on Fed policies under each of the chairmen I worked with or knew during the second half of the twentieth century and early twenty-first, they also include encounters and opinions from other times and places that in retrospect are brought to mind by events of a particular period and that by now seem almost integral to them.

Throughout the book, I discuss the analytic and empirical questions in monetary economics that influenced monetary policy debates during the second half of the twentieth century and early in the current century as the issues arise in practice. They include, among other things: the role of the money supply versus interest rates in guiding policy during the period of the great inflation; the monetary base and reserve aggregates versus money-market conditions as a day-to-day operating target; the increased emphasis in more recent years on real variables and inflation expectations rather than monetary variables as policy guides; and finally the role of the Fed in avoiding systemic collapses in financial markets, as highlighted in particular by its behavior in the run-up to and during the great credit crisis with its implications for monetary and regulatory policies and their interconnections. Many of these issues are rather technical, not to say arcane, but I attempt to explain them in ways that are, I hope, sufficiently jargon-free to make the controversies clear to interested readers who are not professionally trained in the field of economics and yet also to offer some insight from, or formed in, the trenches to professional colleagues.

But much of the book is based more anecdotally on my recollections of personal interactions with central bank leaders and others as they attempted to manage policy decisions and their implementation, sometimes well and sometimes not, and in my interpretations of events to which I was privy. No doubt, policy may look different to others, especially to its makers and shakers, than it did and does to me.

Nonetheless, I trust that this book's approach reveals, among other things, the important role in policy played not by pure economic reasoning or understanding, but by personalities and their responses to the political, social, and bureaucratic contexts in which they find themselves. My experiences at the Fed suggest that a great leader for monetary policy is differentiated not especially by economic sophistication, but by his or her ability to perceive when social and political limits can and should be pushed to make space for a significant, paradigmatic change in the approach to policy should it be required, as well as by the courage and bureaucratic moxie to pull it off.

To help readers who may wish to concentrate on particular aspects of Fed policy, I have structured the book by chapter as follows. After an overview of monetary policy and its management in the first chapter, the second chapter covers the slightly less than two decades beginning in the very early 1950s during which William McChesney Martin headed the Fed, years in which the institution began to adapt itself to the changing postwar world and to modern economic thinking. The ensuing three chapters cover the 1970s and most of the 1980s, the period of the great inflation and the Fed's efforts to deal with it—not too successfully under Arthur Burns and William Miller (chapters 3 and 4) and, finally, successfully under Paul Volcker (chapter 5).

The sixth and seventh chapters, devoted to the chairmanships of Alan Greenspan and Ben Bernanke, respectively, cover the Fed's policies in more recent times, beginning in the latter part of the 1980s. The period featured a lengthy interval of stability in the early years of Greenspan's quite long tenure, but instabilities associated with asset bubbles predominated in later years, culminating in the great credit crisis during the first decade of the new century that severely tested the Bernanke Fed.

The eighth chapter discusses the influence of all these experiences—the failures and the successes—on the Fed's stature and image, taking into account, among other things, the seminal financial legislation adopted in the summer of 2010 in response to the credit crisis. The last chapter concludes with a comparison of the various chairmen's performances and also, looking ahead, with observations about how the Fed's institutional structure and the conduct of policy might be better adapted to evolving circumstances in the future, especially in light of more recent experiences and financial evolution.

1

Overview of Policy Management and Managers

If you believe the national media, the head of our nation's central bank—the chairman of the Board of Governors of the Federal Reserve System—is thought to be the second most important person in the country. This position carried no such status in the early 1950s when I first reported for work through the C Street entrance of the Fed's headquarters building in Washington, D.C., a white marble, rectangular, faintly classical structure that fronted Constitution Avenue and, across the road, the extensive green mall with its affecting monuments to the nation's history.

At that time, monetary policy was very far from a national watchword, and markets were far from being obsessed by the Federal Reserve System's actions. A few economists thought the Fed was important. Some, especially those often termed monetarists, even had the temerity to blame it for conditions leading to the stock-market crash of 1929 and the ensuing economic depression, for the economy's extended failure to recover, and for the secondary recession in 1937–1938, when the Fed took action that arguably cut short a promising revival in economic activity.

By and large, the Fed escaped being closely and causally linked with the deep and lasting depression of the 1930s by the press, the public, and the political world. Instead, errors in the conduct of the nation's fiscal policy came more into focus. As the story went, the need for enlarged government spending to revive the economy during this dreadful, long economic slump was not understood at the time either by politicians or by fiscal experts, many then prominent in academia, so the economy did not escape from its doldrums until spending was literally forced upon us by the coming of World War II.

This explanation, although far from complete, does have much validity. It is what I internalized from my studies as an undergraduate at Harvard College. After the war, with GI Bill in hand (and some parental supplement), I had transferred there from Southern Methodist University in Dallas, where my family had moved during the Depression when I was going on eleven years old.

Not until the great inflation that began around the mid-1960s in the United States and lasted about fifteen years did the Fed's central role in the economy become clearly and perhaps irrevocably impressed on public consciousness. The persistent, detailed research and broad educational efforts of modern-day monetarists such as Milton Friedman and others were in part responsible for helping to convince the U.S. Congress and the public of the Fed's crucial role in permitting, if not originating, the inflation. Because the Fed was the sole institution in the country with the power, as it were, to create money, and because everyone readily understood that too much money chasing too few goods caused inflation, the Fed's influence and responsibility were quite evident.

During a depression, the Fed or any other central bank can often hide its responsibility for continued economic weakness behind the old saw that "you can lead a horse to water, but you can't make it drink." Central bankers can and do in effect say, "Don't blame us if people won't borrow enough or use enough of their cash to spend and get the country out of a depression." Although that position is not a terribly unreasonable one to take, it does not really get the central bank off the hook because it begs the question of how the nation gets into such a position in the first place and what the central bank's responsibility is for getting it there.

In any event, the idea that the Fed's chairman is the second most important person in the country increasingly took root in the public's understanding, insofar as I can judge, when inflation was finally suppressed in the early 1980s by an aggressive anti-inflationary policy under Chairman Volcker. It seemed to remain in place subsequently even as Fed policies in the latter part of Greenspan's tenure and Bernanke's were tarnished by speculative bubbles and the great credit crisis, which turned out to be as, or even more, disruptive than price inflation.

Volcker's and Greenspan's immediate predecessors, Arthur Burns and Bill Miller, presided over a Fed that failed to control inflation, and the country was quite sensibly reluctant to bestow a complimentary sobriquet on leaders who were not performing well, certainly not as well as they should. Neither of these two chairmen acquired the kind of credibility and prestige associated with successful policies that would make private market participants hang breathlessly on their every word.

In the last analysis, the immense power of monetary policy resides, of course, not in the individual chairmen, but in the institution of the Fed itself. Chairmen become powerful to the extent they can influence the votes of their policymaking colleagues. A chairman's influence is generally more limited than one might in the abstract expect. It waxes and wanes with the chairman's particular skills and charisma in the internal management of policy, as well as with his own credibility with the public and Congress, which in turn strongly affects his internal credibility. Nevertheless, a chairman can have an outsized impact on policy, especially at crucial times, if he has sufficient nerve, internal credibility, and a kind of unique, "artistic" feel to see and take advantage of the potential for increased policy maneuverability within a constellation of economic, social, and political forces.

The Federal Reserve Act, originally enacted in 1913 and amended frequently over the years in response to changing economic and financial circumstances and experience, established the central bank that the chairman leads. As many readers may well know, the Fed comprises the Board of Governors in Washington and twelve Federal Reserve Banks headquartered in cities around the country to provide conventional central-bank and closely related services for their regions, such as bank supervision and clearings and payments in connection with interbank money flows. Although this regional structure appears a bit anachronistic by now as the rapid and revolutionary advances in financial technology of recent decades, along with the advance of nationwide banking through bank holding companies and interstate branching, have further eroded the role of purely regional payments and banking systems, it does continue to serve as an important channel for engaging the country as a whole in the formation and understanding of monetary policy through the participation of the reserve banks in the policy process.

The president of the United States appoints the chairman of the Board of Governors of the Federal Reserve System and the other six board members with the Senate's consent. A board member's term is fourteen years, and one term expires on January 31 of each even-numbered year. The chairman and vice chairman have four year terms, and since 1977 the two are also subject to approval by the Senate.[1] Appointment of an additional vice chairman for supervision, with specific responsibility for developing policy recommendations in the Board's supervisory and regulatory areas, was required by the wide-ranging financial stabilization act (the Dodd-Frank Wall Street Reform and Consumer Protection Act) passed in the summer of 2010 in response to problems throughout the nation's financial and related regulatory structure raised by the great credit crisis. But once the Senate approves presidential appointees, the executive branch plays no role at all in the Fed's traditional domestic monetary policy decisions.

However, in certain areas beyond its monetary policy functions, the Fed's independence in practice is much less than complete. In foreign exchange operations, the Treasury is dominant. And in bank supervision and regulation, coordination with other regulators, such as the comptroller of the currency and the chairman of the Federal Deposit Insurance Corporation (FDIC), is needed for efficient and equitable market functioning.

Moreover, the under the Dodd-Frank Act, the newly established Financial Stability Oversight Council to be chaired by the Secretary of the Treasury (and which includes the heads of all major regulatory agencies as members) has oversight responsibility for promoting a regulatory process that contributes to over-all financial stability. This includes, among other things, requirements and recommendations for enhanced prudential standards to be set by the Fed for certain large nonbank financial companies and large, interconnected bank holding companies (at a minimum over $50 billion in size) that are deemed to represent threats to financial stability.

Finally, as shown in the Fed's use of the discount window for emergency loans to nonbanks during the great credit crisis, the support and participation of the U.S. Treasury seemed desirable to demonstrate political unity in programs that placed the U.S. budget at risk and raised major political and social issues of fairness and equity. The Dodd-Frank act has encoded that in law by requiring specific approval of the Secretary of the Treasury for the Fed's emergency lending programs (redefined in the new law to represent programs established for the purpose of "providing liquidity to the financial system" and "not to aid a failing financial company").

Monetary policy is basically set in the FOMC, a body established by the Federal Reserve Act to govern the system's operations in the market for U.S. government securities and certain other instruments. The committee is composed of twelve voting members, including all seven board members, the president of the Federal Reserve Bank of New York (New York Fed), and four of the eleven other reserve bank presidents, who serve in rotation.[2]

Oddly enough, the law leaves it up to the FOMC to determine its own leadership structure. By long tradition, the chairman of the Fed Board of Governors is annually elected to serve also as chairman of the FOMC, and the president of the New York Fed is elected as vice chairman of that body. I always sensed a certain amount of tension in the room when the vote was to be taken on the FOMC's leadership structure, including its official staff, as needs to be done once a year because a change in membership takes place annually.

The Fed is essentially a creature of the Congress and responsible to that arm of government. As a result, the most important national political figures for the Fed are the chairmen of the House and Senate committees that deal with banking and central banking. The president clearly is secondary in importance for the Fed, and the Congress is extremely sensitive to any hints that he might be seeking or that the Fed might be ceding to him any role as an influence on the central bank's decision-making responsibilities, especially in the area of monetary policy.

When accompanying a Fed chairman to congressional hearings, as I often did when monetary policy was up for discussion, I would, on an occasion or two, hear a senator or representative ask the chairman how frequently he met with the president. I had the distinct impression that the less contact the better, especially if the questioner was in the opposite party from the sitting president. The amount of contact was, so far as I could tell, rather modest, though it varied with conditions of the time and with the interest and attitudes of individual presidential officeholders. The dreary technicalities of monetary policy were certainly of no interest to presidents, and any such discussions were left to other interactions.[3]

With the chairman at its helm, exerting more or less influence depending on his credibility and talents, the Fed as an institution independently makes monetary policy decisions that are crucial to the macroeconomy's behavior in regard to inflation, the ups and downs of economic activity, interest rates, and the financial system's stability. But its independence is obviously far from absolute. Bill Martin, the Fed chairman when I first arrived, used to say (whether original to him I do not know)[4] that the Fed was independent within the government, a formulation that has often been repeated. The phrase's practical meaning is not easy to discern, but it is evocative and somehow reassuring. One reasonable interpretation is that the Fed, like the other elements of government in a democratic country, chooses policies from a broad range of options that are or through further explanation can be made generally acceptable to the country as a whole, recognizing that disagreements of more or less intensity can hardly ever be avoided.

Apart from any particular interpretation, the phrase itself stood me in good stead a number of years ago in Indonesia during a discussion with one of that country's many and apparently ubiquitous former finance ministers—this particular one, at the time, a very influential informal adviser to a new Indonesian "reform" president coming to office following Suharto's downfall. The country's legislature was then in process of enacting a law that would give the nation's central bank more independence. As a way of helping to explain what might be involved in this process to a gentleman who seemed to have some doubts about the law's wisdom, I used the Martin phrase "independent within the government." It was as if a bulb lit up in his mind, and he reiterated my words and added, in reassuring himself, "not independent from the government."

I made no effort to discuss the issue further, thinking it best to let unspoken differences of interpretation remain submerged. Given the political situation in Indonesia, which was still in a state of transition from a dictatorship to a more democratic form of government, and the historically delicate relationships between the Indonesian central bank and the Ministry of Finance, it seemed best at the time to refrain from further efforts to explore the exact meaning of "independence." It was a good bet that our views of what it meant to be "independent within, but not independent from the government" would, as a practical matter, turn out to be different—no doubt as such independence related to the degree, frequency, and effectiveness of influence that the political authorities could be expected to bring to bear on the central bank's decision-making processes.

Although the Fed's legislated independence helps shelter its decision making from interference by the administration, the decisions themselves are inevitably subject to certain constraints. The instruments of monetary policy are generally powerful and far-reaching enough to keep inflation under control and the overall economy on a fairly even keel over a reasonable period of time. But in some extreme economic circumstances—such as those that might be and often have been associated with very large oil-price shocks, wars, financial collapses, highly irresponsible fiscal policies, and other similar forces that are largely exogenous to current policy—the effective deployment of monetary powers raises serious political issues for the central bank. For instance, the bank's powers may not be deployable in a way that keeps both economic growth and the rate of inflation within acceptable bounds, at least for a while (sometimes a rather long while).

In such circumstances, Fed policymakers, being very well aware that they are part of a government established to be democratically representative of the people, are themselves likely to be constrained in the policies that they find it practical to consider by their sense of what is tolerable to the country. Of course, they may be right or they may be wrong in their judgment of the country's attitudes. Or they may fail to understand the degree to which they, through convincing argumentation, can affect public attitudes and enlarge the scope for monetary policy actions. However that may be, I am convinced that such judgments, or perhaps such feelings, whether expressed (essentially they are not) or recognized, lie deep within the individual policymaker's gut. The policymakers are independent, but they are making decisions from within the government and within what they perceive to be certain societal bounds.

The impact of such virtually unavoidable covert judgments surfaced, for example, in the 1970s when the Fed, in the wake of huge oil-price increases, accepted a sizeable inflation rather than risk the possibility of a deep and unduly lasting recession that may have been required to fight inflation even harder and more effectively in the circumstances of the period. The stars reflective of current economic conditions and of political and social attitudes were simply not in proper alignment—or at least leadership at the time could not discern them.

The stars were in better alignment toward the end of that decade and in the early 1980s after it became clear that inflation was itself harmful to growth and to the country's overall well-being. Evolving changes in financial-market structure had also helped level the economic/political playing field. For instance, because of market innovations, small savers were becoming increasingly able to benefit from the high interest rates that were temporarily involved in the fight against inflation. This benefit served to counter pressure on the Fed from powerful congressional support for the agricultural, small business, and home borrowers who were hurt by the higher rates. In brief, the contextual cost–benefit calculus for policymakers became more socially and politically balanced.

Within such a broad understanding of what it means to be independent, the Fed over the past half-century has often, and with varying degrees of success, altered the process by which it formulates, implements, and explicates monetary policy. The exact nature of these adaptations has been influenced by the growth in knowledge about economics as gained from the Fed's own experience and from academic research (both inside and outside the institution), by a changing political and social environment, and by ongoing structural changes in the nation's banking and financial system. Particularly as seen from the inside, the evolution in the policy process has also involved power dynamics within the Fed's own bureaucratic processes, including very importantly the temperament, experience, and leadership capabilities of the various chairmen.

With regard to macroeconomic stability, inflation is, of course, a major concern of a nation's central bank. Some would say it should be the only concern, but it is certainly not the only concern in the United States. I doubt it is ever quite the only concern anywhere in the world, no matter how statutes are written or what public statements the central bank may issue. No central bank can simply ignore what is happening to other aspects of the macroeconomy, such as unemployment, growth, and financial stability.

In any event, for the United States, the monetary policy objectives as stated in the Federal Reserve Act (as modified in November 1977 and retained since) require the Fed to "maintain long run growth of the monetary and credit aggregates . . . so as to promote effectively the goals of maximum employment, stable prices, and moderate long-term interest rates." In the real world, the counterparts to these objectives have changed over the years as both the Fed and the public have become more economically and financially sophisticated, helped along not only by advances in economics research, but also, perhaps more especially, by the cold bath of actual experience. Nonetheless, the potential for conflicts among objectives remains.

The principal area for conflict in practice centers on two crucial objectives: maximum employment and stable prices. Especially in the short term, these two objectives often seem to run up against each other, and the Fed in practice is always adjusting its short-term policy stance in an attempt to reconcile them. At one extreme, when inflation threatens, the Fed attempts to keep the economy from weakening unduly when it has to restrain upward price pressures by doing what it can to force businesses and consumers to hold back on their spending for goods and services. At the other extreme, when the economy is slack, the Fed attempts to avoid arousing inflationary forces that may be dormant in a slack economy while doing what it can to encourage spending on goods and services and hence economic growth.

Fed policymakers have usually resolved the problem of making the twin objectives of maximum employment and price stability appear consistent by shifting the time focus for judging their success away from the short run to the intermediate or longer run. They seem to have interpreted maximum employment as the highest sustainable rate of employment (lowest sustainable rate of unemployment) and price stability as inflation low enough on average so as not significantly to affect the decisions of households, businesses, and investors.

If price stability is maintained on average over that longer horizon, then, so it is argued, the Fed will have done what it can do to create the conditions for the economy to grow at its potential—which essentially depends on productivity and labor-force growth, both supply-side factors well outside the Fed's reach—and thus to attain the maximum rate of employment that can hold persistently. Moreover, if prices are indeed reasonably stable on average over time, expectations of inflation will not get out of hand, and, as a result, longer-term interest rates will generally remain in a moderate range.

Because price stability is in any event the only macroeconomic condition the Fed can be expected to control over the longer-run, the Fed chairman is mainly judged by the extent to which inflation has been contained on his watch. But in practice he is also judged by whether the economy has been reasonably well employed during his tenure—a point not to be forgotten except at peril of one's reputation. If inflation seems to have gotten out of hand, he is deemed a failure. He has permitted too much money to chase too few goods, or, put more pedantically, to chase more goods than the economy can produce when output is growing at its potential and when employment presumably is at its maximum sustainable level.

Over the past half-century, the Fed as an institution and the roles of the various chairmen who have led it are most revealed and probably best understood by how with varying degrees of success they altered the guides for monetary policy and adapted the internal policymaking process in response to instances of growing inflationary pressures, to evolutionary changes in financial technology and the structure of banking and other markets, to crises that threaten the underlying stability of the financial system, and to increasing and well-justified demands for public accountability.

As seen from today, the Fed for much of the second half of the twentieth century made policy in the face of a rising tide of inflation, a tide that crested and was clearly the dominant influence on policy during my institutional tenure. In the early part of the twenty first century, as financial markets and institutions became increasingly more sophisticated and interrelated, threats to financial stability and how they should best be handled became a major concern.

Inflation began to rise late in Bill Martin's term as chairman (1951 to early 1970)—a term most notable, though, for the steps taken by the Fed to modernize its approach to economic research and to reorganize its internal power structure and operational processes for making monetary policy. Nonetheless, within such a structure, inflation gathered more momentum during the 1970s in Arthur Burns's time and in the interlude with Bill Miller, when markets were battered by two large oil-price shocks, one around mid-decade and the other late in the decade, all at a time when society was still riven by domestic political conflicts from the preceding years' wartime protests and social revolutions. The inflationary tide peaked and then ebbed in Paul Volcker's tenure during the 1980s, when the Fed embarked on and succeeded in an innovative policy program aimed at curbing inflation and inflation expectations.

During Alan Greenspan's term of office from mid-1987 to early 2006, inflation remained generally quiescent; indeed, on occasion late in that period, the Fed seemed to fear that a quite slow pace of inflation might turn into deflation. However, in the latter part of that period and continuing into Ben Bernanke's subsequent tenure (beginning in early 2006 and extended to a second four-year term in 2010) the seeds were being sown that fructified in damaging stock and housing market bubbles and eventually serious threats to systemic financial stability.

Thus, while inflation and how to control it were the main problem for Fed monetary policymakers in the second half of the twentieth century, the development of speculative bubbles in asset markets created the principal problems for Fed policy as the twenty-first century began and through its first decade. With very little exaggeration, one can say that inflation in the price of goods and services was the bane of monetary policy in the second half of the last century, while asset bubbles have been the bane of policy in the first decade of the current one. The recessions that followed when inflation got out of control and the ensuing economic contractions when asset price bubbles inevitably burst were at the least equally damaging.

In its effort to contain inflation, the Fed during the second half of the twentieth century dealt with troublesome issues raised by growing concerns both inside and outside the institution about the role to be played by money supply in policy decisions and policy operations. To control the great inflation, the Fed was more or less forced to pay increasing attention to the role of money in policy. It did so not without trepidation and some little contention.

The chairmen thus had to deal with issues about how money should be controlled. Should it be controlled as directly as possible by affecting the quantity of bank reserves made available to the banking system (and held by banks as reserve balances either at the regional Federal Reserve Banks or as vault cash)? Or should it be controlled indirectly by continuing in effect to make policy decisions about the level of short-term interest rates, but also being more sensitive to money-supply developments in doing so?

Equally crucial and obviously closely related were the continuing attempts to find a convincingly workable definition of money to be controlled. These efforts were greatly complicated by the accelerating structural changes in financial technology and public attitudes toward money and money-like assets that were taking place in the latter half of the twentieth century.

It has never been very easy to define money, with various definitions on offer over the years, from a narrow concept embracing currency and demand deposits in the hands of the public to various broader views encompassing other deposits at banks and similar financial institutions along with certain money-market instruments. The concept of money became even more difficult to measure satisfactorily as new financial technology, including credit cards and the development of a wide variety of highly liquid market assets, eroded the need for and usefulness of traditional forms of money such as currency and bank demand deposits.

Nonetheless, even though financial technology and the public's attitudes toward money were beginning to change rather noticeably by the 1970s, the failure of monetary policy to reduce inflation during that decade was, it seemed to me, not especially hindered by definitional problems. Several money measures were developed at the time, and some were in fact employed as policy targets of a sort. Rather, policy was hindered by policymakers' fears of damaging consequences for markets and the economy if they paid too much attention to money and not enough to interest rates.

The FOMC did begin to set monetary targets in the middle part of the 1970s, but shied away from them in practice and thus lost credibility. It was not until the 1980s under Volcker, when the Fed adopted a new policy approach and convinced the market that the Fed would stick to preset monetary targets without regard to the consequences for interest rates (at least over a much wider than usual range), that the pace of inflation was at last successfully slowed—though at the cost of a sharp recession.

However, the pace of change in financial technology seemed to accelerate as Volcker's term wore on. By the latter part of the 1980s, money in its various statistical measures came to be seen as having at best a quite secondary role in policy—a factor to be given some weight in assessing policy and the potential for inflation, but not one by which policy should be slavishly guided.

During the Greenspan years, in evaluating the potential for inflation the Fed focused much more on real factors—such as the extent to which economic growth was tending to exceed or fall short of its potential when the economy was in the neighborhood of or approaching full employment of labor and capital resources—rather than on money. In gauging the potential for inflation during the Bernanke period, the Fed has continued to rely on assessment of the real economic conditions and has also paid particular attention to indicators of inflation expectations.

Nonetheless, while conceptual and statistical issues in measuring money held by the public abound, the Fed, through market operations at its own initiative, does provide to the economy a rather clearly definable and measurable money-like substance, known as the "monetary base." The rise and fall of the base is reflected through changes in the Fed's overall balance sheet, which consolidates the individual reserve banks' assets and liabilities. On the liability side, the base is composed mainly of currency in circulation (the bulk of which represents currency held by the public) and of the banking system's reserve and clearing balances (representing the sum of balances held at the Fed by member banks and other depository institutions to meet reserve requirements and for clearing purposes). On the asset side, the base is represented mainly by the Fed's holdings of U.S. government securities, though it also includes lending through the discount window and holdings of foreign exchange. The composition of the asset side of the base was radically changed and the base also greatly enlarged during the Bernanke years, as the Fed undertook major and virtually unprecedented steps to avert a major financial collapse in markets by, among other things, making loan against a wide variety of collateral under special lending programs.

The Fed's ability to alter the monetary base and its balance sheet pretty much at will through open market operations (i.e., the purchase and sale of securities) – or, in more recent years by more active use of its discount window, including emergency lending to necessitous borrowers—is the ultimate source of its enormous power. It can easily affect the overnight cost of bank reserve funds borrowed from other banks (the federal funds rate) by actions affecting the base and thus the total amount of reserves available to the banking system. But the extent to which the base is transformed into an amount of liquidity in the hands of banks and the public that bears a reasonably predictable relationship to economic activity and prices no longer appears to be easily agreed upon, if it ever was.

The years in which the Fed was enmeshed in policy problems generated by the great inflation (of course, in the inflation's early years, we did not know how long lasting and great it would be) were also years in which the Fed was engaged in bureaucratic struggles that altered the locus of policy power, the guides to policy, and the structure of control over policy implementation. As it turned out, I became closely involved in the process of resolving these issues.

In the latter part of Martin's tenure in the late 1960s, it was slowly beginning to dawn on policymakers that they should begin paying more attention to the behavior of money. At one point, I was asked to go along with Martin to a congressional hearing. That invitation seemed quite flattering at the time because he was not in the habit of taking economists, let alone such a junior one, with him.

As we drove to the Capitol, I remember Martin's saying something like, "Money supply is going to become an important issue in the years ahead. If they raise questions about it, you will have to respond." The question never came up. That was fortunate. Being even younger than my years at the time and quite innocent (that did not last too much longer), I probably would not have managed a bureaucratically adequate response if Bill had followed through on his threat to put me on the spot. In any event, my long and direct association with the "innards" of the monetary policy process began around that time.

It was in Martin's era that the Fed Board of Governors in Washington began to assert its primacy in policy relative to the New York Fed and its president, whose influence had been quite strong and sometimes dominant before World War II and for a time afterward. This turnaround was accomplished in large part through procedural changes in both the formulation of policy instructions and in the oversight of their implementation in the market. These changes were designed to ensure that interpretation of any FOMC decision would be in the hands of the board's chairman in Washington, who was the Fed's designated policy chief, rather than in the hands of the system account manager, a high official located at the New York Fed, or of that institution's president. By Burns's time, the greater power of the Fed board's chairman in Washington relative to the New York Fed's president was well established.

Being so closely involved with two such strong-minded men as Burns and Volcker as they led the Fed's efforts to contain powerful inflationary forces made it very clear to me how central the chairman's role is in influencing the Fed's policy posture. In particular, the chairman's attitudes and temperament are crucial for the institution's capacity to contemplate policies outside the box—that is, outside its traditional patterns. Alone among the Fed's policymakers, the chairman has the stature (although he may or may not choose or be able to realize it) to promote successfully innovations that significantly alter the shape of the policy process. He is the person who has to defend policies; his reputation is most on the line; he is closest, presumably, to the country's political and social pulse; and he is in reality the only Fed policymaker with both a public bully pulpit and an internal position that make him capable of effectively urging imaginative or innovative policy approaches. If not he, then who?

Chairmen, like the Fed as an institution, are bound to an important degree by the social and political context of their times, but those bounds are by no means rigid. They have some give. And from my perspective, a chairman's ability to detect how much the bounds can be loosened and his willingness to exert an effort to persuade his fellow policymakers to do so depend to a great extent on his artistic bent. By "artistic bent," I mean an ability to sense the times, an ability to act a persuasive role both in public and within the institution, and the kind of nerve and vision often seen in creative artists. Intelligence helps, but it is far, far from sufficient.

Workplaces, bureaucracies, social venues, and public events contain and can be influenced by participants who exhibit a kind of artistry. I have often thought to divide the members of my often all too dour profession of economics between those whose approach might be very loosely considered to be poetic (not too many of them) and those who are basically scientific in their attitudes (large in number). The former are more intuitive, more prone to the sin of "casual empiricism," and often more involved in the practical aspects of economics, such as (as in my case) interactions between, on the one hand, monetary policy and, on the other, the behavior of often skittish and unpredictable market participants and of the public more generally.

I would say that a capacity for artistry of that kind influenced, in one way or another, the performance of three of the four chairmen of the Fed Board of Governors whom I came to know rather well in the course of my work. The three were artistic in different ways. Two of them—Volcker and Burns—seemed to take on the role of stage performers on certain occasions, effectively acting a part in a particular scene and before a particular audience. Martin displayed from time to time a kind of intuitiveness in policy insight that was often apt to surprise the more rational, scientific economists surrounding him. His approach to policy seemed more poetic than grounded in a chain of logical reasoning, but at the same time, and not unrelated to sensitive personal qualities that lay behind his intuitive approach to policy, he managed the decision-making process with a certain ease and agreeableness.

Words and their meanings can be confounding, and usage in differing contexts can seem to stretch their meaning out of shape and raise puzzling interpretive problems. Of course, from one viewpoint, it flies in the face of common sense even to think of comparing bureaucrats such as Fed chairmen with creative artists such as painters and poets. Perhaps they should be compared instead with actors who create characters.

The wellsprings that give rise to creativity seem very different from those that feed bureaucratic motivations, even though artists, like bureaucrats, face the common problems of getting ahead and adjusting to the dominant powers that be. No matter, one likes to believe that for artists, the artistic part of life is not a role assumed under and adapted to particular circumstances, but rather represents the person herself in virtually unavoidable artistic action driven not by the necessities of power and worldly success, but by an inner sensitivity and vision. That description is more than a bit idealistic, no doubt, and does not adequately account for the wide and varied motivations that give rise to particular works of art, or at least to works that the world decides to call art.

One might say that a genuinely creative artist is driven to create her own stage and audience (sometimes successfully, sometimes not, but unavoidably trying). By contrast, a bureaucrat, capable of playing a particular role with all the zest of an artist, is generally dependent on the availability of a suitable stage. Unlike an artist, he is not driven to exert his artistry as a way of creating the stage on which he performs. But if the stage and audience are there, his artistic-like tendencies will help him perform much more convincingly than would a more mundane bureaucrat. (Politicians, especially very talented demagogues and charismatic public figures, are evidently more directly comparable to artists who create their own audience and set their own stage.)

The contrast between creative artists and bureaucrats with certain artistic capacities is too simple, of course. A creative artist may also do no more than attempt to adapt her art to a stage and audience that already exist; in that instance, the artist has become more like the bureaucrat who has an artistic bent for certain roles. The artist and the bureaucrat perhaps can be found to one degree or another in almost everyone. Nevertheless, a bureaucrat's artistic side may better suit certain roles than others, just as some artists may not have a bureaucratic side that is usable for their advancement or may not be willing to employ it if they do have it.

If a bureaucrat's artistic talents are effectively to come into play, he must have access to a stage setting and implicit cues suitable to the particular role that most readily engages his creative juices. If his talents do not fit the stage that happens to be set, he will simply miss the cues; he will be unable to notice what is being asked of him, much less to perform effectively. As a result, in the very practical institutional world in which public policies are formulated and implemented, he may well mishandle major issues or handle them less well than they should be.

Such dramas were played out when the artistic sides of Burns and Volcker—the former more adapted to performing on a private stage and the latter better adapted to performing a major role on a demanding public stage—interacted with and influenced the formulation of monetary policy during the inflationary period of the 1970s and 1980s, in Burns's case unfavorably and in Volcker's favorably. Burns's talents simply did not seem suited to taking on the risks of creatively commanding a public stage set in turbulent inflationary times. Volcker, in contrast, was well able to assume and convincingly act out a major role on such a public stage and to command it with authority, even though he was essentially very shy in interpersonal relationships.

As earlier noted, Martin employed a different kind of artistic bent that encompassed a talent for smoothing the process of decision making—a quite minor art it might be said, but an important one that was not a particularly strong point for either Burns or Volcker. One will never know whether Martin's lesser and quieter talents would have helped him very much if he had been placed on the same public stages as Burns and Volcker—or, much later, Bernanke—when times were much more turbulent and the public audience, as a result, was much more critical and hard to please.

So far as I can judge, Greenspan, as an artist of policy, seemed in some degree similar to Martin. His economic insights appeared to have an important intuitive component, though they were based more on an intense scrutiny of a wide and often disparate array of economic data rather than (as with Martin) reliance on extensive contacts with the financial and business community. Because Greenspan was such an avid consumer of data, however, I suspect that he believed his economic insights stemmed more from analysis than from gut instinct; that is, he probably saw himself more as a scientist than as an artist. Judging from the problems in the latter part of his tenure when markets and the economy became more turbulent, his intuitiveness and analytic insights did not seem well attuned to the significance of underlying shifts in market attitudes.

I know Bernanke much less well than the preceding chairmen. He is from a different generation of economists whose training had become more mathematical and analytically rigorous—perhaps, one might surmise, attracting personalities that were less comfortable with interpreting the potential behind shifts in market sentiments and with fully understanding the broad demands of public policy communication. However that might be, Bernanke's willingness and ability to take actions "outside the box"—indeed, well outside—to alleviate the great credit crisis that fell to his lot demonstrated a very necessary flexibility in response to unanticipated, dire events.

2

In Bill Martin's Time

When I arrived at the Fed in the early summer of 1952, William McChesney Martin had been chairman for a little more than a year. Over the course of his long tenure, I rose from the lowest professional rank to officer level, with my responsibilities shifting more and more into areas closely connected to monetary policy. Thus, although not as close to him in a professional way as I was to his three immediate successors, I did after several years come to have a firsthand view of him in action at Board of Governors and FOMC policy meetings.

The name "Bill Martin" was familiar to me before I came to the Fed, but it was only a name, and I had no prior sense of the man at all. The very first comment about him that I heard was from a very close family friend whom I knew over the years as Uncle Ben—a very decent, down-to-earth man who was a specialist on the New York Stock Exchange, one of those fabled people who took a job as a messenger before finishing high school, learned the market, and eventually was able to buy himself a seat and establish a specialist firm that was later run by his oldest son and then by a grandson. When Uncle Ben found out where I was going to work, he said something like, "Oh yeah, Martin, de guy who sold us down de river to de SEC (Securities and Exchange Commission)." Not a comment I took very seriously, but one that has stayed in mind as a small commentary on the way of the world and the differing perspectives that reveal truths in all their partiality.

Martin had been the youngest president of the New York Stock Exchange, brought in to help reform the place during the 1930s in the wake of the stock-market crash. He was also the man who, as assistant secretary of the Treasury in the early postwar years, negotiated in 1951 the so-called Accord with the Federal Reserve, by which the Fed was freed of its wartime agreement with the Treasury to support the U.S. government bond market—an obligation earlier taken on to ensure that World War II could be financed at low interest rates.

Such an agreement limited the Fed's ability to subdue inflationary pressures should they arise because it meant that the Fed would have to buy bonds from the market whenever longer-term interest rates threatened to rise above the agreed-upon level. As a result, the Fed could effectively lose control over the money supply. The market could turn bonds into money on demand instead of the Fed's deciding on how much money to create at its own volition. This agreement became a real concern during the Korean War period, when it was feared that the Fed would need its full battery of weapons to ensure that it could contain any potential inflationary consequences as heightened military spending was added to the postwar economic recovery already well under way.

Thus, by the time Martin came to the Fed in the early spring of 1951, he had contributed to restoration of public confidence in the stock exchange and to the Fed's ability to employ all its powers to fight inflation. They were no mean accomplishments, though hardly ones that made him a household name at the time. They did give a substantial boost to his stature within the organization, making him better able, for example, to further the transfer of power away from the New York Fed and its president to the Fed headquarters and chairman in Washington, D.C.

Be all that as it may, I at first viewed Martin as little more than a pleasant man with reasonable administrative skills, but without a strong understanding of the economics behind policy. Later, as already noted, I came to view him as something of an artist in policy, a man with an intuitive sense, and a man perceived, at least from my perspective, by his colleagues as fundamentally fair—all of which helped make him a very effective leader in the decision-making process.

From my observations at FOMC and board meetings, he never appeared to alienate his colleagues. It was something of a joke that at FOMC meetings, after everyone had expressed their views in the preliminary discussion of policy, he would always say, "Well, we are not far apart," no matter how far apart the participants in fact were. But the "joke," of course, had a point. It conveyed that each person counted as much as anyone else; and even if you were in fact far apart from the rest, the distance could not be too far because you really were a thoughtful and well-meaning member of the group.

Perhaps I am reading too much into Martin's use of the phrase, but I have come to believe that he deliberately, not just habitually, employed it to help the group feel close together and thus as responsive to each other as possible. It looked as if he strove for something like the cohesiveness required in the crew of a large sailboat if the helmsman's efforts were to have the best chance of succeeding.

Martin's influence on the substance of policy was grounded largely in his colleagues' belief that his sensitivity to market psychology (that is, to the evolving attitudes of key participants in credit markets and businesses) was unusually apt. He was convincing in part because he did not come on as the kind of egotistic man who assumed that others must of necessity think like he did. He seemed more able than most to appreciate others' perspectives.

Moreover, because of his experience and background, his exposure to the opinions and attitudes of key decision makers in the private sphere was vast and based on relationships that went well beyond his position as chairman. Perhaps, therefore, he was less at risk of being exposed to views that were slanted simply by the self-interest of informants who related to him only as a man of power—though I may be stretching a bit here. In any event, the whole web of social and financial connections did seem to provide Martin with an aura that exuded assurance and conviction. Together with his modesty, these characteristics went some way toward enhancing his credibility within the Fed as a man whose intuitions—distilled through anecdotes from social and economic sources often outside other FOMC members' reach—might be relied on.

I first saw Martin's intuitiveness and sensitivity to how the policy game should be played at work on a tennis court. It was shortly after arriving at the Fed that I was invited (through the intercession of an early carpool mate who was a regular participant in the game) to participate in the daily doubles match that took place at around noon on the courts then located in the above-ground parking lot that was for a long time across the street from the original Board of Governors building. A second building, aptly named the Martin Building, was later built on the space devoted to that parking lot and, in my mind, to the noontime tennis match. The tennis court was reconstructed just to the north of the Martin Building.

It took about a year for me to become a regular in the tennis match. Another staff person and I would normally play against Martin and J. Louis Robertson, the vice chairman at the time, though occasionally an outsider would alter the mix. Those games came to be one of the highlights of my long (probably excessively long) career at the Fed. They also inspired a number of reactions within the board, although if one of these reactions was envy that the games would aid my professional advancement, I could not detect it. (I have always assumed that the board was too obviously a meritocracy—political appointees apart—for any thoughtful person to believe seriously that you could get ahead by playing tennis with the boss.)

Only once did anything like envy appear, and that was of a rather odd sort. I worked in the Fed's Division of International Finance in my first years. The division head was a well-known economist of the day named Arthur Marget. The problem was that I saw the chairman much more than he did. At the time, the Fed paid almost no attention to international conditions in the formulation of the country's monetary policy (even in our so-called globalized world now, they are generally of limited importance, although there are exceptions, such as the Asian and Russian financial crises of the late 1990s), so Marget was all too rarely consulted for his views about policy and his insights about the world at large.

It so happened that one day, as I was walking down the hall, our paths crossed. Marget stopped me, which was flattering, but to my surprise I heard neither a pleasantry (which I expected) nor a question (as I might have hoped) that recognized my undoubted brilliance in evaluating the capital account of the U.S. balance of payments (my area of responsibility at the time). Instead, he looked at me long and hard, waggled his finger, and said, "Never let me catch you on the tennis court," then after a significant little pause, "except with the chairman." And he walked on.

It surely would not have occurred to him to say instead, "Never let me catch you with the chairman, except on the tennis court." Marget might have been overtly concerned about such a situation if I had been more senior, but not with so young a man whom the chairman would certainly not be consulting on business. Still, as I think back, in the encounter there must have been for Marget a tinge not of bureaucratic competitiveness, but of regret about his particular situation.

In any event, for years Martin never saw me except in tennis attire. Then one day (probably around five years into my career), I happened to be in the corridor of the board members' wing of the building when Martin walked out of his office as I was passing by. He looked, paused, and looked again—something familiar there; after a bit, the light dawned, a smile and a greeting, the first interchange with him when I was in mufti, so to speak.

On the tennis court, Martin's intuitive side came out in his sense of placement—not so much placement of the ball as placement of himself, somewhat analogous to how he dealt with monetary policy. As a tennis player, he had neither real power nor speed, but his decisions more often than not put him in the right place at the right time, which made up for much. How he got there seemed intuitive to me, though it was evidently based on long years of experience. Artistry compensated, up to a point, for certain inherent physical weaknesses.

When wielding the instruments of monetary policy, the player does not need deft, artistic placement so much to compensate for a deficiency in power, but rather to ensure that the huge power at his disposal is most effectively and efficiently employed—in other words, that it does not ruin the economy through either prolonged inflation or recession. Timing is not quite everything, but it is crucial.

If policy—which affects the economy with lags—adapts too slowly when the economy happens to be turning strong and inflationary pressures threaten to emerge, there is a real risk that an attempt to compensate by hitting hard later may devastate the economy through a deep recession. And if timing is too delayed when the economy is turning weak, an attempt to compensate by hitting hard later (i.e., strongly easing) may fail because by that time there is nothing to hit. The economy may be so far in retreat and businessmen and consumers' attitudes so negative that there is little response to policy. Japan's experience in the 1990s and the very first years of the twenty-first century is a prime modern-day example of bad timing.

Because of the inherent difficulties in getting policy decisions right, some experts simply do not, or at least did not in the mid- to late decades of the twentieth century, believe that central bankers should be exercising discretionary judgments at all. They do not believe that the central bank can be relied on to time policy moves in the best way. Prominent among those with this view during my tenure at the Fed were certain monetarists such as Milton Friedman, whose research demonstrated that lags in the economy's reaction to money supply were long and variable. In part for that reason, he seemed to feel it would be just about miraculous if policymakers were able to time their decisions in a way that would be positive for the economy. Rather, he argued that monetary policy should be limited to doing no more than keeping some measure of the money supply growing at a predetermined constant rate.

Other economists who advocate an automatic pilot for monetary policy believe in a gold standard or its first cousin in today's world, the so-called currency board, both of which would essentially limit monetary policy to a rule of maintaining the domestic currency at a predetermined fixed value relative to an external standard, such as a fixed price of gold or a fixed value of a foreign currency (or collection of currencies).

For such people, judgment is too fallible, economic forecasts too unreliable. They prefer for policy to be guided by rules rather than by judgment, on the thought that well-functioning labor, product, and financial markets free of unnecessary restrictions and other rigidities will on their own adjust quickly enough to keep an economy working satisfactorily, or at least more satisfactorily than if the economy also has to deal with the strains inflicted by bad monetary policy judgments. Those who tend to believe—probably most of us, I suspect—that policymakers can improve matters through deliberate policy adjustments are probably considered hopelessly naive, given the scarcity of people with the needed intuitiveness and sense of timing, the waywardness of the political appointment process, and a task that proponents of rules probably believe to be well-nigh impossible anyhow.

There is something to all these objections, especially at certain times for certain countries, but my experience by no means convinced me that rules should dominate judgment. Nonetheless, rules might play a background role that helps temper judgments. They can help policymakers think hard about whether their discretionary policy decisions are well and truly justified, are going too far, or are not going far enough. But even this supporting role presents difficulties because the basis of the rules themselves can easily become outmoded and thus undermine their usefulness. Economic and financial structures change over time. People's attitudes and motivations change. What was previously of value in the rules, such as the virtually exclusive focus on some measure of money supply, may no longer fit evolving economic conditions, not to mention changing social and political imperatives.

A well-known economist, John Taylor, later devised what could be interpreted as a more flexible rule—one that seems better designed to guide judgmental monetary policy decisions. He showed how and under what circumstances (based on the behavior of a few key economic variables in his econometric equations) the interest rate targeted by policy should be adjusted. Although an improvement on other rules that would tie the hands of policy in respect to domestic interest rates, his rule requires knowledge of, for instance, the present state of the economy in relation to its potential as well as an empirical counterpart to the concept of the neutral short-term rate of interest adjusted for inflation, both of which are uncertain and often subject to considerable revision. It also assumes that the Fed has clear specific long-run inflation objectives. And it further presumes that the economy will react to policy changes today as it did in the past, in my opinion always a dubious assumption in light of attitudinal and structural shifts over time that almost never fail to alter the how and why of business or consumer decision making.

Faced with an ever-changing and politically complex economic world, policymakers at the Fed and at other major central banks have rather steadfastly maintained a judgmental approach to policy. My first close encounters with how the Fed as an institution thought about issues in the formulation of monetary policy—including the role of interest rates, attitudes toward bank reserves, and the gradual infiltration of money-supply concerns—occurred early in my career within the board's Division of Research and Statistics. I had transferred there after about four years in the Division of International Finance—a first move away from the margins of policymaking toward the center. Continuing the not quite conscious but seemingly determined effort to get to the center, I subsequently shifted to the banking section within the Research Division and then became head of the government finance section.

The banking section was responsible for, among other things, measuring, keeping track of, and evaluating (though not with any clear policy focus in those early days) measures of money supply as well as the bank reserves and monetary base that supported it. The government finance section was responsible for fiscal policy analysis and, more important for my own future, analysis of the market for government securities, in which the vast bulk of the Fed's open market operations took place. This section also paid close attention to related markets such as those for dealer loans and for federal funds (uncollateralized and usually overnight loans between banks).

Along the way very early in the 1960s, Ralph Young asked me to work with him on a revision of *Purpose and Functions of the Federal Reserve System,* the board-published book that embodied the Fed's official view of itself. Ralph had been director of the Division of Research and Statistics when I first transferred there, but had then moved on to an office in the board members' wing from which he headed up the Division of International Finance and took on other tasks.

As it turned out, I seemed to be adept at writing official positions, so that, as the years and decades passed, I could never quite entirely distance myself from this document, though my involvement of course became more managerial as time went on. With so much involvement in the book and its development, I became well educated in, and perhaps to some minor extent even contributed to, the evolution of institutional thought as the document was transformed edition by edition. Over time, the Congress mandated new duties for the Board of Governors (such as for bank holding companies and rules governing the appropriate description of interest rates charged for consumer debt and housing). At the same time, the Fed's attitudes toward monetary policy and related questions were also being adapted in light of experience, changing economic and financial circumstances, and congressional interest and oversight.

Though *Purpose and Functions* covered all facets of the Fed's operations, its presentation of monetary policy was central and of most interest to the college students of money and banking who were viewed as its prime audience. I came to know Ralph much better as we sat together at his large working table bringing up to date the policy sections of the book's earlier postwar revision—I wielding the pen and he of course having the last word. In the process, I began to feel comfortable enough with him to do something that probably surprised him and in retrospect surprises me.

We were working on a passage to justify the Fed's then "bills-only" policy, a policy adopted at the time to make it clear that open market operations were to be conducted only in Treasury bills (short-term market instruments maturing in one year or less). It was a mildly controversial policy, at least in my mind, which had been adopted after the Fed was no longer bound by the World War II agreement with the Treasury to maintain low interest rates on long-term U.S. government securities. Within certain parts of the Fed, however, the policy did seem to be more controversial; the New York Fed was strongly opposed to it early on, which led to some internal contention between the Fed chairman and that bank's president.

The policy's purpose, I assumed, was to make it very clear that the Fed had no intention of interfering in any way with market determination of longer-term rates and would let these rates reflect purely private-market supply-and-demand forces. Moreover, the bill market in any event exhibited the necessary "breadth, depth, and resiliency" required for Fed open market operations—the jargon I quickly learned for describing markets considered liquid enough to absorb seamlessly the very large amount of buy-and-sell transactions required almost on a daily basis to implement monetary policy.

Longer-term markets, by contrast, were considered to be "thin," so that Fed operations ran a high risk of unduly and undesirably interfering with interest-rate levels in those markets. In short, the Fed wished to avoid obscuring informational content embedded in the collective market attitudes and actions of private investors and borrowers that might provide useful signals to policymakers about, for example, the strength of credit demands and perhaps even about underlying economic activity (no one thought very seriously about inflation expectations in those days).

My first effort at drafting an explanation of and defense for the bills-only policy was apparently not strong enough. I always had a lingering sympathy for the idea that the Fed and the Treasury should be flexible enough in their approach to debt management (Fed operations in securities markets are essentially a form of public debt management)[1] so that market operations could be employed in an attempt to affect the yield curve, at least transitorily, for economic purposes. For instance, it might well be useful for the Fed to purchase longer-term bonds when the economy is weak in an attempt to exert some added downward pressure on long-term Treasury bond rates in the market. Such an effort just might make it a bit easier at the margin for businesses to finance capital spending. There seemed to be little harm in it and some possible good to be gained. I suppose such weak-mindedness must have crept into the way my draft was phrased—though, of course, I no longer remember the exact wording at issue.

Ralph suggested different language that made it sound as if it were unthinkable for the policy ever to be changed. I recall saying that I could not write it as he suggested; I did not believe in it. Ralph insisted. I, strangely enough, continued to resist. He then said that if I would not do it, he would bring Charlie down tomorrow to do so. At that point, our session ended. Sure enough, the next day he worked with Charlie. The day after, he and I very pleasantly resumed our collaboration, and on it continued.

Although the bills-only policy later faded away, the Fed as a matter of practice remained generally inactive in longer-term markets for a long time because they were indeed thin, and the risk of misinterpreting Fed activity was viewed as unduly high. During the Greenspan years, however, an effort was made to undertake open market operations across a broad spectrum of Treasury maturities in a neutral manner in the regular course of transactions. And most recently, as will be noted in the chapter on Bernanke's tenure to date, the Fed in response to the great credit crisis, engaged in a large program for purchasing longer-term Treasury securities, certain government agency issues, and mortgage-backed securities guaranteed by such agencies—the purpose being to keep downward pressure on longer-term rates to aid in the recovery of the mortgage market in particular and the economy more generally.

Before our work together on the Fed booklet, at a point when Ralph was still running the Research Division, he walked down to my office (in the division's banking section at the time) and handed me a typewritten document written by a professor named Karl Brunner and requested my opinion on it. As I remember, it simply described—by way of elaborate and logically and institutionally correct relationships put in the form of equations (really truisms or identities in this case)—the mechanics of how operations by the Fed lead to an increase in the monetary base and hence in the money supply held by the public.

My comment was that Brunner was doing little more than explicating in detail the institutional relationships involved in how the Fed supplies money to the public. He was telling us nothing that we didn't already know. At least, I thought we certainly had to know it; anything else would surely have been unthinkable.

It was eminently clear to me that the Fed did not guide its monetary policy by aiming at a predetermined amount of or rate of growth in the money it was capable of supplying to the economy (and of the corresponding totals of bank reserves or monetary base implied by such an objective). It seemed at the time to have no intention of doing so, presumably because it thought policy worked better and more effectively through another route, not because it failed to understand the mechanics of connections between reserves supplied to banks and their transformation into money.

I knew very little about Brunner. I did know that he and a relatively young up-and-coming academic named Alan Meltzer were working with the House Banking Committee and writing a document that evaluated monetary policy at the Fed. What I took away from their work, as it unfolded, was that Fed policy, although fairly good at recognizing the turns in business cycles when they came (e.g., it could be seen taking easing actions that lowered short-term interest rates as the cycle turned down and tightening actions as it turned up), was very bad at easing or tightening policy sufficiently in advance to avoid or minimize such cycles or, indeed, inflationary pressures as they might arise. That occurred, so they seemed to be saying, because the Fed's guidelines for policy operations erroneously placed too much stress on so-called free reserves (which can be measured as the difference between the banking system's excess reserves and borrowing from the Fed) instead of an aggregative measure, preferably the monetary-base, that would be more directly related to money-supply behavior.[2]

Their report was an important step in introducing monetarist thinking into congressional oversight of the Fed and perhaps even in beginning to make the Fed more conscious of the need to give money supply a more important role in policy, either directly or indirectly or seemingly, though a number of years were yet to pass before relevant steps were gingerly taken in that regard.

Instead of focusing on money, monetary policy operations in those early days and in practically all of the ensuing decades were designed to influence pressures on bank liquidity (via free reserves) and associated key money-market rates (the federal funds rate now) and thereby, with some lag as effects spread more broadly through credit and asset markets as a whole, on economic activity and prices. I do remember a brief conversational by-play with the president of the Federal Reserve Bank of Cleveland at the time, a former business school dean named Willis Winn. He rather mocked, in a gentle and polite manner, my tendency always to discuss the demand for money in attempting to explain its behavior. Didn't I know the Fed affected (indeed, in his mind controlled) the supply of money? Well, of course, I knew that the supply of money was affected by what the Fed did in its open market operations, but this far from explained the actual growth that occurred in the stock of money in the public's hands at any particular time.

The size of the Fed's open market operations during a short-term policy period (of, say, four or six weeks) was determined, as noted earlier, by a decision that affected short-term interest rates or, stated more generally, money-market conditions. The principal operating guide for the system account manager in New York was indeed free reserves, but the decision about the level of such reserves was guided to a great extent by the constellation of money-market conditions desired by the FOMC, whether a little tighter, easier, or about the same as before. Open market operations would then provide to or take away from the banking system as many bank reserves as needed to keep free reserves and money-market conditions as a whole in line with immediate policy objectives.

As a result, the stock of money in the public's hands would grow in that period at whatever pace was consistent with the public's demand for money to hold at existing interest rates and also with the demand for money needed to help finance the ongoing growth in the nation's income at the time. So the demand for money was the essential determinant of actual money growth in view of the way the Fed conducted policy. The Fed would supply as much money as was demanded by the market, given income and interest rates.

If the Fed decided, by contrast, to hold money growth to some predetermined pace over a particular short-run period, it would in effect be deciding to make the demand for money in the market conform to its institutional view of what the supply should be at the time. Because money demand is, as earlier indicated, determined by both interest rates and income growth, and because income growth would not be significantly affected by Fed actions over the shorter run (policy affects the economy with a longer lag), interest rates during any particular short-run period would bear the full brunt of such a policy approach. They would have to change by as much as necessary to balance the demand for and supply of money, given the nation's income growth and the associated growth in transactions demand for money.

The relationships have become simplified in the telling, but that is the gist of the story. In brief, you can control an interest rate, and the supply of money to the public will depend on whatever stock of money is demanded at that rate. Or you can instead attempt to control the supply of money, and the interest rate will vary to bring the public's demand for money into balance with a fixed supply.

Such issues and their operational implications for the implementation of monetary policy emerged faintly in the halls of the Fed during the 1960s. They became more and more insistent and noisy as time went on in the inflationary climate of the 1970s and early 1980s. How they were handled in practice underlies much of the policy issues discussed in subsequent chapters on the Burns and Volcker years.

Back in the Martin period, it was very clear to the young me, and I supposed to most everyone else, that the Fed during any particular policy period simply provided whatever amount of money was demanded by the public, given interest rates and economic activity. It did so in the hope and expectation that the amount of money thereby supplied would over time come to be consistent with the goal of price stability. The Fed did not seem to be operating a policy that assumed a close and predictable shorter-run relationship between pressures on bank liquidity (and their related short-term interest effects) and money supply.

Such an understanding was so much in my mind, even after only a few years at the Fed, that I did not quite see why anyone seemed surprised that monetarists found a very weak relationship between pressures on bank liquidity positions (to wit, on free reserves) and money-supply behavior. I was reminded of this response in an encounter with a more senior colleague at the Fed in those days, a gentleman named Homer Jones, as he was preparing to leave his position as a section chief in the board's Research Division (I think it was the section responsible for consumer and mortgage credit analysis) to assume the role of head of research at the Federal Reserve Bank of St. Louis. Once there, Homer set the St. Louis

Fed on its long-held and useful path as a devoted source of monetarist research and analysis within the Federal Reserve System.

As I was passing by Homer's office one day, he called out, asking me to come in. He was poring over some charts and statistical results and wanted to talk about them. "See," he said, "you cannot control the money supply by controlling free reserves," or words to that effect. He seemed to exude a certain amount of relief at finding up-to-date evidence that the world as he remembered it from graduate school remained in proper order. The notion that the Fed's influence on money growth was through its influence on bank liquidity positions was, it is true, a crucial element in an earlier book published in 1930 by an economist named Win Riefler (who focused on the pressure put on banks from being forced to borrow at the Fed).[3] At the time of this conversation Win was the éminence grise at the board and principal policy advisor to the chairman, with an office in the board members' corridor. Perhaps his being in that position contributed to doubts by monetarists about whether the Fed fully understood its own mechanism and failed, so it appeared, to grasp the need to guide policy by aiming at total reserves or, preferably, the monetary base, rather than at such a marginal measure as free reserves in order to control money supply with any satisfactory degree of precision.

However that might be, I remember responding to Homer in a rather offhand way, saying something like, "The Fed's not trying to control money supply with free reserves. It's trying to affect bank credit conditions and, by extension through that route, overall credit conditions and the economy." And in my mind I had little doubt there was a fairly consistent relationship between changes in free reserves and the degree of tightness or ease in bank credit and associated money-market rates. I remember nothing further about the conversation, but I am sure that we did not go into much depth on the subject. I just thought the issue he raised basically misconstrued policy as it was being practiced, whereas Homer must have thought I was either hopelessly naive or gullible.

Beneath that brief banter lay a fairly deep disagreement between monetarists (or at least the stricter ones) and what I took to be the prevailing view at the Fed. If the central bank was to aim at a predetermined target for money by controlling aggregate reserves of the monetary base, it would be giving up its control over the price of liquidity (money-market interest rates), and letting such costs fluctuate over a wider range than was its historical practice. The Fed and most central banks were wary of large rate fluctuations, believing that they would pose an excessive risk of emitting confusing signals and thus destabilizing markets.

In that connection, it needs to be understood that all central banks are quite well aware (or should be) that the need for an institution capable of averting a system financial meltdown is one of the main reasons for their existence. A central bank is in effect the deus ex machina that, as it were, stands outside the financial system, is not subject to the strong and often unpredictable forces that sometimes threaten disarray in markets, and thus can act as a sure lender of last resort when all else is failing. It can be relied on always to supply credit and money as might be required to keep incipient disarray from turning into a full-fledged system-wide breakdown. That responsibility represents a fundamental obligation to the nation, and it is felt strongly by those charged with it.

The Fed's pursuit of a so-called even-keel policy in connection with major Treasury financings in the earlier part of the postwar period could be considered a distant cousin of such concerns about excessive instability in markets. For a number of years, even after the 1951 accord with the Treasury had released the Fed from its obligation for supporting the government bond market, the Fed kept its monetary policy stance unchanged for a short period surrounding regular large quarterly Treasury debt offerings. At those times, new intermediate- and longer-term securities were offered to the public to refund maturing debt and perhaps to raise some new cash. The Fed's even-keel policy helped to ensure that the auctions' went smoothly.

In those days, the Treasury set a price for the issues that reflected existing market conditions. Any sudden change in those conditions, as might occur through a change in Fed policy, risked a failure in the offering; for instance, if the Fed tightened the Treasury might not be able to sell the full amount on offer, at least not without the embarrassment of repricing the issues. Although a systemic failure in the markets was hardly at risk, the Fed seemed to believe that a tranquil Treasury financing was in the national interest and worth any potential small delay that might be involved in adjusting its policy operations. This type of even-keel operation was abandoned once the Treasury shifted toward an auction system where price and yield were set through competitive market bidding.

As a general rule, central banks are disposed to conduct monetary policy in ways that they believe avoid an untoward risk of undermining the financial system's safety and soundness. They are generally conservative in their attitudes toward the market and seek to implement policy without excessively abrupt shifts in market liquidity and credit conditions. In very recent times, such an approach to policy implementation has been accomplished not only through generally modest or moderate adjustments in the key money-market rate that now guides policy—the federal funds rate—but also by much more open indications about the Fed's own attitude about the future of policy and about crucial elements influencing it. In later chapters, I will have more to say about potential negative effects of the latter approach. The three-year period beginning in late 1979, when the Volcker Fed made its frontal assault on inflation through a more direct effort to control money supply by targeting a particular aggregate-reserve measure on a day-to-day basis and by ignoring interest-rate behavior over a relatively wide range, was very much an exception.

As inflation picked up in the late 1960s, the Fed began to adjust its policy stance and thinking to take account of newly emerging economic and financial conditions in the country, as well as of advances in monetary and economic research generally. It was becoming clear that a shift in economic thinking—in the economics profession, in the relevant congressional committees, and in the corridors of the nation's central bank—was taking place.

The Great Depression had receded in memory, and attention was moving away from almost a sole focus on maintenance of adequate spending on goods and services to more concern about the supply side of the economy. Moreover, the tools of the economic trade were being greatly sharpened by concurrent advances in econometric model building and more sophisticated methods of time-series analysis, all of which encouraged more confidence (and often more than was warranted) in the profession's capacity to project future developments, to discriminate among the relative importance of various explanations and hypotheses being offered to understand economic developments, and, to guide policymakers in balancing objectives that often seemed to conflict, such as price stability and low unemployment.

Most of the important supply-side issues affecting how the economy functioned—such as price and wage rigidities, various other impediments to the free flow of resources in product and labor markets, and the impact of tax structure and incentives on economic efficiency and growth—are not under the Fed's direct control, though of course they influence the economic environment and the problems it confronts. The supply of money, however, is—although with varying degrees of certainty and recognizing definitional doubts—under the Fed's control, if not precisely month by month or even quarter by quarter, then at least over intermediate and longer terms.

With signs of resurgent inflation, the Fed began to pay more attention to money's observed behavior, how it might best be controlled, what liquid assets in addition to currency and demand deposits should be included in measures of money, and which particular measures (narrow measures such as M1, which includes currency and demand deposits; broad measures such as M2, which includes time and savings deposits; or even broader measures that encompass instruments such as large certificates of deposits and money-market funds). The number of M's and their composition naturally changed over the years to reflect shifts in financial structure and consumer and business behavior.

At about the same time in the 1960s as money supply gradually entered their consciousness, policymakers also showed more concern about getting a better handle on the lags between policy operations and their effects not only on prices, but also on real economic activity. As Brunner and Meltzer had highlighted, it was not good enough to know when the economy was at a turning point. It was, and of course always had been, more important to anticipate the future as best one could, so that policy adjustments could be made early and looming recessions or inflations either moderated or averted. That policy worked with a lag had of course been long known, but the Fed now began to make institutional changes that would increase the odds of anticipating and offsetting or moderating future recessionary and inflationary developments.

Around this time, the FOMC finally permitted and received numeric staff projections of the likely economic outcome in quarters ahead based on policy operations thus far and on other factors such as prospective fiscal policy. Before then, Fed staff presentations to the FOMC or the board had been limited to evaluating current economic trends, and whatever suggestions they contained about future economic behavior generally remained implicit.

The staff's economic forecasts came to be embodied in a document known as the green book (named for the color of its cover). The Fed as an institution preferred to characterize them as projections rather than as forecasts because the former term seemed more professional and less likely to raise questions about whether they did or did not represent satisfactory outcomes. Whether called projections or forecasts, they required certain assumptions about policy in the future, a practical and presentational problem that was never very easily resolved.

These numeric forecasts (initiated at the time by a very intelligent economist, Dan Brill, then head of the Division of Research and Statistics) were essentially based on judgments from current developments and indicators of future activity (such as surveys of spending intentions), but they also employed the preliminary insights and results from a quarterly model of the U.S. economy that the board staff was in the process of developing. As I recall, the forecasts also normally assumed no change in policy—that is, in those days, no change in pressure on bank reserve positions (typified by free reserves of the banking system).

Of course, if one were cynical about economists' forecasting ability, as many were in those early days (and as a number of people still are, not without reason), it was not crystal clear that policy would be greatly improved by explicit numeric estimates of important economic variables looking several quarters ahead. Much depended not only on how good the projections were, but also on how they were presented and interpreted—their ranges of uncertainty made clear, their assumptions brought into the light of day.

To me, and I assume to many others, it always seemed best to view the Fed's or anyone else's numeric forecasts as essentially indicative. They should be interpreted as suggestive, for instance, of whether future growth would be strong or weak; whether a potential recession would be dire or just a blip; or whether inflation would be within a comfort range, outside of it, or strong enough to risk accelerating into more of a hyperinflation or weak enough to risk falling into deflation. In that sense, it is not the particular numeric values of the forecasts themselves that should carry decisive weight in a policymaker's decision, but rather the qualitative explanations surrounding them. Naturally, there is always the risk that in presentation, whether written or oral, such explanations may or may not be sufficiently emphasized or even well discussed.

Much of a projection's value also depends on how much self-confidence policymakers have in their own capacity for independent thinking. If they have too little, they can end up being no more than captives of the staff's forecasts. If they have too much, they can be at risk of ignoring valuable insights that might contradict their preconceptions.

All that being said, I gained the impression over the years that numeric economic projections became the dominant force in the policy process (except possibly during the few years when the Volcker Fed adopted an approach to policy driven by money supply). It could hardly have been otherwise in view of the huge amount of staff intellectual and statistical resources devoted to the projections and their convincingly full and detailed presentation. Of course, as it turned out, the forecasts of the Fed staff were never very far from what seemed to be the consensus of "sound" outside forecasters and mainstream opinion, the area also naturally inhabited by FOMC members.

The forecasters at the Fed almost cannot help choosing the least controversial and usually most conservative of likely outcomes relative to the general consensus. This approach guards against loss of credibility with their bosses and generally turns out not to be too far off the mark on average. Policymakers, like staff forecasters, also have an inherent disposition to conservatism in decision making. They usually prefer to adjust policies gradually, which is a far from irrational way of operating. Given all of the uncertainties they face, gradual changes more often than not guard them against finding themselves too far off base when circumstances turn unexpectedly.

However, the interaction between policymakers' conservative inclinations and numeric forecasts that require the credibility of being in the neighborhood of a consensus sometimes unduly narrows the channel of policy thinking. The practical substitute, of course, is to take numeric projections for what they really are: best estimates of a likely outcome within a large margin of error. Any policymaker would probably say that is indeed what he or she does, but there remains some doubt in my mind.

Also, in the 1960s the board's head of research participated with representatives from other elements of the government—the Council of Economic Advisers, the Budget Bureau, and the Treasury Department—in preparing the economic projections of the economy that underlay the annual federal budgets and presumably influenced the stance of governmental fiscal policy. One assumes that the Fed's participation in this group, known as the "quadriad," was justified in the name of improving coordination between fiscal and monetary policies. However, the structure obviously raised questions about whether the board staff's own projections of the economy, sent to the FOMC and helping to frame monetary policy debates, were unduly influenced by the quadriad's projections. In theory, they were not, but in practice one might tend to think that in the mutual give and take that went into agreement within the group, a certain amount of Fed "independence" risked being lost, not deliberately, but in the natural course of discussion.

Questions about the reliability of estimates for the government's military spending in connection with the Vietnam War were a very sore subject at this time. Good estimates simply could not be had on any timely basis. Actual results always turned out to be substantially higher than the figures contained in the federal budgets of those days. In my role as chief of the board's government finance section during a few of those years, it became very clear to me that the Budget Bureau, the Fed's natural contact for background information on spending items, seemed to be more in the dark than usual. Efforts to cadge more realistic figures out of the Defense Department were unavailing. And one simply could not arbitrarily add a larger than usual "fudge factor" to official estimates of defense spending just on the hunch, no matter how informed by bitter experience, that realistic spending figures were being suppressed somewhere in the government.

I have always felt that the Fed's inability, or anyone else's for that matter, to obtain realistically strong estimates of military spending in those days may well have led to forecasts of the strength in economic activity and price pressures that were lower than they should have been. If so, this result could well have contributed to the Fed's sluggishness in fighting emergent inflationary pressures as Lyndon Johnson's Great Society and the Vietnam War together drove up the federal budgetary deficit and the total of spending on goods and services in the economy.

It was not that the Fed failed to stiffen monetary policy, despite pressures from the Johnson administration. I was present at the FOMC meeting where Martin, with both quiet drama and a light touch, described his hair-raising ride in a jeep driven by President Johnson over, so it seemed, the roughest terrain that could be found on his Texas ranch. In that way, the message was being underlined that the Fed should not become so restrictive as to risk unsettling the economy and make the president's life more difficult than it already had become. Nonetheless, Martin was returned safely to home base, and the Fed continued on its tightening course, but it was in the circumstances too conservative and cautious.

In any event, the issues connected with the Fed's having too close an involvement in the administration's economic forecast (a forecast that was inevitably influenced at least to some degree by the political context surrounding it) manifested themselves when in the late 1960s Congress (finally) passed a tax increase. The Fed then promptly lowered the discount rate, presumably in response to an implicit, if not explicit, political agreement. Under such an agreement lay the simple thought that if fiscal policy were to become tighter, monetary policy could and should become easier. Monetary and fiscal policy would be coordinated.

Although coordination was a sound idea in the abstract and generally considered a good thing, many in the Fed did not see the practical application of it to be so obvious at that particular time. Getting the rate lowered turned out to be a bit difficult. Most reserve bank boards of directors did not want to do so because inflation was fairly high, and they were not at all sure that the economy would weaken very much as a result of the tax increase.

The Federal Reserve Bank of Minneapolis was finally persuaded to propose a drop in the rate, and the others then followed along, as tradition would have it (buttressed by the Fed board's very seldom exercised legal authority to "review and determine" reserve bank discount rates). Unfortunately, the economy for a while remained stronger than anticipated, and the rate decline then had to be reversed. An internal rumor indicated that some Fed board members, including the chairman, felt that the staff and its projections had misled them. Not long after these events, Dan Brill received a good job offer from the private sector and left the board staff. When Arthur Burns came on the board as chairman early in 1970, the board ended its participation in the quadriad, which then became a troika composed only of institutions that reported directly to the president.

Around 1965, a few years before these events, Dan came into my office and asked if I would take over a statistical document that had been traditionally forwarded to the FOMC and did nothing more than present charts of the behavior of bank reserve and other monetary aggregates, along with a simple descriptive text. Dan asked me to transform it into a useful policy document and in the process to be sure to spell out the statistical parameters of money-market conditions (which particular interest rates, which measures of bank liquidity) so that the FOMC's vote to keep money-market conditions unchanged, tighten them, or ease them would be quantified and thus much clearer to both decision makers and the system account manager at the trading desk in New York.

This initiative took place well before the FOMC settled on the federal funds rate as the key money-market rate, indeed even before the funds rate was the main focus for the market itself. Dealer loan rates, the three-month Treasury bill rate, and nonprice factors (such as the net need for reserve funds by major city banks and the reserve surplus position of country banks who were the main suppliers) were then all aspects of money-market conditions taken into account by the trading desk. When the FOMC told the account manager in New York to do something to money-market conditions (tighten, ease, leave unchanged), neither its members nor he could be very sure of what exactly was meant. There was always some room for suspicion that things had not worked out quite as expected.

Thus began the policy document that (to this day) proposes and analyzes alternative policy postures for FOMC consideration—the so-called blue book (also named after the color of its cover). This report served two purposes. First, money-supply and reserve measures were introduced into a document that discussed the broad interest-rate and monetary factors that ought to be considered in and would be influenced by the FOMC's operating decision about the tightness or ease in money-market conditions during the period between meetings. Second, the flexibility of the manager of the Fed's Open Market Account in New York became more limited. Numbers defining tightness or ease hemmed him in. Moreover, the interpretation of the numbers came through the board staff as well as through the account manager, thus effectively enhancing the power of the board and its chairman relative to the New York Fed and its president.

The blue book stayed with me throughout the balance of my career at the Fed. In addition to preparing the blue book, I began participating in the morning call (around 11:00 a.m. in those days) that took place between the account manager in New York, a reserve bank president representing the FOMC, and a senior staff person at the board. The arrangement was another way of ensuring that the account manager's actions were fully consonant with the FOMC's operating directive issued to the

New York Fed. Immediately after the call, the manager's proposed action for the day, along with relevant statistics, was circulated in a memo (written by board staff, mainly me after a while) to committee members. Everyone was informed. The president on the call could ask whatever he wanted at the time the day's program was being formulated, as could any board member who walked into the staff office where the call was being held (few did). Protests could be registered about the day's approach to operations, though they very seldom were.

By the time I became the senior staff person on the call, beginning in the early part of Burns's tenure, the manager's proposed actions did not generate any controversy—maybe on the rare occasion, but hardly ever. He and I had preliminary discussions every morning. At the same time, I always briefed the chairman quite early about how the day seemed to be developing. I also spoke with him after the manager had given me a preliminary indication of his intentions. The manager then took no market action until I was able to inform the chairman. Volcker in particular was a stickler about that—not always easy if he was abroad or traveling in the United States, but it was always accomplished, even when he was in China, as I recall. Once or twice, the market became a bit upset because the Fed was delayed in its actions beyond the usual so-called Fed time (around 11:35 or so in those days). Rumors of unusual developments began to spread, not too seriously, but there they were. The truth simply was that I had been unable to reach Volcker quickly enough.

Burns was not quite as involved as Volcker in day-to-day market operations, but the difference was not enough to be of any great significance. In my experience, Miller was and wanted to be the least involved in such operations. I have no firsthand knowledge of the nature of Martin's involvement on the operational side.

After Burns left office, we met occasionally for lunch. At one of them, during Volcker's tenure, Burns made the comment that Volcker must have been just like him. With Miller, he said, I could do whatever I wanted, but not with Volcker. There was a certain, but very limited, element of truth in that assessment. He seemed to forget that there was also a committee.

So far as I could tell, the staff leadership position I eventually attained had much more influence when the chairman was strong than when he was not, always assuming that the person in this staff position had a good relationship with the chairman. When a chairman is viewed as weak or uninterested, the FOMC has no coherence. But because committee members always remain aware of and sensitive to their prerogatives, there is no way a leadership vacuum can be filled by anyone on the staff. Nor should it be. Someone on the committee has to step up. None ever did in my observation in the rare years when there was a vacuum, such as during Miller's brief tenure. And, in any event, I rather doubt that, given the Fed's peculiar institutional structure, anyone really could. However that might be, I always had the feeling in Miller's time that the account manager listened to my views on market operations with a bit less intensity and that the committee members were less enrapt by my policy presentations—nothing of earthshaking consequence in all that, but still a little something.

Around the same time that the money supply began coming in from the cold, the Fed also and coincidentally began to worry about what came to be called the membership problem. Membership in the Federal Reserve System was mandatory for banks that chose national charters, but not for state-chartered banks. The advantages to membership were few. Membership did provide direct access to the Fed's clearing and payments system, as well as relatively privileged access to the Fed's borrowing facility (the so-called discount window); nonmember institutions could borrow only under rather stringent conditions, including the requirement of a special vote by the Board of Governors under the Federal Reserve Act's then emergency loan provision applicable to loans made to "individuals, partnerships, and corporations". Institutions had to weigh the advantages of membership—mainly public relations, in my opinion—against the cost of being subject to the Fed's regulations on nonearning cash-reserve requirements to be held against deposits, which some institutions felt to be unnecessarily burdensome. Moreover, a number of institutions preferred state rather than national charters, in part on the thought that dealing with state chartering and banking authorities could be accomplished on a friendlier basis than with federal authorities; and many of these banks, especially but not exclusively smaller ones, had little interest in membership.

For whatever reason, a number of banks at the time took to withdrawing from the Fed, and many newly formed banks chose to stay out of the system. They saw little practical need to take on any of the burdens of Fed membership (minor as they were). Access to the discount window was of no great importance because the interbank market for funds had broadened and could readily be tapped into, and clearing and payments needs could easily be accomplished through correspondent banks at a reasonable cost. It looked as if the value of membership in the Fed, including its prestige, was no longer at a premium.

This drop in value was worrisome to the Fed. Some discussion took place, as I remember, about the point at which attrition of member banks would begin to have an adverse impact on monetary policy. From my perspective, that point was certainly nowhere near at hand and highly unlikely ever to arrive in practice, but it remained a concern to the powers that be. Or at least they thought it was a good talking point to give some heft to the more immediate worry, which was basically political.

Support for an independent Fed was greatly aided by the nationwide network of Federal Reserve Banks and their branches, each with a board of directors representative of a cross section of leading citizens and presumably opinion makers in the area. This network helped promote understanding of the Fed around the country and indirectly helped boost the Fed's image with Congress. No doubt, a monetary policy seen to be serving the economy and public interest well was absolutely crucial to the Fed's prestige and continued effective independence. But it was by no means politically inconsequential also to have a broad built-in support system throughout the nation. The Fed needed as much buffering as possible against those inevitable periods when its monetary policy would prove to be unpopular—by making life quite difficult for small businesses, farmers, home owners, and many other citizens, and in the process arousing the wrath of Congress and in particular the members of the oversight banking committees.

The so-called membership problem later dissipated when the Monetary Control Act of 1980 was passed, and, among other provisions, practically all depository institutions were made subject to reserve requirements set by the Fed and had equal access to the discount window. In the 1960s, however, the political and social environment for such a grand approach was lacking. Instead, at that time, a committee from the Reserve Bank staffs came forward with a recommendation to the board in Washington, D.C., that was designed to make it simpler and less costly for member banks to calculate and meet the reserve requirements imposed by the Fed.

It was a highly technical recommendation, but the issue illustrates some of the diverse interests at play within the Federal Reserve System and also touches on the ambivalence of early efforts to give more weight to money supply in policy deliberations.

The recommendation changed the reserve-requirement structure so that reserves (in the form of vault cash or deposits at Reserve Banks) that banks were required to hold on average during a so-called reserve accounting period (at that time one week, then later two weeks) were no longer to be calculated on the basis of deposits held at banks in that period but on the basis of deposits at the banks two weeks earlier. For obvious reasons the new structure was referred to as "lagged reserve requirements."

The proposal was highly irritating to a number of monetarist economists, becoming almost a rallying cry for them, because it eliminated the direct linkage between the amount of reserves provided by the Fed during any particular reserve-requirement accounting period and the amount of deposits that could be outstanding on the books of banks during that particular period. It looked as if the Fed was gratuitously weakening its ability to achieve reasonably close control of the money supply should it ever wish to do so.

Looked at more realistically, though, the proposal was at worst introducing no more than a two-week delay in the Fed's capacity, such as it was, to control the money supply directly. If the deposits in the money supply were growing at a stronger pace than desired in the reserve accounting period, this growth would be reflected in an increased demand on the part of banks for reserves two weeks later to satisfy the concomitant rise in their required reserves. If the Fed did not supply those reserves, their cost would go up as banks bid against each other for the relatively scarce supply. In other words, the federal funds rate would rise and initiate a string of market adjustments that would work over time to restrain growth in bank credit and money. Delaying the start by only two weeks did not seem to be much of a threat to the Fed's control over money, should it ever wish to make that a center piece of policy, because a time horizon for achieving effective control consonant with basic policy objectives of price stability and growth was on the order of three to six months on average, certainly not a week or every two weeks.

The proposal served two main purposes. First, it would demonstrate to member banks that the Fed was sympathetic to their technical problems and would do what it reasonably could to alleviate them. This was still the early days of computer technology, and banks—especially banks with large branch systems, such as Bank of America at that time—found it quite difficult and costly to ensure that they had full knowledge of their required reserve obligations on a current basis. The proposed lag would provide some relief for them. Second, the proposal, by eliminating uncertainty about the amount of reserves that the banking system was required to hold would in a degree simplify open market operations for the system account manager and avert the potential for market misinterpretations. The manager would be more certain of the amount of reserves that needed to be added or subtracted by open market operations to meet the FOMC's objective for the degree of pressure on bank reserve positions in an operating period. And subsequent revisions of the initially published measure of free or net borrowed reserves, which the market took as an important indicator of the stance of monetary policy, would be minimized.[4]

The proposed introduction of lagged reserve accounting had in the normal course been put out for comment from interested institutions and citizens. At the end, I was given the task of summarizing the comments, which were largely quite technical, at the final board meeting on the subject. As I remember, I also took the occasion to make sure that the board understood that the lagged reserve-requirement structure, if adopted, might well appear inconsistent with greater emphasis on closer control of the money supply should the Fed move in that direction. I do not remember if there was much discussion of the point, which I doubt had been brought up to them before or at least in any pointed way.

I do recollect that Bill Martin, chairing the session, made sure to take note of the point in his summary remarks at the end, but continued on to indicate that there was already considerable momentum behind the proposal, moving it forward toward final approval. So there was, and so it was. I do not believe that the chairman of the committee originating the proposal, who later became president of the reserve bank where he spent the bulk of his productive career, ever quite forgave me for inserting a basic monetary policy question into discussion of an issue that was clearly being guided by member bank relations.

Looking back on Martin's tenure, I would say that insofar as the internal bureaucratic structure of policy was concerned, he made a number of important and lasting changes. He went some distance in modernizing the use of economics as a tool for policy at the central bank, succeeded in ensuring that the Board of Governors and its chairman were clearly established as central to the power of the Federal Reserve System, and successfully asserted the chairman's primacy as the Fed's spokesman and symbol of the Fed. I am sure he felt that it was right and just to work toward ensuring that the board in Washington played as strong a role in policy as the law permitted. He understood well that the Fed was a nationwide system (his father had been at one point president of the Federal Reserve Bank of St. Louis) and that the broadness of the Fed's constituency was symbolized by the location of its headquarters in Washington (the nation's political capital) rather than in New York (the nation's financial capital).

Although Martin may or may not have expressed it this way, he probably wanted it to be very clear that the New York Fed and its president, with deep roots in the heart of U.S. financial markets, did not by any means represent the broader concerns of the Fed as a whole. Be that as it may, he never convinced Congressman Wright Patman, then chairman of the House Banking Committee, that the Fed was not the handmaiden of large banks and, to use a very old term, of finance capitalism, which made it very difficult, if not impossible, to implement constructive legislative changes in those days.

Over the years, especially after Patman's departure, times and attitudes changed. The Fed came to be viewed mainly through its national policy role for fighting inflation. For a long while, there also seemed to be less suspicion in Congress and elsewhere about the Fed's supposed excessive sympathies for high finance. But the Fed never managed completely to avoid such suspicions, and they appeared again to come into full flower in response to the Fed's actions to help bail out large financial institutions in the wake of the great credit crisis of 2007–2009. In chapter 8, I attempt to assess influences on the Fed's image over time, including the powerful impact of the recent, explosive great credit crisis.

I am not so sure Martin would have felt very satisfied about his role in introducing modern economics into the policy process, though I do recall hearing him express some faith—he did have moments of naiveté—that economists in the future might come to rival the growing ability at the time of engineers for precision in rocket guidance. In any event, the introduction of economic forecasts into policy formulation did not show early signs of success. By the time he left the Fed, inflation was on its way up. The staff had stumbled now and again in its efforts to forecast the economy. An old-fashioned soul, with a much more intuitive than scientific mind, Martin might well have come to believe that all the newly introduced precision about the economy's future had done more damage than had the wild and woolly ride on Lyndon Johnson's bucking bronco of a jeep.

Although Martin may have felt a twang or two of regret about the impact of a modernized presentation of the economy and its outlook on policy setting, I doubt he felt any qualms—well, almost any—about his role in introducing more precision into the specification of day-to-day operating objectives for monetary policy. Doing so helped make the whole internal monetary policy process work more coherently and smoothly—and with the Fed's chairman more clearly at the helm. That role tended to expand over time under Burns and Volcker as the nation's monetary and financial problems became much more complex and demanding—and in consequence bringing considerable excitement into my own professional life.

By the end of Martin's term, I had become one of the two associate directors of the Division of Research and Statistics (Lyle Gramley was the other). Chuck Partee was head of the division. My job was mainly in finance and particularly in issues connected with the formulation and implementation of monetary policy. That was the structure when Arthur Burns arrived at the end of January 1970.

Roles and positions changed over the next sixteen years or so that I was at the Fed—the Burns and Volcker years (with the Miller interregnum). Chuck became a governor, as did Lyle later, after he had first left the board and become a member of the Council of Economic Advisers under Jimmy Carter. I remained at the board in various positions, first leaving the Research Division and becoming adviser to the board in a separate office, with Chuck as managing director in overall administrative charge of the Research Division as well as the International Finance Division. That structure did not work very well, especially in the international area, where old traditions of independence were not easily dented. My role as the principal official for domestic monetary policy questions and oversight continued as it was.

After Chuck became a governor, I became staff director of an office with substantive responsibilities for monetary policy and related issues,

responsibilities that were later extended (by the board under Miller) to encompass certain international issues, such as exchange-market operations and Eurodollar questions. The Office of the Staff Director for Monetary and Financial Policy, as it came to be designated, had few direct employees—one deputy, two secretaries, and the FOMC administrative staff. Necessary staff for exploring substantive economic and financial issues came as needed from the other board divisions, including research, international, legal (relative to certain reserve-requirement and discount-window questions), and reserve bank operations (relative to actual administration of the discount windows).

The setup was something like having dessert without needing to swallow all that awful broccoli and spinach beforehand. It worked well, in part for historical reasons, I suppose. After I left, one year before Volcker's departure in 1987, it was abandoned, and a more conventional framework reestablished, as noted in chapter 6 on the Greenspan years.

3

Arthur Burns and the Struggle against Inflation

Arthur Burns was very unfortunate in the particular decade, the 1970s, where fate placed him as chairman of the Fed. He served in years of quite strong inflationary winds, not only prevalent in the United States but also in other major developed countries.

In the United States, it was also a period of rather persistent downward pressure on the dollar in foreign-exchange markets, which intensified domestic inflationary pressures and signaled a developing loss of confidence in the dollar as a currency. There was the devaluation crisis of 1971–1973 when the United States in effect went off gold and stopped supporting its price in the market. This crisis was followed by further dollar weakness in the wake of the first huge oil shock of the decade in 1973–1974. This shock and a second one coming toward the end of the decade shortly after Burns left office dealt a far greater direct blow to U.S. economic costs and prices then than such shocks would now. The various structural adjustments mandated by federal and local governments, along with private-sector initiatives, have subsequently muted, although certainly not eliminated, as recent experience has shown, the potential for a serious inflationary impact on our domestic prices and costs from a sharp rise in the oil price.

During the 1960s when Martin was in the last half of his long tenure, inflation in our country averaged about 2½ percent (as measured by consumer prices), a pace that tripled to close to 7½ percent in the next decade. Perhaps not all of that acceleration should be attributed to monetary policy under Burns. Some of it may have reflected the rise of inflationary momentum (and presumably expectations) in the last four years of the Martin chairmanship, when inflation rose to about 4¼ percent on average. But it seems apparent that monetary policy under Burns aimed more at containing rather than suppressing the worsening inflationary situation.

Money-supply growth accelerated rather sharply in the early stages of the 1971–1973 devaluation crisis, and the federal funds rate in real terms (measured as the nominal rate less the concurrent rise in the consumer price index) moved lower even as real gross domestic product (GDP) growth was rising. From 1974 through 1977 (Burns's term ended early the next year), a period when the inflation rate picked up strongly on average, the real funds rate actually turned negative—thus, from that perspective, exerting no real restraint on inflation. The market soon perceived that the Fed was doing too little to contain money growth to a pace that would significantly restrain inflation, and the institution's anti-inflation credibility substantially eroded.

In the circumstances of the 1970s, the Fed was indeed very hard pressed to devise policies that would both reduce persistent upward price pressures and keep employment and economic growth on a socially and politically acceptable path. In an effort to gain control of inflation, the Fed, under Burns, did begin to pay more attention to money supply in setting policy, but that approach was bedeviled by only a half-hearted belief in its efficacy, a belief partly, though not entirely, influenced by a great and far from irrational fear of quite unpleasant economic and financial consequences if such a policy were carried out firmly and dogmatically in the institutional and market conditions of the time.

On the financial side, policymakers were well aware that swiftly rising market interest rates could easily become a serious threat to the viability of a number of financial institutions and to the stability of the financial system as a whole. Both banks and thrift institutions were then subject to ceiling rates on deposits.

If the ceiling rates had to be raised rapidly so that institutions could retain depositors, it was feared that banks and thrifts would be faced with potentially severe losses and bankruptcy because their costs could quickly outrun the return on assets they held. Thrift institutions were especially at risk because their assets were so heavily concentrated in mortgages, which mainly bore fixed returns in those days. Yet if the ceiling rates were not raised rapidly enough, thrift institutions' capital would still be threatened because they might be forced to sell assets at a loss to meet deposit drains. As capital eroded, a deposit drain could easily become a deposit run.

The course ahead for policy seemed very treacherous. The Fed suddenly found that Scylla and Charybdis were looming large and narrow and turbulent was the way in the waters where policy was sailing.[1] The hazards from the continuing financial pressures on banks and thrifts—always well in mind because of the Fed board's role in making regulatory decisions about the level of deposit ceiling rates at banks—reinforced a normally cautious step-by-step approach to policy. And that approach was further sustained by the apparent absence of public and political support for a monetary policy sufficiently tight to reduce inflation back to something like the pace of the 1960s.

Indicative of public concerns in those days, I drafted many a letter (for the chairman's signature) to explain to Congressmen that high interest rates did not raise costs that added fuel to inflation. Rather, high rates were anti-inflationary because on balance they helped restrain the spending that was running in excess of the goods being produced and brought to market. Whether the Congressmen were convinced I do not know, but at least they could show evidence of their concern to constituents faced with the higher borrowing cost of buying homes or autos.

In short, there was no appetite for any kind of radical monetary policy adjustments, which was consistent not only with the risks to the financial health of depository institutions and the lack of wide popular support, but also with ingrained attitudes toward policy within the Fed itself. Arthur Burns fit in well in that respect. Conservatism and caution were built into his personality—by no means a bad thing for a central-bank chairman in normal times, but a real limit for the times in which he found himself.

Under Burns, the Fed did nonetheless succeed, I believe, in containing inflation to some degree, minor and unsatisfactory as it may have been. The relatively modest price increases of 1971–1972 were in part associated with the wage-price controls instituted by Nixon at the time, but were clearly unsustainable in face of the gathering upward price pressures and had to be abandoned.[2] After averaging 10½ percent in 1973–1974 in response to the initial oil shock, the annual inflation rate fell back to a 5 to 7 percent range in the next three years. It did not burst forth more strongly again until the second oil-price shock toward of the end of the decade, when William Miller took office as chairman.

By that time, with monetary policy having shown no signs that it was determined to reduce inflation to more tolerable levels and efforts at money-supply targeting being viewed as a pretence, the Fed had almost completely lost its credibility as an inflation fighter in the market. The psychology of inflation expectations was becoming an ever more important element in the evolution of actual price increases and in complicating the Fed's efforts to control inflation.

Arthur Burns was the first chairman who had made his reputation as a professional economist. He had been a professor at Columbia, had headed the National Bureau of Economic Research, and had been chiefly known, at least in my mind, for his compilation and thoughtful assessment of U.S. business-cycle statistics and indicators. Burns, as I remember from discussions with him after he came to the Fed, seemed to have little use for theoretical analyses of the economy, whether Keynesian or monetarist, to explain its cyclical propensities.

Rather, he viewed each cyclical episode as embodying a unique set of events. One experience differed from the other by whatever particular imbalances—whether in inventories or other economic sectors—had arisen in the process of an economic upturn and leading, more or less unavoidably, to the succeeding downturn as the economy rebalanced itself in preparation for the next spurt forward.

In one of our many conversations on the subject of monetary policy (most of which were related to technical monetary operations of the day), Burns expressed strong doubt about whether one need worry very much about the particular amount or stock of money in the hands of the public (and thus by implication about the growth of money at least in the short term or perhaps even the intermediate term). After all, he said, the same amount of money could support either more or less economic activity. If the economy were strong, an existing stock of money would just be turned over more rapidly, with any rise of interest rates attributable to the strength of credit demand relative to supply.

His careful reading of business-cycle experience seemed to convince him that there was a powerful inner dynamic within the U.S. economy that was independent of monetary policy and of the level of the money supply within a fairly wide range. Such fairly relaxed views about the importance of money might well have also influenced his attitude toward the timing and intensity of policy adjustments (that one need not rush into things because any particular stock of money and credit supplied by Fed operations was not itself crucially important).

Burns's attitude toward money contrasted with the views of his at one time very good friend Milton Friedman, who emphasized the key role of money growth in affecting, with a lag, fluctuations in the economy. Thus, in Friedman's opinion, the Fed's effectiveness in smoothing out cyclical fluctuations in the economy was severely limited by its apparent, almost willful, lack of attention to the money supply. In my view, he may well have overemphasized the role of money in his eagerness to make his points clear to the public and Congress, but there was something to what he was arguing.

The effect of money growth on prices—with full effects tending to become evident with a lag of perhaps a year or two—was less subject to dispute. Even those who downplayed the causative role of monetary policy in the business cycle believed that inflation over the long run was a monetary phenomenon and, thus, the Fed's responsibility.

Although I knew something about Burns's professional economic reputation and contributions before he arrived, I knew nothing about his personality. It was rumored to be a bit on the rough side. Well, it was and was not.

I recall Chuck Partee, a man of considerable sangfroid, returning just the slightest bit shaken from his first meeting with Burns. Chuck apparently had mentioned a few problems about something our new chairman was requesting. Burns promptly informed him that he knew any number of economists available in New York who would be happy to come down and do the job here. Not so terrible really for a new boss who had already commanded a large research organization and was probably a bit uncertain about the quality and—more important in his mind, I suspect—the loyalty of the group he was inheriting; nonetheless, a bit crude.

Burns continued to be quite demanding professionally. He could be fearsome in questioning economists who made presentations to the board on various economic or other issues, especially if he sensed that the person did not have full command of his material. Not infrequently a lazy thinker, I personally found that working closely with Burns forced me to stretch and dig deeper to keep up my grades, as it were. He made me a better analyst—more precise and more willing to push thinking into third and more drafts before permitting something like satisfaction to set in. Although a taskmaster, he could also be very polite, even gracious, to those whom he viewed as having fully mastered their subject and who were usefully contributing to the task at hand (read, "ensuring that the chairman received all the support needed to help guide the board and the FOMC").

Nonetheless, he did have a temper, sometimes a fierce one. I came to believe that for the most part it was deliberately employed for purposes of control in interpersonal situations. The forcefulness and power of his temper were let loose mostly, insofar as I could see, in private or semi-private discussions. They extended in a degree to board and FOMC deliberations, but only through a covert sense that something might erupt, though at what potential peril one could not know. However, his temper did not seem to extend at all to a broader public stage, on which it ironically turned out to be really needed, if transformed constructively, in the conditions of the time.

He did not seem willing or able to step forward and make a strong effort at persuading the country or his colleagues to accept a broad program for action by the Fed to keep inflation more under control. There just did not appear to be a significant supportive constituency, and public enemies appeared to be much more vocal than supporters. Of course, he, as chairman of the Fed, necessarily talked a good anti-inflationary game. However, for the most part the talk consisted of proposing actions to be taken by other branches of government, such as reducing fiscal deficits and—especially in light of the failure of the Nixon wage-price controls—taking various measures to make pricing in the labor and product markets more flexible, all normal and perennial favorites of central bankers.

Key policymakers almost unavoidably take account of public and political responses to their policy stance in some degree as a matter of course, partly for personal reasons related to their own self-images and partly for policy reasons related to the broad public and political support needed to sustain the long-run effectiveness and viability of the institution they lead. Worry about such responses turns out to be more important for some leaders than for others. While all tend to be quite sensitive to the need for avoiding the unnecessary risk of making enemies in high places or broadly in the public sphere, the problem comes when they cannot quite take the risk of making such enemies when conditions warrant that they should.

Serious opposition to the policies that have been adopted is normally generated from a fairly diffused, generalized, and comparatively benign category of opponents. The "enemy" are to be found among a broad range of consumers, businesspersons, elected officials, and others who may at times object to a particular policy because of adverse economic and financial impacts in their areas or industries, making their feelings known through the large number of channels available in an open society.

The conflict takes place on a broad, public stage. It is widely known and publicized. Many people who will risk and even stage conflicts in their personal life are fearful of doing so in the public sphere, where they are more openly exposed. Shying away from public conflict, they then tend to miss the cues that call for risking bold policy action.

Nonetheless, even though Burns was not able to take on the public responsibility and conflict involved in implementation of a stronger anti-inflationary policy, he did, insofar as I could tell, resist pressures on him emanating from the Nixon White House. If memory serves, it was early in the run-up to the 1972 presidential election that the White House encouraged newspaper gossip that Burns was seeking a pay raise—an early "dirty trick," so it would seem. Those reports had no legs and faded away. Around that time, with the administration attempting to exert influence in any way it could, Burns asked Chuck Partee and me to go to the office of Peter Flanagan, an assistant to the president in the White House, to explain the technical side of monetary policy.

It seemed that the White House had somehow gotten it into its head that money-supply behavior was important to its reelection prospects. We were to explain how in practice money supply related and responded to the Fed's open market operations and how variable and uncertain was the connection, especially over the shorter run. I do not recall the details of our discussion. At any rate, they were certainly not received with any great interest and actually were, as it turned out, no more than tedious preliminaries in the meeting.

John Ehrlichman's arrival toward the end of our visit was the main event, unadvertised as it had been. He had something very definite to say to us.

His speech went something like this: "When you gentlemen get up in the morning and look in the mirror while you are shaving, I want you to think carefully about one thing. Ask yourselves, 'What can I do today to get the money supply up?'" That was it; that was why we were there—not to explain, but to hear.

Interest rates of course mattered much more politically than the money supply's day-to-day behavior because their effects on the economy and finance were more immediate and obvious. The White House people might have been very well aware of that, but, if so, were blessedly loath to embarrass all of us by mentioning it. Nevertheless, I also think they did believe that money-supply behavior in and of itself could be of some little importance to reelection prospects (perhaps because they were overly influenced by monetarist thinking in certain Republican political quarters). Odd it was: a state of mind that saw far too many trees that needed tending, some of no real consequence to the very short-term health of their political forest.

Be all that as it may, to the extent that Burns manifested his considerable qualities as an actor, it was, as noted earlier, in roles assumed on an interpersonal stage, not on the larger public stage. Burns's artistry took the form of deliberately employing a heightened form of anger at certain times when this interpersonal stage setting called for a kind of drama. A number of instances of what I believed were role-playing anger remain in my memory. It may not have always been role-playing, of course. Anger as a trait seemed to be a feature of Burns's basic temperament, and it was not always controllable. I mention here only one instance, a relatively mild example, which involved me personally.

Before sending the monetary policy alternatives to the FOMC via the blue book, I would as a matter of course show them to the chairman, who was chief executive of the FOMC and responsible for its proper functioning. None of the three chairmen with whom I worked very closely on monetary policy, including Burns, interfered in any way in the formulation of these alternatives. One and all recognized that the staff should objectively formulate policy alternatives that were realistically consistent with the ongoing discussions of and approaches to policy by all FOMC members. If the members began to believe that staff objectivity was being compromised by the chairman, not only would the staff's credibility be impaired, but also, and more important from the chairman's point of view, the backlash would greatly undermine his ability to exert any special influence on the outcome of policy deliberations.

Only once did Burns, in the privacy of his office, greet a particular set of policy alternatives proposed by the staff (in essence me, though based on extensive discussion with other staff at the board) with a rather sustained burst of anger, claiming with drama and pungency that I was needlessly and thoughtlessly making his job that much harder. In those days, the policy specifications were based on expected relationships among various measures of the money supply and interest rates emerging during the period between meetings. Because both of us recognized that little could or should be changed in the presentation, which reflected essentially technical judgments based on past practical experience and a number of econometric models, a truly trivial, insignificant change quickly dissipated his anger (something like reducing a forecast of M1 growth over a two-month period from 10½ to 10 percent).

Burns was undoubtedly and genuinely disturbed by the policy problems and the probable bond, currency, and broader market disturbances that loomed ahead. He also recognized that the staff's judgments about future relationships of the key variables could very well be wrong, as they often were.

Nonetheless, even though the staff was projecting financial relationships where the range of estimating error was unavoidably quite large, it was up to policymakers, not the staff, to make the very difficult practical decision of determining which actual emerging behavior of money supply or interest rates would in any event be desirable or acceptable in light of policy's broader and longer-term economic goals. It was not up to the staff to shade their best judgment about likely money-supply and interest-rate tendencies, given existing economic and financial conditions, in order to make the FOMC's or chairman's job of policymaking easier.

The intensity of this chairman's reaction represented a response made, I suspect, somewhat half-heartedly and out of habit—the actor responding rather automatically in an interpersonal context to cues suggesting that life was going to become very troubled and in the hope that his acting skills might alter the situation. He had not come to a considered judgment about the need for this particular scene. He quickly subsided when he had an excuse for realizing the pointlessness of the act. Perhaps I am being naive, but it is also my belief, based on eight years of close contact with Burns, that he neither wished for nor expected the scene to exert any undue influence on the staff's continuing professional judgment about current and prospective financial relationships that were crucial to the discussion and formulation of monetary policy at the time.

As inflation intensified in the 1970s, the economic cues calling for action were apparent. He recognized the economic problem, of course, and took some positive steps, but he was unable to respond in any creative or charismatic way, as noted earlier. For instance, it was not within his character to attempt to exercise powers of persuasion and logic dramatically and compellingly enough in public speeches and congressional testimony so as to evoke the public support that might have made it easier for the Fed itself to pursue a stronger anti-inflationary policy.

Such an approach might have altered policy to some degree if it could have helped change the political and social attitudes of the period, including prevailing economic beliefs and themes that have a powerful determining influence on the range of options that policymakers admit as practical possibilities. Stated that way, the task may seem too Herculean, but the effort remained worthwhile and, if it had been undertaken during the 1970s, might just have influenced a few key people. It is notable that in the Per Jacobsson lecture that Burns delivered shortly after leaving office—a famous lecture series at the annual International Monetary Fund meetings in which notable speakers are expected, among other things, to distill for those still in power the wisdom from their past experiences—he emphasized how a country's monetary policy is almost necessarily limited by conditions generated from the political, philosophic, and social ethos of the time.[3] Quite possibly true, certainly to a degree, but his statement was also perhaps either a recognition that he had not risen to the occasion or a rationalization for not having done so.

It was not that Burns, like almost every other chairman I observed in action (except one whose personality was simply too alien to the structure), did not make a, sustained effort to be a leader and to influence policy decisions made by the FOMC. He most certainly did. Without such efforts by a chairman, policy formulation tends to become even more of a mushy compromise and less effective in meeting the country's needs. Burns worked hard at it. But his actions were, as the now common expression has it, "inside the box." They were basically maneuvers, not a grand performance that might have persuaded an audience (his fellow policymakers, for instance, not to mention the country as a whole) to see the economy and policy from a paradigmatically different viewpoint.

Burns's policy influence, also like every other chairman's, was inescapably limited because the eleven other voters on the FOMC had independent views and oaths of office that they took very seriously. A chairman did have a bit more leverage as compared with other members because he had the task of presenting and defending the policy before Congress and to the public. As a result, the FOMC gave a little—sometimes very little—more weight to his views, in part, I believe, on the grounds that he should not needlessly be saddled with a policy he could not convincingly defend.

If a chairman is fortunate enough to accrue more and more public credibility as time went on, as did Volcker and later Greenspan, his personal influence would be enhanced, but it would still be more limited than most of the public seems to think. Moreover, if he attempts to extend his personal influence on the formulation or implementation policy beyond what was acceptable to the FOMC, he may well lose much, if not all, of the additional power he has accrued. However, if a chairman never makes a special and personally convincing effort to exert leadership, he will rapidly become a neuter and no more relevant to policy than any other committee member—and possibly even a bit less so because he will have lost some respect as a result of his failure to fulfill a role traditionally allotted to and expected of him.

I observed instances when a chairman successfully added to his capacity to influence policy or overreached and lost power or underreached and did not achieve the power or influence the office merited. Outcomes were affected by a chairman's sensitivity to the dynamics of a bureaucratic process, to the nuances of policymakers' motivations and self-images, and to a sense of limits. It is not too much of a stretch to interpret such a sensitivity, which for best results required an intuitive and almost poetic feel for a situation, as evidence of the need for an artistic side to a chairman's persona—though artistic in a minor key perhaps.

Thinking back, I would say that Burns and Volcker's personalities were too strong in their very different ways to make effective use of such minor arts. It was not really in them, and their colleagues perceived them as domineering. These chairmen were able to play the leads on the stages suitable to them, but they were not as sensitive as they might have been to the temperament and feelings of their fellow voters on policy, who often feared that they were deemed to be no more than a supporting cast.

All chairmen did engage in bureaucratic ploys of one sort or another, some more successfully than others. Burns initiated a few positive and lasting changes in the format of FOMC discussions, mostly to make them more free flowing and to the point. For instance, almost immediately after taking office, he changed the meeting's traditional set order of initial presentations about the economy, most of which had been read from prepared texts by board members and reserve bank presidents in fixed rotation. The latter generally had included in their presentations a quite dull and not too relevant description of regional economic conditions and statistics. Instead, Burns asked to have these regional presentations submitted in writing prior to the meetings; they were collated and distributed with a red cover to all members.

Later in the 1970s, as one of the Fed's first responses to the increasing demand by Congress and the public for more openness in policy, that particular document was made public about two weeks prior to a meeting. It was chosen largely on the grounds that, of all the material submitted to the FOMC, it gave the least insight into policy considerations. The color of the cover was changed to more neutral beige, it being deemed that, in those Cold War days, red simply would not do.

At an FOMC meeting, the evaluation of conditions in the national economy and prospects for the future—which included a presentation about the economy from the head of the research staff—was then followed by discussion of the appropriate policy response, the main business of the meeting. The gathering culminated in the committee's discussion of and votes for a particular policy directive (to be implemented by the system account manager at the New York Fed) proposed by the chairman and seeming to represent majority opinion. The directive was usually one of the alternatives originally presented by the staff or a modification thereof. It was also one that seemed most likely to be adopted with very few dissents if any. The wording might need a little more tuning for that. The chairmen I knew generally abhorred dissents, some much more strongly than others, but all preferred only one or two at most because a large number of dissents reflected badly on the chairman's stature—that is, on the public and congressional belief that he was the prime mover in monetary policy.

In Volcker's time, the discussion of a particular policy directive generally took place after a coffee break. He used the break as an opportunity to consider which policy alternative or possible modification was likely both to get committee approval and to reflect his own preferences. As evidence that the committee's decision-making process was far from cut and dried or preordained, I remember some one-on-one conversations during those breaks where Volcker would ask my opinion about the probable policy outcome (this was after the committee had already discussed the economy and policy issues for two hours or more). I would then make some response, not infrequently with some uncertainty; he seemed no more certain; and we would go on from there to no very clear conclusion.

In attempting to micromanage the policy decision, Burns employed a variety of minor tactics. He sometimes kept the committee in session without a coffee break. On occasion, if the committee was being especially obdurate, he would also ignore the usual time for lunch breaks should the meeting last that long—on the theory, I suppose, that an opportunity to relax over lunch would tend to dilute the energy behind and the persuasiveness of his arguments (sandwiches would instead be delivered to the meeting).

A bit more than other chairmen, Burns also was not averse to structuring meetings so as to minimize influences that might conceivably infringe on his ability to influence the policy outcome or that might divert the committee's energies and time toward topics that were not central to policy. He did away with oral presentations on international issues and conditions (except for the report on exchange-market conditions regularly given by the officer in charge of foreign-exchange operations in New York). I presume he believed that they were not central to policy (which they clearly were not in those days), took up precious time at the meeting, and offered the remote possibility that some members might be unduly influenced by irrelevant information and opinions. He also requested me to inform the manager for domestic operations at the New York Fed that he was to shorten his presentation, to confine it to past operations, and not to speculate on future money-supply or interest-rate behavior. All of these changes made a certain amount of sense to me, in part, I suspect, because my role was left inviolate and in some way enhanced by the subtraction of others' roles.

But I underestimated how far the chairman was willing to go to purify the policy discussion of, to him, extraneous and potentially dangerous influences. At one point, Burns in private suggested that my oral presentation on the domestic policy alternatives—obviously at the core of policymaking, not a sideline like international issues—was unnecessary, that I had said all that was needed in the blue book circulated prior to the meeting. Gadzooks! He had a point, of course. Nonetheless, it was still quite an unexpected blow for someone who well knew that loyalty to the chairman (along with objectivity in relation to the committee) and evidence of the chairman's confidence were the sine qua non for survival in my position and more particularly for the kind of stature and influence that would make survival enjoyable.

As noted earlier, I was responsible for the policy document. After I reached a high enough level on the staff, it had become traditional for me also to make an interpretive oral presentation about the policy alternatives and respond to any technical questions committee members might have. Naturally enough, this presentation took place just prior to the committee's own policy discussion.

Unfortunately for me, Burns had decided to make his own introductory comments about policy as a way of starting off the discussion and, to the extent that he could, of defining its parameters. In his mind, therefore, there was always some risk that Axilrod's preceding presentation would muddy the waters and potentially dilute his influence on policy. Needless to say, in my view it certainly would not because I was well aware that it was not my role to provide background interpretations that distinctly favored one policy alternative over another.

Although interpretive analysis might make one alternative sound better than others, given the existing market situation, it was nonetheless very unlikely, indeed almost unthinkable, that it would be one unacceptable to the chairman. As a matter of fact, one committee member once quietly praised me for presentations that often subtly led the group toward what seemed to be the chairman's view (or something very close to it). Knowing that man very well—he was both very ambitious and somewhat innocent—I very much doubted that he was being ironic.

In any event, I demurred from Burns's suggestion that there was no need for my oral presentation at the meeting, averring, as I remember, that it was a useful supplement and helpful to the committee—all the while thinking that I certainly wanted to avoid such a blow to my considerable prestige within the Fed. He did not press the point at the time. A few weeks later, a special meeting of the FOMC was quickly called in between regular meetings because of a sudden shift in economic and market conditions. In part because of time constraints, much less documentation than usual was prepared. The policy alternatives were presented quite summarily in a very few pages without the traditional blue cover.

Given the meeting's special and rather obvious purpose, Burns told me that there would be no need for my oral presentation. To my mind, the camel's whole head was now under the tent, not merely its proverbial nose. But help unexpectedly arrived. In the course of the meeting, just as the discussion of the economy concluded and Burns turned to policy without referring to me, one of the more independent-thinking governors, Andy Brimmer, asked if we were not going to hear from Steve. "Why, of course," said the chairman, as if it had been planned all along and had just momentarily slipped his mind. I went along with the gag by staring at a blank piece of paper and making a valiant effort to look as if my presentation had been written out (as it always had been). The chairman thanked me fulsomely. A day or two later, I met Andy in the corridor, and he asked if I had really prepared a briefing. I said no, and he said, "I thought so."

That was the end of it, or so I figured. But Burns persisted. He raised the subject with me again. I finally took my best shot. "Mr. Chairman," said I, "I know you have confidence in me, but if I do not make that presentation before the committee, Mr. Holmes [then the high official at the New York Fed who was designated to implement the committee's policy in the market and with whom I spoke at least two or three times per day] will no longer really believe that I have your confidence, no matter what is said. He will no longer believe that you back what I say. I will not be able to influence him as you might want."

I do not remember my exact words, of course, but they were to that effect. Burns said nothing in response, and the subject never came up again. This whole episode was conducted most politely. I evidently did not prove to be such an interpersonal threat or irritant that would represent a cue for the actor to stage a fearsome performance, but it was another example of what every bureaucrat at the Fed must surely know: your degree of influence depends on whether the chairman appears to be on your side and, most important, on the extent to which he himself is a strong leader.

During that period, I used to joke that I had the simplest job of the top three staffers on the economics side. I just had to communicate a few times a day with the FOMC's manager for operations in New York and make sure that he took no market action that conflicted, in the chairman's view, with the policy adopted by the committee. Burns, like other chairmen, believed that his position called for him to be the guardian of and ultimate arbiter in interpreting policy once it was adopted. Over the years, this attitude gave rise to some conflicts between the chairman and other FOMC members, though surprisingly few in my experience. But

Burns also wanted to be certain that the manager in New York clearly understood and accepted the chairman's paramount role. The manager in practice did, though there was possibly space for a little "legal" doubt because the policy directive was officially issued to the Federal Reserve Bank of New York as agent for the FOMC.

To make sure that the manager understood the practical situation, Burns very early in his tenure had me call and inform the manager that the views of the president of the New York Fed, the account manager's immediate boss and also vice chairman of the FOMC, merited no special consideration in deciding on daily operations. This action reflected the chairman in a normal bureaucratic mode, no need for drama at all. Indeed, he was simply participating in what had been a long-standing internal struggle for dominance within the Federal Reserve System between the Board of Governors in Washington and the Federal Reserve Bank of New York, the Fed's operating arm in domestic and foreign-exchange markets. Burns apparently wanted to be doubly certain that the Washington side had indeed won the struggle.

All of the worry about how to make sure that Washington and not New York was the center of interpretive authority in implementation of the policy directive is now ancient history. Since my day, the FOMC has made it virtually impossible for current policy operations to be misinterpreted by the public or to be fudged in one direction or another either by the account manager (that battle was won early in Martin's tenure) or by the FOMC chairman (an issue that never quite died even into Greenspan's tenure).

The specification of monetary policy's current operating objective was finally clarified about as much as it could be for the public in 1994, almost halfway through the Greenspan period, when the FOMC took to making a public announcement of its policy decision immediately after its meeting. Moreover, the decision was clearly represented by a single money-market interest rate, the much aforementioned federal funds rate, so that there could be no room for interpretation by the account manager in New York or for mistakes in the timing or size of operations that might in turn lead to market misinterpretations of policy decisions, as had occurred on an occasion or two in the years before the policy decision was immediately announced.

But back in earlier days under Burns and later under Miller and Volcker—well before immediate announcement of the operating objective—one of my principal roles as a high-placed attachment to power was to ensure that the policy process functioned cohesively and efficiently and also, to be sure, as consistent with the chairman's role as chief arbiter in interpreting the FOMC's policy decisions. Apart from questions about policy implementation, it was always up to a chairman to consult the committee as required if he thought the direction of policy should be changed between scheduled meetings. The committee sometimes gave him discretion to alter the policy stance by a little without consultation. Needless to say, there was a time or two when some committee members and the chairman disagreed, politely but not without a little sense of contention, about when consultation was required.

It was not always easy to know when consultation was necessary. In Volcker's time, I remember one day carefully poring over with him the literal transcript from the tape kept of FOMC meetings—I was also secretary to the committee as well as staff director by that time—to see if the previous meeting did or did not provide him with a certain minimal flexibility to alter policy before the next meeting. We could not come to any definite conclusion. Discussions can be vague, tape systems do not always clearly pick up everything said, and transcribers with the best will in the world sometimes do not get what is or might be there.

In any event, bureaucratic maneuverings of one sort or another do not control inflation. That takes a distinct and determined shift in policy. As inflation worsened in the 1970s, some constructive policy innovations did indeed occur in the Burns period—some, after 1974, in response to action by the Congress. However, consistent with his personality and the times, they were incremental and stopped short of drama on the public stage. They also stopped short of significantly reducing inflation, though they dulled it some.

During the 1970s, the Fed responded to the growing pressure for giving money supply more prominence in policy by adopting ranges for money growth in formulating monetary policy and by making the behavior of money a little more influential in ongoing policy operations in the period between meetings. This step was indeed small and in practice no more than minimally effective.

Money-market and bank liquidity conditions, characterized in particular by the federal funds rate, remained the day-to-day operating targets for the Fed. However, the policy directive adopted by the FOMC for the period between meetings came to permit minor additional changes in the overnight federal funds rate above and beyond the initial rate indicated at the meeting. The relevant phrase in the policy directive was known as the proviso clause. It permitted the funds rate to be raised or lowered a bit further if money growth during the period between meetings deviated by some unacceptable amount from the particular ranges anticipated for that intermeeting period.[4]

Complicating, if not diluting, the whole procedure was the fact that the particular range for that operating period normally differed, sometimes substantially, from the longer-run growth rate of money that could be considered, whether in prospect or in retrospect, to be satisfactory enough. In any event, it was not until about midway through Burns's tenure that annual target ranges for money were formally put in place.

In response to the passage of House Concurrent Resolution 133 (something of a triumph for the monetarist staff on the House Banking Committee), the first "year" for which monetary targets were "established" covered the period from March 1975 to March 1976. One-year targets based on each quarter of the year were subsequently put in place. Thus, four new one-year targets were set in the course of each year. Starting with the year ending with the fourth quarter of 1979 (consistent with provisions of the Full Employment and Balanced Growth Act of 1978, often termed the Humphrey-Hawkins Act), monetary targets were set and pertained only to calendar years.

Giving more emphasis to money growth in policy during the decade of the 1970s was not as innovative as it seemed, for several reasons. First, the potential for change in the targeted money-market rate during the interval between FOMC meetings remained limited, generally to either half or three-quarters of a percentage point. Second, we developed at the Fed a number of different money-supply measures, somewhere between three and five at one time or another, that were used internally in varying degrees and also made available to the public, quite probably in the hope that the actual growth in at least one or two measures would turn out to be within the Fed's indicated ranges or could be deemed as satisfactory. Internally, though, the emerging behavior of M1 traditionally carried the most weight for making operational decisions. Third, in any event, the indicated money ranges were not firmly held as targets because the ranges set for a year ahead were rebased every three months, in effect forgiving the actual outcome of the preceding period.

One of the Fed's more determined anti-inflationary governors, Henry Wallich (who frequently cast a dissenting vote), in his speeches helped popularize the notion of base drift to describe this procedure. Needless to say, this description did not help the Fed's credibility. It became apparent that in setting the next annual range, the Fed was not attempting to offset the preceding overshoot (or undershoot, as the case might be). The annual ranges seemed to have no practical significance.

Apart from questions raised in the market's mind about whether the Fed was sincere in its efforts to control money, given what seemed to be an operational approach that looked half-hearted at best and rather deceptive in the bargain, the Fed was also confronted during the decade of the 1970s by difficult analytic questions about the significance of a series of innovations in banking markets. These innovations appeared to be altering historical relationships between money measures and the Fed's ultimate economic objectives of price stability and economic growth.

As it turned out, especially for growth in money narrowly defined as currency and demand deposits (M1), money grew noticeably less in some years (1975 and 1976 come particularly to mind) than would have been expected from historical relationships between money and income given interest rates of the time. Some economists used the phrase "the case of the missing money" to identify the issue.[5]

It took a while for the full dimensions of the problem to be realized. Interest rates had risen rather sharply in 1973 and 1974 around the time of the first oil shock, the powerful inflationary thrust it generated, and the Fed's efforts at containment. During the next two years, interest rates subsided, as did inflation, in the wake of the extended recession (sixteen months according the National Bureau of Economic Research business-cycle reference dates) following the oil-price shock. However, both remained at advanced levels compared with the postwar period through the mid-1960s. Also, especially at the longer end of the yield curve, they remained stubbornly higher than in the more turbulent second half of the 1960s as inflationary expectations began to pervade markets.

Expectations that interest rates would remain on higher ground were strongly influencing depository institutions and their customers. Customers became more and more unwilling to hold funds in deposits bearing either no or relatively low regulatory ceiling interest rates compared with higher market rates available, for example, on short-term Treasury bills and commercial paper. Indeed, a reevaluation of cash-management techniques by businesses and others was widely taking place.

At the same time, improving financial technology made it easier and economically feasible for depository institutions to retain customers in face of the market's increasing attraction. Cleverly designed instruments that could pass muster with regulators were put on offer—such as interest-bearing savings accounts with telephonic and preauthorized transfers into then non-interest-bearing demand deposits, which at least gave the customer the benefit of some monetary return while preserving easy access to checking account services.

The process of market adaptation and innovation rolled on for another decade or so, deepening and becoming ever more widespread, culminating in a proliferation of money-market accounts against which checks could be written and offered by mutual funds, securities firms, and others. Finally, by around the mid-1980s, in the interest of market efficiency and competitiveness, ceiling rates on all types of saving and time deposits were finally abandoned completely, and explicit interest on checking accounts came to be permitted.

The mid-1970s was still early in the transformation process, however. To begin getting a handle on the extent to which structural changes in finance and banking posed a problem for interpretation of money-supply figures, the Fed undertook surveys of varying degrees of formality through its regional contacts with banks. In addition, econometric equations relating money to income and interest rates over a long time span were carefully monitored to see if and to what extent the demand for money might be shifting away from past norms.

I remember that an early estimate based on information obtained from a sample of banks suggested a shift in funds out of money (M1) equivalent to about two percentage points. As time went on, money demand equations estimated for the whole economy suggested an even larger shift on the order of three to four percentage points in each of the two years 1975 and 1976.[6] That is, the equations predicted significantly more money growth than was actually occurring.

Taking such a large shift of preferences into account, the Fed's monetary policy was much more expansive than thought. For instance, the actual growth of M1 averaging around 5½ percent a year in those two years would have practical effects on economic activity and inflation more consonant with growth on the order of 8 to 10 percent once allowance was made for the shifts out of cash that were attributable not to any lessened desire for instant liquidity but rather simply to the availability of new cash-management techniques. These developments were not ignored as they were occurring, but it naturally took some time before they could have any kind of real impact on policy formulation. There were unavoidable bureaucratic lags.

Subjectively speaking, I would guess that it might have taken at least up to a year before the staff felt reasonably certain that a shift out of money of lasting significance for the formulation and interpretation of monetary policy was in fact taking place. A failure of money-demand equations to predict the actual money-supply growth (within an acceptable range of error) for a quarter, given interest rates and income, was not particularly unusual; the failure was not extremely unusual for a full year; as it consistently extended into a second year, one was literally forced to stand up and take notice.

Then, of course, there was a further lag before policymakers themselves might be convinced of the policy significance of the new institutional developments. Indeed, actual M1 growth for the two years 1975 and 1976 turned out to be running generally within the targets adopted for it, so that there was little incentive by harassed policymakers to believe ill of such figures. Anyhow, real GDP growth was still on the weak side in the early part of those two years before resuming its pre-oil-shock rise—more reason for policymakers not to worry too much about such seeming technicalities as money demand shifts.

More weight was given to M1 in policy operations at the time than to broader measures such as M2, as previously noted, because the latter included funds held for purposes of longer-run saving rather than for financing nearer-term transactions. But, as it turns out, the broader measure—which included time and savings deposits as well demand deposits and thus was not affected by shifts of funds out of demand into such deposits—was probably a much better reflection of the expansionary force of monetary policy in the 1975–1976 period. This measure's growth had accelerated rather sharply into the low double-digit rates.

At the same time, in discussions about whether policy was too tight, too easy, or just about right (it always seemed to be the latter once policy was put in place), there did not seem to be much consideration, if any, of the real federal funds rate (the nominal rate set by the Fed less the concurrent increase in the average price level for goods and services) as an indicator of the policy's stance. As noted at the beginning of this chapter, the expansiveness of monetary policy would have been very clear if it had been judged by the real funds rate, which was negative on average (and therefore quite expansionary by historical standards) in the 1975–1976 period. It remained negative or around zero over the balance of the 1970s as inflation persistently rose, stimulated greatly by the second oil-price shock toward the end of the decade.

By the time that shock hit, Burns had left the board. He was not reappointed by President Carter as chairman when his term was up in early 1978. He was, I believe, disappointed, though that response was not very evident to the outside world. Among my last conversations with him, he did ask if there was anything he could do for me before leaving, though he quickly noted that there was not much time left to get any significant change through the board. He seemed a little sad, a bit deflated. I demurred, merely saying that I had enjoyed working with him and thought that I was in a pretty good position to work with the new chairman.

A high-level political appointee of Carter's later told me that they could not understand how Burns could have expected to continue on in the new administration. Neither could I, but not because I thought the outcome of policy was unconscionably far beyond the pale at the time. He probably did about as well as, or maybe only a little worse than, any other likely choice would have done in the circumstances. Policy just looks much worse in retrospect from the perspective of almost three decades of reasonable price stability.

I simply thought that a new Democratic president would be much more comfortable with his own appointee in charge of the Fed. In any event, Arthur Burns had not achieved the kind of public stature that would make it difficult to replace him. Confidence in both domestic financial and foreign-exchange markets remained quite shaky because of the persisting inflation-bred uncertainties that the Fed had failed to subdue under his leadership.

Carter chose G. William Miller to be chairman of the Fed. Burns, a good soldier, kept saying, when the opportunity arose, that the president had chosen "wisely and well."

4

The Miller Interlude

During Bill Miller's year and a half in office, the Fed's credibility in markets was further eroded as inflation intensified, impelled in part by the second oil-price shock. The belief that the Fed's commitment to monetary targeting was essentially a sham became more pervasive. Doubts about the Fed's anti-inflation credibility were adversely affecting both the domestic and the international value of the dollar. At home and around the world, the belief grew that U.S. dollars were a depreciating asset. Something rather dramatic and ultimately convincing had to be done.

This something was not accomplished under Miller and, given his temperament, probably could not have been. He was an extremely smart and able man, but central banking, central bankers, and the ins and outs of monetary mechanics and policy just did not grab him where he lived. Although he had been for some time on the Board of Directors of the Federal Reserve Bank of Boston, he never quite seemed comfortable with the give and take of negotiating monetary policy at the Board of Governors of the Federal Reserve System in Washington. Prior to his appointment as the Fed's chairman, he had been the successful chief executive of Textron, a large conglomerate of the day. I assume that, as CEO, he had become accustomed to feel that the reins of authority were securely in his hands, that he understood how they needed to be tugged for the race to be won, and that it was in his power to do so with no more than a minimum of interference.

The situation at the Fed in Washington must have seemed very different to him, or so I imagine. The whole monetary policy process involved a bureaucratic apparatus that was unfamiliar and in many ways trying. Depending on whether a decision was to be made by the board or by the FOMC, either six or eleven other people beside the chairman had an equal say in it. His colleagues' underlying motivations often were not clearly expressed, if expressed at all. Implementation of a decision relied on policy levers that—because of economic uncertainties, market complexities, unpredictable attitudinal shifts, and long lags—were not well or clearly linked to the institution's ultimate objectives. Even if long-term goals might be easily stated (it took no effort to favor price stability and growth, for example), how to approach them, what objectives should be emphasized in the nearer term, and how best to reconcile possible conflicts among them were always up for negotiation.

As I recall, in one of our first conversations Miller seemed to be suggesting that the board needed an overall chief of staff. I explained that was not in our tradition. The organization in place was basically one in which the board looked for staff leadership to individuals separately responsible for each significant area of activity. Individual board members also had a degree of administrative oversight, formal or informal, for certain areas. There was no need for a chief of staff to oversee the work. Power was diffused, but incentives for cooperation were clear and effective enough among the staff and were built into tradition and board oversight. That was how the board seemed to want it. After my explanation, Miller said something to the effect that our conversation might be sufficient. If there was a more aggressive subtext in that comment, I never really acted on it.

Once, under Burns, the board secretary at the time (Bob Holland, who later became a governor) was apparently given—or so it was perceived by the rest of the staff—the authority to act as a staff chief rather than simply as the guardian of the schedule for issues to come to the board. From what I later gathered, the board as a whole did not take this apparent assumption of power well. The chairman had enough power without having it enhanced by a staff chief (beholden to the chairman) who might attempt, so the suspicion went, to control not only the scheduling, but also the content of material to be presented to the board for decision.

Shortly after Miller arrived, he did directly ask me to make an overt oral recommendation to the FOMC about which of the policy proposals before it should be adopted. Odd were the ways of the world. Burns had feared even a barely recognizable covert recommendation, and here was Miller more or less demanding an overt one. One man wanted as much control over the process as he could get; the other wanted, perhaps, a stalking horse. I thought that my making such a policy recommendation to the FOMC was a bad idea mainly for practical institutional reasons.

I had long believed that the FOMC staff should stay away from making definitive recommendations about whether overall monetary policy should be tighter, easier, or stay the same. Recommendations by staff on more technical issues—such as securities eligible as collateral for repurchase agreements or whether open market purchases should be made in short- or longer-term sectors of the market—were a different matter. But the FOMC's bureaucratic structure seemed to work most smoothly if the staff avoided making an overt recommendation on the guts of policy—that is, on whether bank liquidity and the related money-market conditions should be eased or tightened. Although the FOMC voters encompassed both the board members and reserve bank presidents, the principal economic, legal, and secretariat staff support for the committee was drawn from the Fed Board of Governors. It had always seemed to me that reserve bank members of the FOMC were sensitive to a perceived threat of policy dominance by the committee's Washington-based core. Some may have been overly sensitive, but I never thought they were entirely wrong.

In that context, the division of labor that seemed to work best for the committee's decision-making process was for the staff to focus entirely on its own objective assessment of the outlooks for economic activity and prices, and of the likely market and economic reactions to various policy options. There was no need for the staff to make policy recommendations. Live and let live. The committee did not interfere with us, and we did not interfere with it. The nineteen voters and potential voters who were designated by law to decide on policy certainly represented a sufficiently wide spectrum of opinion to cover all options and come to a decision that was well thought through. (For a while, Burns asked Chuck Partee, who was then number one on the staff, to give his policy preference at some point in the course of discussion. I never noticed that his contribution had any effect, good or bad. It just seemed useless.)

Despite all my instincts about what best suited the institutional situation, I felt that my relationship with Miller, which turned out to be quite good, would certainly get off on the wrong foot if I protested to him about making a policy recommendation at the FOMC meeting, something that very clearly fell into my bailiwick. Given his background in business and certain other discussions I had with him, I thought he would simply conclude that I lacked conviction or a willingness to take on responsibility. (Burns and Volcker regularly asked me in private for my own monetary policy view, which I gave frankly and readily, as I assume did other staff members who might also be asked. Other FOMC members generally were sensitive enough never to ask me for a policy opinion.) It should be clear that I did make specific policy recommendations within the different institutional structure of the Fed Board of Governors on matters within my province there—for example, on discount-rate and reserve-requirement questions, policy instruments still of some importance in those days and under the sole control of the board, not the FOMC.

In any event, my recommendations to the FOMC under Miller (they stopped with Volcker's arrival) were, as befit my position, well within the mainstream of Fed thinking at the time. They certainly did not advance the committee's capacity to think beyond its long-established norms. They were not especially useful. If they had been more adventurous—for example, argued for an even stronger anti-inflationary policy—maybe an eyebrow or two would have risen, but most likely to question whether the objectivity of my analysis of policy alternatives was in danger of becoming a bit suspect.

With monetary policy failing to take a stronger stance against inflation, the Fed's credibility in markets remained weak, especially so in the highly sensitive foreign-exchange markets where the dollar remained under attack. Efforts were continually being made through intervention in the exchange market to shore up the currency, as had been the case at times under Burns. Such efforts were at best usually no better than holding actions, if that.

In practice, the volume of dollars that foreigners and U.S. citizens could sell into exchange markets was almost limitless relative to the limited amount of foreign exchange that monetary authorities in the United States had available to acquire such dollars and to the amount of their own currency that foreign central banks and governments were willing and able to employ in buying the dollars without risking adverse effects on their own domestic policies. What was needed, of course, was a basic change in the stance of monetary policy that demonstrated a clear commitment to containing and actually reducing inflation—which, if convincingly implemented, would turn businesses and other exchange-market participants into much more willing holders of dollars.

The Fed was not yet in that mode, however. Instead, it continued with efforts to soften any damaging exchange-market effects of its domestic policies through use of direct intervention in those markets (sometimes unilaterally, but preferably and more effectively as part of multilateral cooperation). To enhance its ability to intervene in support of the dollar, the Fed had over time made efforts to widen its access to foreign exchange, most importantly by developing and expanding its so-called swap network with key foreign central banks. The network became quite extensive, including all the major developed countries and eventually a few others. Through it, for example, the Fed could obtain German currency (deutschmarks in those days) from the Bundesbank (the German central bank) by "swapping" dollars for them—something like a loan agreement in which German currency would be available up to an agreed amount with dollars used as collateral.

In that way, the Fed and the Treasury would have on tap from all participating countries a fairly sizeable amount of foreign currency (though still not much more than a drop in the huge market bucket) that could be employed to help support the dollar on exchange markets. This amount would help supplement the meager outright holdings of foreign exchange by U.S. monetary authorities (in this context inclusive of both the Fed's and the U.S. Treasury's monetary accounts).

With regard to the Fed's actions in and attitudes toward the foreign-exchange market, it should never be forgotten that the secretary of the Treasury had come to assume principal responsibility for intervention policies. By law, he could not control domestic monetary policy, of course, but he was by common consent the U.S. government official who had the final say on how or whether exchange-market operations should be undertaken in response to developing exchange-market conditions, in what currencies, and with what exchange-rate objectives, if any, in mind.[1] The Fed carried out operations both for its own account and as agent for Treasury accounts at the same time (with its own accounts normally taking the larger share), but the maximum size of operations in total was governed in the end by Treasury decision.

The Fed was in a sense the government's operating arm in this area, bequeathed more or less flexibility depending on the attitudes of the particular Treasury regime in power, though the Fed was not without independent influence. Especially in the years before the Reagan administration, the Fed did have a strong impact on the strategies adopted because of its closeness to and knowledge of the market. Moreover, no operation at all by the Fed for its own account could be undertaken unless it was authorized by the FOMC. This legal technicality helped to buttress the Fed's influence on governmental decisions and strategy in relation to the exchange market. But that the Fed would intervene for its own account without at least informing and seeking the Treasury's consent or refuse to intervene if requested by the government was not, in my view, very likely.

During the Reagan years, when Volcker was in charge of the Fed, the Treasury was philosophically predisposed against any market intervention (with an exception for force majeure, such as at the time of the assassination attempt). I remember calling the then Treasury undersecretary Beryl Sprinkel on any number of occasions (after first checking with Volcker) to suggest the usefulness of some exchange-market operations at a particular juncture. The invariable response was, "I'll check with Don (Don Regan, the secretary at the time) and get back." I would promptly walk down to Volcker's office to say that they weren't interested, but just didn't want to say no right away.

He knew that of course, as did I, before the call was made. Still, it seemed desirable to make them aware that sometimes the market could usefully be toned up a bit, especially, from my parochial viewpoint, if it involved an exchange-market transaction that phased in with our domestic security market operations. Once exchange-market attitudes got of hand, either on the bullish or the bearish side, experience suggested that intervention alone without supporting changes in monetary policy was not especially effective, and that unilateral intervention was in any event much less effective than multilateral action coordinated with other major countries.

It was in Miller's time that the United States attempted to increase the amount of foreign exchange available for intervention by issuing foreign-currency bonds, the infamous Carter bonds. This was done as part of a package (including also increased commitments under swap lines) put together in 1978, when another exchange-market crisis was brewing, in an attempt to encourage the markets to believe that the United States was really garnering enough ammunition to keep the exchange market under reasonable control.

Among the Carter administration's many missteps, the foreign-currency bonds are hardly a blip on the radar screen, but they left in their wake a feeling within that administration and other administrations that never again would such a politically ill-judged action be undertaken. It may have been a good idea financially, but politicians came to believe that it was tantamount to a public confession of failure by the government. It seemed to admit that the United States was without enough credibility to finance itself at home and that it was being forced to seek succor from, of all people, foreigners. Not a good posture politically.

I actually thought it was a pretty good idea at the time. I pushed it with Miller, but am not certain how it actually came to be supported by the government policymaking group responsible for putting together the package to support the dollar. At one point, the undersecretary of the Treasury, Tony Solomon, asked me to come over to his office. The purpose was to expose me to the views of senior Treasury officials who advanced arguments that such bonds were operationally very difficult to manage, of doubtful legality, and, in any event (as emerged mostly by implication), not really worth the effort considering their political risks. Upon returning to the Fed, I reported to Miller that the Treasury staff had put forth all their objections, but that they did not sound extremely convincing to me.

Either the next day or the day after, the package was announced, including in it foreign-currency bonds, although in practice no more than a relatively modest amount were actually sold in the German and Swiss markets. While I do not have first-hand knowledge about who in the administration was instrumental in the bonds' inclusion, I suspect the approach had the support of Charles Schultz, the influential head of the Council of Economic Advisers at the time, and perhaps of Tony Solomon. It looked as if the administration wanted to do everything possible to avert the prospect of a major foreign-exchange-market crisis. Its underlying fear concerned the strength of the domestic economy, and I tend to think that it feared that in an effort to thwart such a foreign exchange crisis, monetary policy might get too tight for its liking. Making some concession to the Fed's support of foreign-currency bonds might be viewed, so I imagine, as tossing a bone that might help keep monetary policy from tightening beyond the modest firming that was part of the broad intervention package under consideration.

It was also around this time that the Fed became involved in the issue of reserve requirements on so-called Eurodollars. They were deposits held in banks abroad that were denominated not in the currency of the local country, but in dollars. They had become very popular with British banks and were growing apace in Germany and certain other foreign countries. To foreign banks, the instruments were competitively attractive. By and large, they were not subject to reserve requirements, so that the foreign banks could offer a slightly higher dollar interest rate to the account holder than could be obtained in the United States, where banks had to allow for the cost of holding some of the funds placed with them in non-interest-bearing form to meet reserve requirements.

Some analysts of U.S. monetary policy felt that because Eurodollars were not subject to reserve requirements set by the Fed, they were outside the control of monetary policy and thus might weaken the Fed's control over inflation. But to others, including me, they did not seem much of a threat. They earned U.S. interest rates, so that whatever control the Fed had over such rates at home (through the knock-on effect from the influence of its open market operations on the federal funds rate) would also influence dollar interest rates on instruments issued abroad to virtually the same degree. Nonetheless, from the Fed's viewpoint, there might be something to be gained from placing reserve requirements on Eurodollars if the market came to perceive that the Fed was showing a bit more resolve as an inflation fighter—a small step no doubt, but with credibility so weak, any little step seemed helpful.

Miller was persuaded that the Fed should propose to the G-11 countries[2] that Eurodollars be subject to reserve requirements at least equal to the dollar reserve requirement on certificates of deposit held mainly by businesses at major banks in the United States. Although domestic monetary policy and exchange-market conditions were a concern, I have the distinct sense that an important impulse should be attributed to the Bundesbank. It was worried because many of its domestic banks were establishing subsidiaries outside the country—in, for instance, Liechtenstein—and thus evading to a degree its regulatory control. The United States was sympathetic in part because it wanted to encourage German cooperation in exchange market intervention.

The effort to persuade other major countries that reserve requirements should be imposed on Eurodollars was an interesting exercise, but doomed to failure. That inevitable failure was not quite as evident as it should have been at the beginning, though. Miller did get in touch with Fritz Leutwiler, head of the Swiss National Bank at the time and chair of the G-11 group of central bankers that would consider it. So far as I could see he encouraged Miller to bring the idea forward, or at least did not discourage him. However, he neglected to mention how strong the opposition was; he must have known, being very well connected for many years and considered to be something of a sage and an insider's insider by this point in his life.

I accompanied Miller to one of the group's regular monthly meetings held at the Bank for International Settlements (BIS) in Basel, Switzerland, where he was to introduce the subject. I was not in attendance at the meeting of principals, but the reception must have been cold and unsympathetic, if I can judge from the genuine fury of Miller's reaction when he exited the meeting. Perhaps his anger was more intense than it diplomatically should have been, but it was not unjustified because he must have felt that he had in effect been led up the garden path only to be presented with a bouquet of thorns.

In the end, the group decided to establish a committee to discuss Eurocurrency issues and their regulatory and other implications as a whole; it also agreed to a subcommittee that would focus on Eurodollar reserve requirements specifically. The secondary status of the Fed's proposal was thus clearly recognized. There was no broad-based sympathy for the idea, in large part because it was seen as an unnecessary regulatory and cost burden on foreign banks, which would reduce their edge in competing for large deposits against domestic U.S. banks. I am sure many could see little reason to introduce structural changes in their banking markets to suit the convenience of the Fed, which was viewed as not doing enough on its own to combat U.S. inflation and a weak dollar.

I was made chairman of the subcommittee. Alex Lamfalussy, then head of research at the BIS and designated to chair the parent committee, explained the committee structure to me in the course of a pleasant auto ride around Basle. He must have thought that such a quiet expedition, far from tensions pervading the meeting rooms, would help assuage the Fed's wounded feelings, or at least mine if I happened to have any. So far as I was concerned, his effort seemed unnecessary, though I understood that it was well meaning. In my recall, Bill never attended another session at the BIS.

Our subcommittee met at various times over a longish period and presented its report to the parent committee early in the Volcker era. As a technical matter, the subcommittee found a way, in the course of interesting and very pleasant technical discussions, to set up a viable reserve-requirement system for Eurodollars. Unfortunately, the system necessarily also involved reserve requirements on other Euro-currencies because, for example, a Euro-deutschmark, such as might exist in Liechtenstein, could easily be sold forward into dollars at the time of creation and thus in effect become a Eurodollar.[3]

The majority of the subcommittee voted against recommending the plan. That outcome was no surprise at all to any of us involved in the process. I was very well aware of the intensity of opposition from a number of quarters. Indeed, one person at a very high level seemed to believe that I personally was intent on undermining London as a center of banking (or so I came to be told on equally high authority). This belief seemed most odd to me.

That strange and unreal fears were at work, however, was brought home to me when a quite senior official from the Bank of England arrived in my office toward the end of one very hot summer day in Washington. He was evidently hurried and a bit discomforted from a long day of meetings. What he wanted to know was how we could make sure that anything as foolish as a Eurodollar reserve requirement would not be put in place. I ignored the peculiar use of the word "we" and explained that our group was working on a practical though complicated plan, but that, as he must know from his own people, there were not sufficient votes for recommendation.

He left, and I was left with uneasy feelings about the underlying sources of their very excessive worries. These worries were presumably dominated by the fact that the City of London was in those days about the only thriving part of the British economy, which was still in its pre-Thatcher doldrums. In such a situation, they feared any structural changes in banking that had the potential for being even the least bit damaging. Such a fear was understandable, of course, but attributing motives and so much personal influence to me specifically was not. It was not quite rational. In any event, the parent committee duly ignored the subcommittee plan and limited itself to prudential exhortations and data gathering, time-proven choices for evading contentious issues.

In August 1979, seventeen months after his arrival, Bill Miller left the board. He had accepted Carter's offer to become secretary of the Treasury.

I feel sure he was much happier and more productive in that position. It was much better suited to his temperament. Within the obvious political constraints, he could experience something like a hands-on effect at work. Specifics were more his thing. So far as I could see, he was very effective in implementing, for example, the financial aspects of the sanctions on Iran that helped lead to the eventual release of the kidnapped Americans held under duress in our embassy there. Monetary policy was just too amorphous for someone of his temperament, no matter how highly intelligent he was.

To replace Miller at the Fed, Carter nominated Paul Volcker as chairman. At the time, Volcker was president of the New York Fed. Perhaps more important, he had a strong reputation in international financial circles that stemmed mostly from his constructive work in the international area as undersecretary of the Treasury during the early 1970s. At that time, as noted in the previous chapter, the U.S. dollar was also under severe pressure internationally, and the gold standard of the day could no longer be held. His international reputation for soundness, high intelligence, and commitment to financial stability made in the process of the complex multi-country negotiations that ensued were, I would think, crucial to his appointment.

Markets were again roiling, and Carter's economic and political credibility were at or close to their lows. He needed someone like Volcker, whether that person was or was not well connected politically. I remember Volcker describing the appointment as a "bolt from the blue."

5

Paul Volcker and the Victory over Inflation

During Paul Volcker's eight-year tenure as chairman of the Fed, beginning in August 1979 and lasting until August 1987, policy changed dramatically. He was responsible for a major transformation—akin to a paradigm shift—that was intended to greatly reduce inflation, keep it under control, and thereby restore the Fed's badly damaged credibility. This transformation involved a new approach to open market operations that was designed to assure closer control over the money supply by focusing day-to-day operating decisions much less on interest rates and much more on an aggregate level of reserves, an approach that was in its full flower from late 1979 to late 1982.

It was an exciting period, and, as heightened by Volcker's artistic performance, it can also be called a glamorous time. I thought of myself as the chief engineer of a shiny new machine with enormous and as yet untried power. It was almost solely because of Volcker that this particular innovation was put in place—one of the few instances in my opinion where a dramatic shift in policy approach could be attributed to a particular person's presence rather than mainly to or just to circumstances.

He was the essential man for a combination of reasons. He combined great sensitivity to shifting trends in political economy (he could see what the country would now accept) with a willingness to take dramatic action. Moreover, he was technically very competent in the nuts and bolts of monetary policy, which made it much easier for the FOMC and the chairman himself to feel confident that the new approach, although not risk free, had a reasonably good chance of working.

Moreover, it was clear that the chairman could be relied on to exercise sufficient day-to-day oversight to ensure that policy, with its rather complex statistical underpinnings, was implemented as intended and was not, to put it delicately, overly interpreted by the staff. From Volcker's perspective, much more was involved than merely keeping informed. This was not only because of his personal temperament and strong technical background but also because he was very much aware of what was on the line for him as an individual, as well as for the institution he headed. Although he did not quite micromanage, his interest in policy operations might best be described as avid and, indeed, penetrating. From my perspective, that approach was a good thing. It made one feel like part of a very important, challenging, and nationally constructive moment.

Political, social, and economic attitudes supportive of a strong anti-inflationary policy were more apparent early in Volcker's tenure than they had been in Burns's. The costs of inflation had been becoming more and more evident to the public and, by extension, to politicians as the economy stagnated, jobs were lost to foreign competitors, and the real value of savings was eroded. With another foreign-exchange crisis also in process, it was left to Volcker, in the fall of 1979, to perceive that the time was ripe for dramatic action to contain inflation.

Because of such an attitudinal shift within society it was in a real sense easier for Volcker to take this stance than it was for Burns in his different circumstances. It was fortunate for Volcker and for the country that conditions had so changed that his capacities as an actor—which were well suited to a public stage—could be given full play in the new context. He was well prepared for the part. The stage was set for him, and he made the most of it.

On a private stage, Volcker, unlike Burns, was generally quite shy, one would almost say insecure, if that were not such an odd thing to say about someone who was so very intelligent and who exhibited a clear mastery over the tools of his trade as a central banker. Nonetheless, the combination of this odd sort of shyness-bred insecurity and remarkable intelligence on occasion manifested itself in an impatient sarcasm, followed, depending on his relationship with or respect for the other person, by a small retreat into a kind of sheepishness. None of that was evident, however, on the public stage.

There, Volcker the actor was in full display. He was totally in command of himself and the subject matter. He spoke with force and conviction. He responded to questions from Congress and the public with certainty—

perhaps not with total clarity all the time, but instances of obscurity for the most part seemed deliberate to me. If one contrasted this display with the shy, sometimes gauche, social and personal behavior of this extremely decent man, it seemed clear that he was a consummate actor taking on a part made for him.

Volcker, because of his background in finance, was intensely interested in the technical analyses that underlay monetary policy and its operations. So was Burns, by the way. I used to joke with a colleague or two that Burns and I had just spent another session rediscovering the wheel, but that was too flip an expression. He simply would not settle for fuzzy ideas and concepts or easy acceptance of the common wisdom. I also suspect that he wanted to be very sure that I, at the center of policy implementation and proposals, knew exactly what I was talking about. Volcker, in part because of his prior positions as Treasury undersecretary for monetary affairs and president of the New York Fed, brought with him a vast store of experience in aspects of banking and finance that were crucially connected with the Fed's operations. He had much more firsthand familiarity with the ins and outs of finance than did the other chairmen before or, indeed, after him.

This trait was especially important for the chairman to have at the time. The policy approach adopted by the Fed in the fall of 1979 and effectively abandoned in the fall of 1982—once inflation had been suppressed and the Fed had to turn its efforts to getting out of the recession at the time—was heretofore untried and rather complex in its mechanics. Moreover, the statistical basis for determining the target for reserve aggregates consistent with the FOMC's policy decision entailed considerable leeway for staff judgment. As noted earlier, I am not at all certain the FOMC would have adopted the approach if its members had not had great confidence in the chairman's ability to oversee the mechanism and the implied policy discretion that was necessarily required by ongoing statistical adjustments as new data became available.

Also, I rather doubt that any other chairman I knew would have proposed this approach to the FOMC because it required a willingness, in practice, to bow more strongly than the system ever had in the direction of the monetarists and thereby to revolutionize the Fed's approach to the market by giving up a substantial degree of control over money-market interest rates in the course of day-to-day operations. Indeed, Volcker had for some little time before he became chairman been advocating the value of practical monetarism as an approach to inflation control.

I do not intend to bore whoever happens to be reading this account with detailed technical explanations about how the Fed's approach to policy operations from 1979 to 1982 differed from what the Fed had done before and after, or for that matter how it differed from what has ever been done (to my knowledge) by any other central bank in history, except perhaps the Swiss Central Bank.

But some explanation of the methodology by which the policy was implemented cannot be avoided. It should help make the policymakers' motivations and worries more clearly understood. It should also provide a context for better understanding issues germane to the public's reception of and attitudes toward the policy, as well as the sometimes contentious interactions with professional economists at conferences, not to mention an occasional dig from behind the back.

It is well recognized in economics that one can control the price of a good or its quantity, but not both at the same time (except by coincidence).[1] Central banks throughout history have essentially, in one way or another, attempted to control the price of a good. Sometimes it was the price of gold, sometimes the price of foreign exchange, and sometimes the price of money (e.g., a short-term interest rate, chiefly the federal funds rate in the United States).

Prior to the Volcker policy change, the Fed had in essence been controlling the price of money for a number of decades—not always being very explicit, even to itself, about that or about which particular rate. In any event, with the price of money controlled, the amount of money in the economy depended on how much was needed by businesses and consumers at that interest rate, given the volume of economic or financial-market activity that had to be supported, as explained earlier in chapter 2. So if an inflationary amount of money was demanded because the public wanted, for example, to purchase more goods and services than could be readily produced, the Fed willy-nilly supplied it. This modus operandi encouraged, and sanctioned, the excessive rise in the average level of prices that characterized inflation, at least until interest-rate policy could be changed. In view of the innate conservatism with which policymakers wielded policy instruments available to them, interest rates were often changed too slowly, too incrementally, to avoid a buildup in inflation.

Under Volcker, for a three-year period during which inflation was wrestled to the mat, the Fed stopped aiming at the price of money and instead concentrated on deliberately limiting the amount of money in the hands of the public in a single-minded effort to curb upward pressure on prices of goods and services. As a result, if the public needed more money to finance spending than the Fed had targeted, interest rates would promptly rise (money would become more expensive) because the Fed would refrain from supplying the money through its market operations. (And vice versa: if the public wanted less money than the Fed was aiming at, interest rates would go down.)

In implementing this policy, the FOMC at each of its meetings would specify a short-term target path for money believed to be consistent with attaining a specified annual objective for money growth. The market manager in New York was then held responsible not for an interest rate, but for providing to the banking system an aggregate amount of reserves under his control (the nonborrowed reserves provided through open market operations) judged consistent with that money path. Under this approach, in the normal six-week period between FOMC meetings, the price of money (as indicated by the overnight federal funds rate) was permitted to fluctuate freely within a wide range (usually four percentage points from two up to two down around the rate at the time of the meeting, though sometimes the width of the range was six points), so that interest-rate changes over the course of a year could accumulate much more quickly than under the previous policy regime.

This new policy approach was "practical monetarism" at work. The hopes were that it would help overcome the Fed's loss of market credibility by demonstrating renewed and enhanced seriousness in the institution's approach to inflation control; that inflation would in practice come under control more quickly and more surely than otherwise as the policy was implemented; and that the potential for damaging economic side effects, such as deep recession, from a powerful anti-inflationary thrust to policy would be moderated as credibility was restored and business, labor, and financial markets adjusted rather quickly to expectations of lower inflation.

In the end, the inevitable recession was quite deep and lasting (divided into two tranches based on the generally accepted business-cycle reference dates published by the National Bureau of Economic Research), one of six months in the first half of 1980 and a second of sixteen months from around mid-1981 through late 1982. The first recession was related mostly, in my opinion, to the Board of Governor's acquiescence (hardly avoidable in practice) to Carter's request (politically inspired and economically unnecessary) for the imposition of credit controls.

These controls were announced in March 1980. I was in charge of staff work for preparing the nonbank part, including consumer credit controls in particular. Because we all were aware that the economy looked shaky at the time, the controls were written, or so we thought, in a way to avoid an undue drop in consumer spending. Unfortunately, consumers instead interpreted them quite adversely. By early summer that year, the controls were quickly dropped at the administration's request, as the presidential election date was closing in.

In the course of the two recessions immediately following the Fed's new, stern anti-inflation policy the rate of inflation dropped by more than was originally expected (at least by me). Moreover, the basis was laid for a long period of relatively well sustained economic growth through the end of the 1990s. Since then, this extended period of reasonably stable prosperity has come to be seriously threatened in the aftermaths of a misbegotten stock market bubble that burst at the beginning of the current millennium and of the severe overall credit market crisis of 2007–2009, when the collapse of a housing bubble and mortgage markets spread more broadly through unduly leveraged markets and financial institutions. The role of monetary policy in relation to these latter developments will be discussed in chapters 6 and 7 that evaluate, respectively, monetary policy under Greenspan and his successor, Bernanke.

Once the Fed had broken the back of inflation, it retreated from practical monetarism and returned, in effect, to close control of the federal funds rate. The initial retreat in the early 1980s was undertaken to keep the recession from worsening and to encourage a return to growth. However, as time went on, continued innovations in financial technology and unpredictable shifts in the public's attitudes toward money and near-monies made it increasingly difficult to settle on a satisfactory measure of money to guide policy—that is, a measure that seemed to bear a reasonably consistent and predictable relationship to economic activity and prices. Thus, the support for a monetarist or even for a quasi-monetarist approach to policy eroded. Money played a gradually diminishing role over the balance of Volcker's tenure and, as indicated earlier, just about faded out of the picture entirely by Greenspan's.

Back in late 1979, however, the new policy initiative announced by Volcker on Saturday, October 6, 1979, was revolutionary and unanticipated by the market. Many have wondered about the timing of the announcement and related matters. In October 2004, at a Fed conference celebrating the action's twenty-fifth anniversary, three economists presented a useful paper that examined the how and why based in large part on their reading of published commentary by participants and on a time line of events. At the same conference, I was invited to comment on their presentation. Thorough and fair as it was, it did not, from my perspective, give enough credit to the uniqueness of Volcker's personality and vision in the evolution of the policy. Also, it tended to give too much stress to particular market events instead of to the cumulative dangers from the markets' persisting instability and the Fed's declining credibility over time. It also tended to neglect the timing and impact of the bureaucratic and consultative process involved in clearing the decks for such a radical shift in policy and its processes.[2]

Insofar as the public was concerned, a new policy world was unveiled that Saturday when a special press conference took place in the very impressive board room on the second floor of the Board of Governors building in Washington, D.C. FOMC meetings were regularly held around the massive oval table that dominated the room and that seemed to exemplify at least solidity, if not quite authority.

From the doorway at one end of the room connecting to the chairman's office, three people emerged to face a large gathering of the financial press. The chief person was Paul Volcker, who stood a full foot taller than the two helpers flanking him—me in my capacity as the chairman's man who would oversee the practicalities of the new policy, and Peter Sternlight, who was to implement the new policy in the market in his role as the FOMC's account manager in New York. Our entrance is about all I remember of that press conference. It was a signal event, no doubt, but I recall nothing of what I heard, though something of what I felt. I mainly remember a feeling of bemusement at the symbolism of such a tall man flanked by two such short guys—the actor whose time on the main stage had come and the very small supporting cast he gave the appearance of needing.

Perhaps that sense of bemusement screened the rest from view, recognizing that it was not my scene. Moreover, my memories of events leading up to that scene are sporadic at best, for the most part being limited, egotistically enough but perhaps not so unusually, to those instances in which my personal involvement was outside the routine.

For instance, I at one point forgot that the full FOMC had been secretly convened that Saturday morning for a final vote on adoption of the new policy (a telephone conference call the preceding day had alerted the members, and they had also just received the staff memorandum presenting the details of the proposal). I was reminded of this sequence of meetings in the course of trading old war stories with Joe Coyne, who at the time was the board's assistant for public relations, on a trip back to Washington a few years after I had left the Fed to work on Wall Street. I had forgotten how really short the time span was between detailed presentation of the proposal to the FOMC, the vote on it, and its presentation to the public. In view of the extreme sensitivity of domestic and exchange markets at the time, the risk of leaks was being strictly minimized.

Going back somewhat further in time, I recall indicating to Volcker, shortly after he took office, that I had an idea how a policy aimed at a more direct and certain control of the money supply could be practically implemented any time he was ready to embark on one. It was not a great mystery. Some years prior to Volcker's arrival I had chaired a staff group that had examined the subject for an FOMC subcommittee (headed by Sherman Maisel, then a Fed governor) in Burns's tenure to study how its policy directive might be improved. The staff group had recommended that a growth rate in money supply, mainly M1, should be the principal operating objective for monetary policy for the period between meetings and that a reserve aggregate, in particular the nonborrowed reserves provided directly through open market operations, should be employed as the instrument of control—a recommendation that was not adopted by the subcommittee, which instead proposed (to no practical effect) another, and rather odd, reserve aggregate, reserves against private deposits, as its preferred operating instrument.

In any event, I cannot recall exactly when Volcker came back to me with instructions to begin thinking seriously about a practical program for implementation of a policy that involved the employment of reserve aggregates to control money. Surely we must have been discussing it in some depth for a while before I was told—a vivid memory—that I would have to remain in Washington and prepare a paper for the FOMC on the policy issues and mechanics of the proposed new policy rather than go to Yugoslavia for the annual meetings of the International Monetary Fund and the International Bank for Reconstruction and Development (where I would in any case be no more than a fifth or even a more distant spare wheel).

I remember incidentally that at one point in preparing this paper, I received a phone call from Air Force Two, the plane carrying Volcker (and other U.S. officials) to the meeting in Yugoslavia. The exact point of the call was a bit obscure, but I think it simply reflected Volcker's anxiety about such a momentous policy change. It was an enormous innovation for policy and certainly merited anxiety. He wanted to make sure that I was doing what had to be done.

I remember saying "yes" or "of course" as the conversation progressed. "Conversation" is not quite the right word to describe our exchange because there was so much static in the transmission that I was able to understand only part of what he said. I was not really certain about every word in the questions I responded "yes" to. The phone call left me with a nagging doubt, in those Cold War days, about whether communication between the president and our submarines and bombers near and around the Soviet Union was in fact adequate to the task should games of chicken and spying turn more serious.

The implementation of the new policy and the process of shifting the economy and financial markets to a more stable environment did not unfold as smoothly as we hoped. The country experienced temporarily very high and widely fluctuating interest rates, a sharp recession, and bewilderment from the misguided efforts at credit controls first requested and then rather promptly abandoned by President Carter, as earlier noted. It was a rockier ride than we had permitted ourselves to contemplate in advance.

Shortly after the new policy was adopted, at a usual weekly Board of Governors executive session in which current monetary operations were discussed, a governor asked me for an opinion on how high the federal funds rate might go. My answer was 15 percent; the funds rate at the time was, as I remember, about 8 percent. The governor blanched. I considered myself very brave. As it turned out, the funds rate, at its peak during the period, reached the neighborhood of 20 percent.[3]

Whatever policymakers' expectations and anxieties, for the policy to work most effectively it was clear that market participants had to believe that the Fed had truly changed its attitude toward the money supply and interest rates; that it would stick to its money-supply targets; and that it would really let rates fluctuate more widely, almost freely. Although the FOMC had initially established a four-point range for the funds rate at its policy meeting on October 6, the limits were subsequently widened for a while to a six-point range, as noted earlier. In any event, the limits were not viewed as absolute, but were taken to represent junctures at which the committee would have the opportunity to reassess progress and conditions. Generally, rates were not or did not need to be constrained—although I remember that during the Carter credit-control program, the funds rate dropped to the lower end of its initially adopted range for an intermeeting period, and the FOMC decided that it should not drop further.

Because the Fed had never given such free rein to money-market conditions and because its credibility was quite low, it would naturally take time to make believers of market participants. Moreover, the Fed's reputation for conservatism in its approach to policy, or to anything else for that matter, was a major obstacle to belief that a revolutionary change was taking place.

Shortly after announcement of the new policy, Arthur Burns (who was then resident at the American Enterprise Institute) invited me out to lunch. I remember mainly the drift of the conversation. He believed that we had overstated how radical the change in policy posture was. "You are not really going to be doing anything different from what we were doing," said he. "Yes, we are," said I, and I went through some of the technicalities that would ensure a very different, quantity-oriented approach to policy, which would lead to a previously unthinkable wide range of week-to-week fluctuations in the federal funds rate unconstrained by Fed intervention in the open market.[4] When the lunch broke up, I had the feeling that he only half believed in what I told him. In those early days, his belief might have even been higher than the market's.

The Fed's efforts to make the market as whole believe in the new policy's essential quantity orientation were not helped when, early on, one of our important officials in New York happened to say in the course of a public presentation that the Fed was in the process of "experimenting" with a new approach to policy. When Volcker heard that, he went ballistic, to put it politely. The idea of an "experiment" was anathema to him because it suggested a lack of conviction at the Fed and would most certainly not help us regain market credibility. I was promptly dispatched to

New York to give a presentation to a key market group—mainly the government securities dealers whose own operations were most immediately affected by the policy shift—designed to make them clearly understand that the Fed knew exactly what it was doing and that the new policy approach was durably in place.

Meanwhile, and much more important for the success of the new policy, as Volcker went around the country giving speeches, he almost always made a point of stressing that the Fed would "stick to it" (i.e., to the new money-supply policy). I initially thought he was overdoing it, but this emphasis turned out to be very necessary. The real aim of convincing the public, through both policy actions and rhetoric, that the new policy would stick went beyond the need to influence the attitudes of dealers in the money and securities markets. If the policy were to involve as little economic disruption as possible, business and labor would have to believe deep in their hearts that the Fed would not let up until inflation was restrained to a much slower pace. I took them to be Volcker's ultimate and most important audience because the more quickly lower inflation expectations worked to moderate pricing decisions and wage bargaining, the more likely that any ensuing economic recession would be less deep and shorter than otherwise.

Volcker and the policy succeeded in that goal to an important degree. Although the recession was hardly mild or short, as noted earlier, inflation turned out to drop more, and more quickly, than we had anticipated. In that regard, however, the Fed also owed much to President Ronald Reagan. His policy toward the striking air controllers at the time—standing against their wage demands and in effect breaking their union—quite probably was, through its demonstration effect, instrumental in the unexpected speed with which the wage-push side of inflation was restrained. This outcome made it easier to bring inflation down without an excessively prolonged period of economic weakness.

The short-term money markets fairly soon became convinced that we were in fact sticking to it, though it took longer for bond markets to be completely convinced. Money-market participants came to understand that if they could make a good estimate of the next weekly published money-supply figure, they would be able to anticipate interest-rate developments with much more certainty (because Fed operations were now designed to lead either to a rather quick rise of short-term rates if actual money growth was coming in strong relative to target or to a decline if growth was weak). The result was a boom in demand for economists trained in the Federal Reserve System.

A new profession, "Fed watching," was born, or at least its profile was raised noticeably. A number of staffers from the board moved to Wall Street—not the top leadership, but midlevel staffers who knew or could quickly learn how we estimated measures of money supply and bank reserves. As the money supply receded in importance, many of these people eventually maintained their highly paid foothold in the private sector by transforming themselves into more general economists and developing a patter good for customer relationships and the news media.

As time went by, the Fed seemed to be having more success in regaining credibility with markets than in convincing certain high officials of the newly elected Reagan administration that we knew what we were doing. The undersecretary of the Treasury for monetary affairs, Beryl Sprinkel, who was the main representative of monetarism at the policy level in the administration, was apparently the most concerned, so it seemed.

I had fairly close contact with Sprinkel because his main areas of responsibility included the government-securities and foreign-exchange markets, in which the Fed was closely involved. So far as I could tell, pleasant as he was personally, he almost could not bear the thought that control over the crucially important money supply was lodged in the independent Fed and thus outside the administration's oversight. Moreover, and much worse yet, he thought that we simply were not up to the task. He believed that our new method for controlling the money supply was flawed and would inevitably fall short, no matter our best intentions. He spent a great deal of time making public pronouncements in one form or another to the effect that the Fed was not performing as well as it should, thus to some degree undermining the credibility we were attempting to reestablish.

Meanwhile, a very informal interagency breakfast was organized in an effort to make him and the administration better understand what we were doing and how. The group—including representatives from the Fed, the aforementioned undersecretary, and a few other administration officials—was not supposed to discuss whether the policy stance was appropriate, but to focus on the engineering.

I have no idea who initiated the breakfast. All I remember is Volcker one day telling me that there would be such a regular meeting (once a month I believe). Two of the republicans on the board (they might have been the only two at the time)—Preston Martin, the Reagan-appointed vice chairman, and Henry Wallich—and I would attend. (This was very early on in the Reagan years before he had the opportunity of appointing more governors and before his appointees became a majority on the board and not infrequently a thorn in Volcker's side.) These particular governors were chosen for the meeting, I surmised, because their party affiliation might help to assure the undersecretary of our good will. I was there as chief engineer to ensure that the technicalities of monetary policy were well understood and presented. From one point of view, the governors were my minders. From another point of view, I was theirs because everyone present knew that I would immediately report the substance of discussion to Volcker.

Because of the subject matter, I did almost all the talking for the Fed in what turned out to be a largely futile effort to convince the undersecretary that our operating method for controlling money supply was not fatally flawed. Logic was on my side, so I thought, but unshakeable belief was on his. We never got much beyond that impasse. In any event, it took a year or two, as I remember, for the administration to see, that Sprinkel's public pronouncements were being counterproductive and to place him under wraps.

Many monetarist academic economists also doubted our ability to control the money supply. Their reasons were roughly the same as those behind the undersecretary's skepticism. Technicalities set aside, their objections concerned the method of reserve requirement accounting at the time (the lagged reserve-requirement procedure noted in chapter 2) and the particular quantitative measure of bank reserves we chose to control on a day-to-day basis (the nonborrowed reserves provided directly by open market operations rather than the other more aggregative and broader measures they preferred, such as the total monetary base). I assume that even if these economists were to admit that the highly volatile week-to-week fluctuations of money were not economically meaningful or controllable, they simply did not believe that our approach could exert sufficient control over a more economically meaningful intermediate term of, say, three to six months.

Even deeper down, though, they must have felt that if the Fed really had adopted the monetarist faith, it would conduct its operations differently, more directly in line with the book as written by the original disciples. They could not quite believe that we would stick to it or, if we did, that the "it" would be strict enough. All this is speculative on my part of course.[5]

The Reagan administration harbored not only monetarist economists at the policy level, but also supply-side economists. Indeed, the U.S. Treasury was home to both. Supply-side economists were not nearly as interested in the details of monetary policy operations as the monetarists were. Tax policy was their principal bailiwick. In that role, they too succeeded in making the Fed's life difficult by helping persuade the Congress and others that the large tax cut the administration proposed would increase productivity and saving rather than just stimulate demand and potentially lead to inflationary spending.

Thus, they could argue that the tax cut would not lead to higher interest rates, but might even—eureka!—reduce them. The cut instead opened the door to explosive budget deficits, as the Democrats in Congress could not resist a bandwagon that was so easy to ride and piled on it some of their own pet projects. The supply-side viewpoint also influenced some newly appointed board members, who occasionally dissented on the side of ease in part because they expected long-term productivity growth to accelerate as a result of the lower tax rates introduced by the Reagan administration (which, so it was believed, would cause everyone to work harder). As a result, they believed that the economy would have a greater potential for growing faster without inflationary pressures, an expectation that was disappointed during the period of growth following the abandonment of practical monetarism.

I remember once riding over to the Treasury from the Fed in the company of the Treasury assistant secretary for economics, a leading supply-sider of the period. He took the occasion to make me understand—somewhat menacingly, I thought—that I should be clear that the tax cut was for supply-side purposes that would enhance productivity (underlined by a determinedly expressive glare on his face) and not (the implicit message) encourage old-fashioned unproductive spending. By this statement, I presumed he intended me to understand that the Fed need not tighten policy. I really could think of nothing substantive to say in response that would not get us into areas best avoided at the time. Somewhere in my head is the phrase, "But the tax cut might have strong effects on demand"; however, I really don't know whether I just thought it or managed to mutter it unheard as we approached the Treasury building.

Central bankers around the world were of course very curious about the Fed's new approach to policy. Through participation in a group of monetary experts established by the Organization for Economic Cooperation and Development in Paris, in another somewhat similar group that met annually at the BIS in Basle to discuss monetary policy implementation, and in other forums, I met many different central bankers. Nothing at all dramatic happened, even in a low-key way, or even conceivably could have happened at such meetings. If any of us had an artistic side, it would not be displayed on such stages. Sober-sided and generally quite straightforward and honest analysis was the order of the day. Of more enduring value were a number of good friendships that evolved, and naturally so, because we were a rather like-minded group dealing with similar problems and trained in a central-bank culture that seemed to encourage mutual respect for colleagues and took the hard edge off any aggressive tendencies.

A number of the foreign central bankers curious about the technical aspects of our new domestic monetary policy operations also showed up in Washington. One of the conversations I most clearly remember was with the then governor of the Bank of France, not because of its substance, but because of its mode. He spoke to me in very slow French, so I could briefly believe what I knew not to be true, that I could understand the spoken language. In turn, I spoke to him in slow English so that he could believe what I also assume was not quite true, that he could understand spoken English.

The foreign official who showed the most detailed interest was the man then in charge of domestic-market operations at the Bank of England. At his request, I took him through all our worksheets used in deriving the aggregate-reserve target and showed him why and how we made adjustments to the original target path—adjustments that reflected a more or less automatic response to new statistics and the exercise of some judgment.

As we went through the whole process—which had come to seem rather mechanical to me—his eyes suddenly lit up, a small contented smile briefly passed across his face, and with a slight sigh of reassurance he said, "Ah, I knew there must be some flexibility." Clearly there was, but I really never thought of it like that. To me, it just seemed that the assembled staff who reviewed the statistical information were doing no more or less than what was technically necessary to make the engine work as desired and directed by the FOMC. I do not think of that attitude as either naive or self-deceptive; the statistical adjustments—which, to be sure, had judgmental aspects—were built into the procedure as adopted by the FOMC.

The initial reserve target path had to be recalibrated as a result of, among other things, continuing changes in the composition of the money supply that affected the so-called multiplier relationship between reserves and money, essentially a purely technical adjustment. In addition, though, a judgment had to be made about whether the initial nonborrowed reserve target path (as technically recalibrated) itself should be changed, either up or down, because money growth was veering too far from expectations. Such a deviation would suggest that the initial path was not working well.

A shift in path for the latter reason would either intensify or reduce the pressures on market interest rates (depending on whether the path was lowered or raised) by changing the amount of bank reserves provided through open market operations as compared with the original target path—an adjustment that was indeed rather more judgmental than purely mechanical, but was made, as I recall, on the basis of a consistent (more or less arbitrary) formula derived from how far money supply and its associated reserve aggregates were deviating from the original path. I reported all adjustments the staff made (but they were basically my decision, of course) and the reasons why first to the chairman, then to the board at a special weekly limited briefing session, and to the FOMC as a whole through ongoing statistical reports and communications related to the daily market call. (The manager for open market operations at the New York Fed also reported the adjustments in the various reports he made directly to the FOMC.)

From my British colleague's viewpoint, there was still some real danger, apparently, that Ms. Thatcher might force the Bank of England into a modus operandi similar to ours. He must have greatly feared that the bank would as a result not be able to exert its traditional close control over the money market. Well, the truth is that it would not have been able to do so. To him, however, anything that might be interpreted as a loophole looked like the proverbial port in a storm. As it turned out, Ms. Thatcher never did get her way; the bank apparently put up fierce resistance.

This was the period when even the British Parliament attempted somehow to become further involved in oversight of monetary policy as the debate about the best approach to monetary control became more and more of a public matter. Unlike in the United States, where the Congress and the president's administration are effectively separate arms of government, in Britain the parliamentary system elides that distinction and leaves the chancellor of the exchequer to represent the government in its relation to the central bank. As a result, the Parliament does not have the same close and continuing relationship to the Bank of England as the U.S. Congress does to the Fed.

Nonetheless, the parliamentary committee that focused on monetary and financial matters, among other things, appeared to be looking for a way to make its presence more keenly felt, though without great support, as nearly as I could tell, from within the Parliament as a whole or from the government more widely. Be that as it may (and it may be quite different than I have depicted because I have no special substantive knowledge), the committee asked, through Volcker, if I could come over to give some expert testimony on Fed operations. Volcker rather reluctantly agreed, with the provisos that no publicity would be given to my presence (he did not want U.S. congressional banking committees to believe that Fed staff could be called to testify on monetary policy), that I would respond only to quite technical issues, and that I would not comment on the British approach to policy operations.

Very soon thereafter, the chief financial official of the U.K. embassy invited me to lunch. We ended up at a quiet corner table in a fairly popular K Street restaurant in Washington. What he really wanted was assurance that I would not be commenting in any unfavorable way on British monetary policy or operations before the parliamentary committee. As I was in the midst of convincing him that I would be making no comment one way or the other on that very sensitive subject, but would confine myself to answering questions about the technicalities of U.S. experience, a third party suddenly loomed up before our table.

Startlingly enough, this unwanted presence was wielding, of all things, a camera, thus becoming more unwanted. He explained that he was a newsman doing a story on power lunches in Washington, thereby becoming even more unwanted. "Would you mind if I take your picture?" he asked. Appropriately misinterpreted to achieve a newsworthy effect, a pretty good story was within his grasp. My British colleague blanched ever so discreetly and with a show of deference referred the question to me. My response, of course, was a straightforward "please do not," made with only the smallest degree of extra hesitancy (that's about as devilish as central bankers get), whereupon the man quickly retreated, and our luncheon resumed its quiet, reassuring way.

Curiosity about this supremely unimportant transatlantic appearance of mine—if it were in any way important, it would never actually have occurred—continued on the other side of the Atlantic. When I arrived in London, the resident U.S. Treasury representative greeted me. Of course, he too wanted to know what I was going to say. Indeed, he went further; he offered to accompany me to the committee hearing. Naturally, I accepted his kind offer.

I was then invited to a lunch attended by key staff at the Bank of England and hosted by its governor, Gordon Richardson. Our paths had crossed on other occasions, and by this time I believe he thought of me as a friendly type. After my usual reassurances that the parliamentary group had agreed not to put questions about British monetary policy or operations to me and that I certainly had no intention of responding if they did, our luncheon discussion passed on to more important matters for the Bank of England. They included such issues as whether, how, and to what extent to bring various monetary and reserve aggregates into the policy process. The bank was under pressure at the time, as previously noted, from the prime minister, who was being closely advised by an economist or two with monetarist leanings, if not doctrinal beliefs. The discussion was interesting and focused, so far as I remember, on how to go halfway toward meeting the prime minister's wishes without actually going quite that far.

As the luncheon broke up, Gordon asked if I would mind if they sent along a young economist to hear my testimony. "Not at all," said I. As it turned out, the hearing, as one would expect, was a tepid affair because we all strictly adhered to the ground rules.

A few weeks later I received a call from a staffer in Congress (oddly enough, as I recall, from some committee other than the Banking Committee) asking if I would send him a copy of the transcript from my testimony before the parliamentary group. "How can I?" I responded. "I was not supposed to have been there." He said something like, "Oh, that's right," and, to my surprise, promptly hung up.

Regarding the Fed's new policy procedure and its implementation, I am still not sure whether all members of the FOMC fully realized the extent to which the procedure entailed certain crucial statistical adjustments, some unavoidably judgmental, as new data became available. I remember one morning when Henry Wallich—a governor whose office happened to be next to mine—walked in with a serious question on his mind, apparently one that had just come to him. Henry and I had a relationship that went far back. Many years earlier, in the mid-1960s, when I was still a rising economist in the board's Division of Research and Statistics, I had been recommended to Henry, who was then a professor of economics at Yale, as coauthor for an article on U.S. monetary policy developments in the post–World War II period. We seemed to think alike on the subject; the article was easily written and eventually published.

When Henry came to the board as a governor, our paths crossed fairly often. In particular, he was the board's representative on many international groups, especially at the BIS. We attended a few meetings together. He was a very pleasant traveling companion, but he had one fault. On our first trip together, he explained that there were two ways to arrive at an airport—one was leisurely with, say, thirty or forty-five minutes to spare, and the other was hastily, with barely a minute to spare. He preferred the latter because, as I interpreted his personality, no time was wasted; airports were made to "disappear" as a complication in a busy life. So that's what we did, an unnecessarily hectic maneuver as it seemed to me. When traveling on my own, I much preferred the leisurely approach and worked crossword puzzles to make airports disappear.

Toward the end of Henry's tenure at the board, the editor of a prestigious project called the *Palgrave Dictionary of Economics* asked if I would write a short article on Henry for them. The dictionary was oriented mainly to highly technical articles on topics in the field (Henry and I coauthored an article on open market operations for it), but it also devoted space to individual economists. For an individual to be included in the publication, he had to be either dead or beyond a certain advanced age at the time of writing. Getting myself to complete the piece was very difficult. By that time, Henry, very unfortunately, was clearly fading from a brain tumor, and I felt spooked, fearing that mailing off the contribution to a publication with such stringent criteria for inclusion would seal his fate. I finally did, of course, and hope it did Henry proud. My vision of Henry is that he approached death—another trip—still thinking about economics, still writing, still reluctant to waste any time in waiting rooms.

All that is by way of explaining that Henry and I had a quite informal and friendly relationship, which enabled him to ask the question as he did that morning and permitted me to respond as I did. "Why," he asked, "do I have to vote to raise the discount rate in order to raise interest rates further between committee meetings, even though you can do it just by shifting the reserve path to provide less reserves?"[6] The implication was that no one had given me a vote on monetary policy, just as no one had given the manager in New York a vote in the bad old days when that person had managed or, to put it more kindly, been forced to impose his interpretation on a policy directive that had been too vaguely constructed. "True enough," said I. "But, Henry, you voted for this policy and what's involved. Don't blame me. Talk to the chairman"—the clear implication being that I had certainly checked such an adjustment with the chairman. I doubt that Henry pursued the matter further. I think he just meant to assure himself that he had fully understood the mechanism underlying the procedure for which he had voted.

Questions are often raised about policymakers' so-called real motives for adopting the new procedure. Many have wondered whether the new policy was simply a cover so that the Fed could raise interest rates while ducking direct responsibility. A policymaker or two made statements that could be so interpreted, but it is a viewpoint that has never made much sense to me.

It would take a pretty naive observer to believe that the Fed is an innocent bystander in the behavior of money-market rates on a day-to-day basis even if the institution claims to be aiming at a different operating target. After all, the Fed is the ultimate supplier of funds to that market, and there is no substantial practical limit to the amount it can supply if it wishes. A belief in the Fed's innocence is something like believing your landlord is not a party to the cold you feel when he claims to be supplying all the heat required by his thermostat setting.

In any event, the public had surely come to understand that the central bank clearly is responsible for inflation. Nominal interest rates necessarily rise along with inflation, so, from that broader perspective, too, the cost of money and credit can be laid at the central bank's doorstep.

To me, the new procedure adopted by the Volcker Fed had the great operational advantage of getting interest rates as high as needed to restrain inflation. The sooner they got there the better. The longer the delay, and the more inflation became embedded in market and business expectations, the even higher interest rates would have to become to turn the situation around. Money supply was a practical target that would achieve the objective of raising interest rates with minimal delay. That is my interpretation of what Volcker meant by his use of the expression "practical monetarism." Whether it is his, I cannot testify.

In retrospect, the Fed might have instead simply embarked on a policy of quickly raising the federal funds rate to a level that in real terms was well above the real return on capital. This policy would have implied a nominal funds rate somewhere in the 15 to 20 percent range in those days, the latter being around the peak level it eventually reached. But the real funds rate was not an active element in policymakers' thinking at the time. Anyhow, raising the nominal rate at a pace and in the sizeable steps that would have been required to achieve the desired effect was well outside the box of Fed thinking.

Because monetary policymakers are traditionally, and usually for good reason, conservative decision makers, they simply were not psychologically capable of deciding to move the funds rate, taken as an operating objective that is up for vote, so far and relatively quickly. Moreover, I suspect the staff did not have the capacity to give such dramatic advice.

Adopting the money supply as an operating target for policy certainly finessed such issues. That the empirical relationship between money growth and eventual inflation had been long studied and generally affirmed was also a great advantage. It gave the target credibility. A money-supply operating target could be set that was not arbitrary, so to speak, but instead was embedded in professional economic thinking and buttressed by research. It also had easy appeal to the public based on the old aphorism, earlier noted, that inflation was caused by too much money chasing too few goods. Moreover, it was a target that could be held for some time; it did not need to be changed frequently like an interest-rate operating target.

The money supply was made operational by being transformed into the aggregate amount of reserves under the control of the Fed that needed to be supplied to achieve the target. As briefly noted in chapter 2, I for one, certainly had more confidence in our ability to estimate this multiplier relationship between the amount of reserves and money supply than I did in our ability to estimate a federal funds rate that would be consistent. The former involved known and set institutional relationships, such as reserve requirements on deposits, though there were of course other complications beyond mere arithmetic that affected the transformation of bank reserves into money supply, such as banks' demand for excess reserves. In contrast, estimating the interest rate that would bring money demand into balance with what the Fed wished to supply required understanding complex and ever-changing economic relationships that involved time lags, demand elasticities, and whatever other subtleties econometricians work into their equations. The odds on being wrong were very high.

With money directly the policy target (as transformed into a reserve aggregate), the funds rate would automatically move in the proper direction if money demand exceeded or ran under the predetermined supply. Within whatever range the FOMC was comfortable with for the period between meetings, no policy decision on the rate was required. And, as already noted, a relatively wide range was indeed set.

Thus, it is almost impossible, not to say practically pointless, to attempt to find a common reason that fits all policymakers who voted for new procedure. Monetarist sympathizers may well have believed that money itself was the crucial element and cared very little for what happened to interest rates. Others may have had much more belief that interest rates were the key variable through which the Fed affects the economy, but went along with the new policy even though they had little confidence in any particular measure of money, especially given the changing structure of finance. Then there were some practical few who might have thought something like, "How can we ever get this committee to move strongly enough?" and for whom money was a very useful instrument. And finally, there were probably those who felt a new approach was needed to convince the public that the Fed was now strongly determined to control inflation.

I personally would subscribe to all of these attitudes, except my purely monetarist sympathies would have been on the tepid side then and have subsequently become more so. Somewhere out there, among the broad and diverse array of assets in modern markets, may be a money supply in the public's hands that fits some reasonable economic criterion—for instance, bears a consistent, predictable relationship over time to behavior of the nominal value of the nation's output of goods and services or to the average price level or to both. But we can no longer find it, if we ever could. It is in effect hidden in all of the world's assets, and the relevant holders are probably no longer limited to U.S. nationals. It is a concept that has now become essentially immeasurable. We can try to approximate it in different ways. Nevertheless, we can have little confidence that any one approximation is better than any other at any particular moment and over any particular span of time, especially so in such free, diverse, and highly liquid domestic and global financial markets as are available to citizens of the United States and other major developed countries.

After the new procedure had outlived its usefulness, it was replaced during the later years of Volcker's tenure by an approach to policy that was very close to targeting the federal funds rate in open market operations, but literally was not. Instead of taking the funds rate as a target, Volcker persuaded the FOMC to use the total of banks' borrowing at the Federal Reserve Banks as its operating target.

However, in the blue book policy document submitted to the committee, an expected federal funds rate, given the discount rate, was associated with particular levels of borrowing. I assume such a roundabout approach appealed to the chairman because, given ever-present uncertainties, he wanted to leave a little market (and perhaps chairman) flexibility in determining the overnight money-market rate. Naturally enough, there was occasionally some confusion in the mind of the manager for domestic operations in New York about what he should consider his basic target if in practice the funds rate were to diverge from expectations relative to the borrowing target. I would clue him in as best I could, based on my more or less continuing contact with the chairman.

No doubt all this seems too arcane and technical, which it is, but there were real market effects and occasional conflicts among FOMC members about whether the market outcome was consistent with what they had understood when they voted at any particular meeting. In addition, because the FOMC was literally targeting borrowing and not the federal funds rate, the Fed Board of Governors itself continued to be able to influence the funds rate (which was fundamentally more important to markets than the level of borrowing) through its control over the discount rate.

In practice, though, there was hardly ever any substantial conflict between the board and the FOMC on interest-rate policy. However, in the latter part of the winter of 1986, the possibility that a discount-rate decrease could be employed to lower market rates led to a major and very unfortunate conflict between the four board members appointed by Reagan and the chairman (who by this time, his second term as chairman, was of course also a Reagan appointee). In the end, all were losers in one sense or another.

The dispute—which was, to me, about as dramatic as things get at the Fed—broke out at a usual weekly board meeting on Monday, February 24, 1986, a day when the staff made its weekly presentation about the latest economic and financial developments. Following the presentation, the board met in a more limited session to consider discount-rate proposals from reserve banks. (Reserve bank boards of directors submitted proposals, but they required approval by the Board of Governors to become effective.) Several weeks earlier there had been a number of proposals for discount-rate reductions on the board's agenda. At each subsequent weekly meeting, the board had decided to table the proposals. Almost all of the proposals were gradually withdrawn. At the time of this fateful meeting, only one or maybe two were left.

Time was running out for the four Reagan appointees, who favored a rate reduction on economic grounds. The chairman was not in favor of such a reduction, in part, as I remember, because he was not convinced of the economic necessity at that point and in part because he feared that a unilateral rate reduction by the United States (i.e., a reduction that was not accompanied by simultaneous decreases in other key countries) would unduly weaken the still fragile dollar on exchange markets. It was not clear whether the differences of opinion were purely economic or the four also wanted overtly to challenge the chairman in order to diminish his stature and influence and to raise their own, but the latter interpretation cannot be entirely ruled out.

As I recall the meeting, Volcker was again prepared to table the remaining proposals, but the four, constituting a majority of the board, insisted on a vote, as was their parliamentary right. Obviously not prepared for such a confrontation, the chairman lost the vote by four to three.

Here is an instance in which Volcker found himself on a stage where his undoubted artistry as an actor was of no help. The confrontation was taking place on essentially a private, not a public, stage. It was a stage in which Burns might have risen to the occasion, recognized the cues that an attack was coming, and possibly fought it off or forestalled it with all the interpersonal ferocity he could muster. But Volcker seemed taken aback, as if he could not believe what was occurring; he must have seen the confrontation as an interpersonal conflict as much as (or more than) a difference in economics; he was just not quite ready to deal with it and, given his personality, perhaps could not have been.

After the vote, he retreated to his office. I do not specifically remember whether he mentioned the possibility of resigning. Maybe he did. The idea was certainly in the air. He did not attend the follow-up session held in the board members' library where the rest of the board and a few key staff, who felt duty bound to attend, convened to draft the press release on the discount rate action. That drafting session, chaired by Preston Martin, was unbelievably tense. Wording suggestions from the staff were received with some suspicion in an atmosphere where "regime change" was in the air. It was almost impossible to believe that Volcker was not masterminding the fine points of the press release, as was his wont.

As it turned out, at some point and through machinations that were never convincingly made known to me, cooler heads prevailed. I have to believe that the administration had no desire for Volcker to resign. There was no political gain in it. Moreover, a resignation, if it came to that, raised all the complications of explaining it and of finding a successor capable of bringing the very considerable international and domestic stature needed to mitigate the probably strong adverse impact that Volcker's resignation under such circumstances would have for dollar values on domestic and foreign exchange markets.

In any event, another meeting was held in the afternoon, and the board voted unanimously to rescind the rate decrease. I was in the boardroom waiting for the meeting to begin when Pres Martin arrived. I went to him and said something like, "I don't think I really need to be at this meeting." He responded, "No, you don't want to be here."

In the Board of Governor's annual report for 1986, it was stated that the earlier decision to raise the discount rate was rescinded on the same day "following a review of prospective actions by key central banks abroad to reduce their lending rates" (p. 81). Two weeks later the board again met and voted to lower the discount rate. At the same time, the central banks of Germany and Japan also voted to lower their rates. Face was saved all around, but it was also lost.

This confrontation on interest rates took place about five months after the Plaza Accord was announced in September 1985, and, in my opinion, it was not unrelated to issues that had arisen, at least in Volcker's mind, as the accord was being implemented. This agreement—signed onto by the finance ministers and central-bank heads from the United States, Germany, Japan, the United Kingdom, and France—was designed mainly to drive down the dollar relative to the yen. And a very substantial drop in the dollar against the yen did take place; indeed, it seemed to be threatening to get out of hand. This drop subsequently spurred another agreement, the Louvre Accord, adopted by these major countries in February 1987, to restore stability to the market.

The Plaza Accord seems to have been the brainchild of Jim Baker, Reagan's secretary of the Treasury. It had an economic basis, but political pressures were telling. The dollar had risen sharply in value following the Fed's successful program for containing inflation, but at the same time U.S. exports were having a harder time competing in the international market. The latter was happening not merely because of the rise in the dollar, but also because of real factors such as the outmoded management practices and production processes in some major U.S. industries. In particular, the auto industry was losing out to foreign imports, especially from Japan.

In that context, enormous political pressure was being put on the administration from Detroit. Both labor and capital were strongly lobbying for action to stem the incoming tide of Japanese cars, and Congress was getting into the act through threats of trade restrictions unless foreign importers, in particular Japan, stopped discriminating against U.S. goods.

The first I knew about the Plaza Accord was about a week before it was signed. Volcker asked me and Sam Cross, the official at the New York Fed who at the time ran foreign-exchange operations for the Fed and (as fiscal agent) for the Treasury, to accompany him to a meeting at the Treasury with Baker and his top political appointees and staff. The accord had been negotiated in great secrecy, and I am not sure at what point Volcker had been brought into the process (it was certainly before this meeting).

The purpose of the meeting was to establish general guidelines agreed upon by the Treasury and the Fed on technical operating issues once the accord was effectuated. As I recall, the discussion covered questions such as under what conditions the United States would intervene in exchange markets and when foreign countries would. In general, it was agreed that the United States would not sell dollars to force our currency down; foreign countries would do that job. The United States would for the most part limit its intervention to times when the dollar might be tending to rise. It seemed like a very bad idea to be seen as overtly and clearly "bearing" one's own currency. Rather, the idea was to let other countries take the initiative in doing so through efforts to strengthen their own currencies (by selling dollars); an effort by the United States to join that particular fray might lead to an uncontrolled and unacceptable panic-type flight from the dollar.

As I recall, in the course of Baker's reading a draft of such an internal operating agreement, out came a sentence that said something about the Fed being willing to consider lowering interest rates. It may even have said that the Fed would lower rates. My memory is simply not that specific. Anyhow, the protest from Volcker was instantaneous, and the sentence was promptly removed. Baker surely could have expected no less. Maybe he thought of the sentence as a trial balloon, or maybe he was attempting to deliver a message. To me, the effort seemed rather misplaced, even a bit jejune.

To make foreign currencies more attractive and the dollar less so, it would be helpful, of course, if interest rates rose in foreign countries relative to the United States. The Japanese government agreed in the Plaza Accord to a flexible management of monetary policy, with due regard to the yen foreign-exchange rate. The central bank of Japan rather soon did raise its discount rate (at which Volcker expressed some surprise at the subsequent FOMC meeting in early November). Everyone concerned probably hoped that U.S. interest rates would decline. The U.S. government agreed to cut its fiscal deficit, which, if implemented, would be a step in the direction of reducing interest-rate pressures. As for U.S. monetary policy, the Fed agreed only "to provide a financial environment conducive to sustainable growth and continued progress toward price stability." In essence, U.S. monetary policy agreed to nothing special.

The U.S. economy at the time was a bit shaky, and there was some sentiment at the Fed for giving consideration to lower interest rates. In my opinion, Volcker probably had no inclination to do so in any significant way at the time, certainly in the aftermath of the Plaza Accord, where lower interest rates could be seen as part of a program to "bear" the dollar and could encourage an undesired dramatic drop in the currency that could easily destabilize the economy. I suggested to him that I develop a chart show, using key international and domestic staff, for the early November FOMC meeting that would discuss dangers for both inflation and economic weakness if the Plaza Accord thrust to a lower dollar got out of hand. The charts and text would in effect buttress the argument for keeping the dollar decline gradual and reasonably well contained and, by implication, for the FOMC to resist any substantial change in policy for now.[7]

Worries about the potential for market instability and adverse effects on the economy, similar to those Volcker exhibited in the aftermath of Plaza Accord, were, as noted earlier, apparently still on Volcker's mind at the time of the February 1986 dispute with other Fed board members.

However that may have been, the dispute had some interesting side effects from my perspective.

For one, there was an incident when I happened to be at the Bank of Japan a few months later. In the course of conversation with a friend who was then in charge of the bank's international department, I was told that the bank would not again let itself be put in that position; he was clearly referring to the recent simultaneous discount-rate cut with the Fed. I relayed the conversation to Volcker, as was their expectation. He looked innocent and said something like, "What can they mean?" Surely we both knew, but I went along with the game and explained my interpretation. What I did not mention was that the Japanese central bankers, aside from irritation at being asked to do something they were not ready for, were perhaps still ticked off at having raised their interest rate after the Plaza Accord only to find that the Fed was delaying any steps to lower interest rates as long as possible even though the economy was rather tepid. The latter point is purely speculative on my part.

It comes into my head, however, in part because in late 1986 Shiguro Ogata, the deputy governor of the Bank of Japan, retired from his position somewhat before his scheduled time, as far as I could tell. He seemed to have been the person designated to take the fall—a common Japanese tradition for avoiding group responsibility—for the unfortunate, though at the time transitory, weakness in the Japanese economy after the nation's adherence to the Plaza Accord. Indeed, on the very day this happened, he was a guest at the first dinner I cohosted in Japan as vice chairman of

Nikko Securities International. As I recall, at one point he left the room to take a phone call, whispered in the ear of one of his colleagues upon return, and calmly finished his meal. His resignation was announced the next morning.

A second side effect comes to mind in connection with a conversation I had with one of the four Fed governors involved in the confrontation with Volcker. He expressed some wonder about why the chairman did not originally suggest postponing the vote on the excuse that he needed time to see if coordinated actions could be worked out with other major central banks. He said that they, meaning the four, would have gone along with such a delay. His comment, intended to convey the idea that only economic questions were at stake, actually tended to reinforce my suspicion that an interpersonal power conflict was at least equally in play (although this particular person, a decent man essentially, had a temperament that could easily have permitted him to avoid acknowledging such a conclusion).

The dispute, from my perspective, also poisoned the policymaking atmosphere enough so that the fumes even penetrated the idyllic little world in which I pretended to think I was working. It inspired me to take a step or two toward leaving the board, half-hearted steps as usual, though, by serendipity as it turned out, this time effective.

In the late spring of 1986, I informed Paul of my intention to resign from the Fed and accept a senior position in New York City at Nikko Securities International, the U.S. subsidiary of the then second-largest Japanese securities firm (though in the process of rapidly losing that position to Daiwa Securities). Among his responses was the suggestion that I ought to consider teaching because, according to him, that was what I had in effect been doing all those years in Washington. Although probably a fair description of the essential thrust of my activities, I had never thought of myself in that way. I enjoyed engaging with the academic part of the economics profession at conferences and otherwise, but I felt no call to be a more active participant in it and never really had when, much earlier in my life, that seemed a real possibility.

In any event, by now, at my fairly advanced age at the time, soon to be sixty, I seemed short on either the professional reputation or political prestige to be attractive to a top academic institution. A position in the market appeared to be the best bet. The pay was very good, not as ridiculous as it would later become on Wall Street, but high enough to help make eventual retirement more comfortable by compensating in a significant degree for the quite low salaries then being paid to senior central bankers in the United States. (That situation improved considerably after Greenspan's arrival.)

Just as important, the Japanese offer represented a chance to change completely our family's pattern of life, to engage with what we thought to be and were the wondrous cultural opportunities in New York, to enter a more active and dynamic kind of world. That opportunity was by no means easy to come by late in an existence that, although intellectually interesting and socially useful, had heretofore by and large been staid in the extreme. It seemed like an adventure—a little one to be sure, relatively safe, but still in all, something of a venture into the unknown.

6

The Greenspan Years, from Stability to Crisis

I had been out of the Fed about a year before Alan Greenspan took over as chairman in August 1987, so my view of him, and of course his successor, Ben Bernanke, is only from the outside—nonetheless a view that can hardly avoid being heavily influenced, for good or ill, by the long years spent inside, sometimes like a caged mouse running on a policy treadmill and sometimes like a fly on important walls.

From one perspective, the value of inside-out knowledge of the Fed should tend to become gradually less relevant and potentially, one might think, even misleading as time passes and economic circumstances, leadership structure, and the social and political environment that influence policy and policymakers mutate. But it should never become entirely irrelevant. Knowledge of institutional continuities—such as attitudes toward the Congress, the construction of bureaucratic language, group decision-making dynamics, and the profound desire and need for institutional credibility—certainly helps in the evaluation of new policy developments as they occur and in interpretation of the thinking behind policy.

I cannot remember exactly when I first met Alan Greenspan. That encounter is lost in the mists of time. Our first planned meeting occurred shortly after he was nominated as chairman, when I received a call in my office at Nikko in New York City asking if I would meet him for breakfast to discuss the Fed. No doubt he was having similar discussions with a number of others. Before that, our paths had crossed only rarely. I do have a memory of chatting briefly with him at a large-scale meeting, possibly the Gerald Ford administration's ineffective conference optimistically entitled "Whip Inflation Now." That encounter occurred long after I had heard of Greenspan and, I also assume, he of me—though I believe I would have heard of him much earlier than he would have known of me.

He had made his name in the private sector as an economic forecaster and a consultant to businesses. Having come to a quite conservative economic and social philosophy well before its popular time, he seemed to gain the confidence of Republican Party power brokers. Partly for that reason, but more especially, I think, because of his innate intelligence and demonstrated economic competence, he was a natural to take on important and diverse public economic policy roles as the conservative movement gained momentum, culminating in his appointment as chairman of the Board of Governors of the Federal Reserve System.

So far as I could see, many, if not most, economists of my generation, coming to the subject after being brought up during the economic hardships of the Great Depression and entering or reentering college in the years immediately following World War II, were more in tune with the economic attitudes of the Democratic Party. Maybe that is an overstatement. I have done no survey.

In any event, as an undergraduate at Harvard I was exposed to the Keynesian revolution, which sought to explain the macroeconomic relationships that can lead to an economy's persistent underperformance,[1] through the teachings of one of his first and most prominent American followers, Alvin Hansen (who coincidentally was also my undergraduate adviser). Following Keynes, he stressed that the economy in practice might well not exhibit a natural tendency to full employment, that monetary policy was a limited instrument during depressions, and that fiscal deficits were needed for cyclical economic recovery and possibly, under some circumstances in Hansen's own view, for sustained satisfactory growth.

Most of the new, exciting research in economics that was talked about in the late 1940s, the 1950s, and for some years after focused on or was related to major macroeconomic issues raised by Keynes's insights and the associated desire to find a way through demand management—that is, by making sure there is sufficient domestic spending by businesses, consumers, and, if not them, governments—to avoid any more huge economic depressions, assure economic growth, and maintain full employment. Inflation was not stressed as any great concern. In class discussion of macroeconomic issues, Hansen did of course point out that over the long run too much money growth would lead to inflationary price increases, but that was old theory, not new, not glamorous, not exciting. It seemed that the Democrats in the immediate postwar years were more in tune with the latest in economic thinking than the Republicans, who generally supported a balanced government budget, were less interventionist, and believed more that free and flexible markets were self-correcting.

Because I ended up doing graduate work in economics in the very early 1950s at the quite conservative economics department of the University of Chicago, where Milton Friedman was beginning to get into full stride and Frank Knight already had made his name, I was well exposed to a more conservative view. Nonetheless, active demand management, through monetary or fiscal policy, to ensure economic growth and full employment continued to be my major interest in economics. Avoidance of another great depression was what mattered. I had little interest in the supply side of the economy in those years—that is, about how to improve the efficiency of markets through which the supply of labor, capital, and other resources were made available for economic production and growth.

Later on I became more appreciative of certain aspects of Chicago school thought. Friedman's emphasis on more stable and predictable money-supply behavior and the associated search for monetary "rules" brought into clearer focus questions about the extent to which the conduct of monetary policy itself can contribute to periods of economic distress and had done so. From Knight, I recall coming to some understanding of what basically and essentially, in my mind, made the economy go, of what brought it to life: innovation and risk taking, together with an encouraging market environment. That idea was probably not exactly central to Knight's summer graduate course on price theory and microeconomics, which I half-dreamed my way through, but it is what I retain. Still, it took a large number of years before I fully internalized the practical importance of competitive, price-responsive labor and product markets for enhancing the nation's capacity to achieve sustainable growth without inflation.

My dual economic training at such institutions as Harvard and Chicago, which featured economic departments with vastly different economic philosophies, in any event did seem to make me much less ideological in my approach to the field. On occasion, I used to introduce speeches with a story about the different answers required to a similar question on the honors exam for the undergraduate degree at Harvard and then on the doctoral exam for a graduate degree at Chicago.

At Harvard, so memory serves, I wrote that monetary policy becomes ineffective after interest rates reach very low levels because there is a liquidity trap; no matter how much more money is provided by the central bank, interest rates cannot be pushed lower since it is not worth anyone's while to purchase bonds; they might as well just hold the cash (or, in the case of banks, just add to excess reserves as short-term rates approached zero). Thus, fiscal policy—direct spending or tax cuts by the government—would clearly be needed to stimulate the economy.

At Chicago, one had to note that Keynes was wrong about monetary policy and the liquidity trap. He neglected to see that even if interest rates are so low that they cannot practically decline further, additional money provided through central-bank policy will in any event create more real wealth (something I remember as the so-called Pigou effect) and thus will have a positive effect on spending.[2]

In the end, which one of the answers is right or wrong, or to what degree, is an empirical question. Judging by Japan's experience in the 1990s, one might believe that Keynes had a point. And judging from the fears expressed by Greenspan in the early years of the new millennium that monetary policy might run out of ammunition at very low interest rates, something similar might have been at work in the thinking at the Fed.

At the time, the Fed and presumably the Bank of Japan were especially worried that the central bank would not be able to move interest rates low enough to stimulate spending in a period of deflation (i.e., declining prices) should one arise, which it had in Japan in the late 1990s and which seemed possible in the United States—though barely so in my opinion—early in the first decade of the new century. In such circumstances, even a zero short-term market rate, the lowest practical nominal rate, would still be positive in real terms. At that point and probably even before it, the central bank would have lost its ability to push real short-term market rates low enough, and indeed into negative territory if required, to encourage significant additional borrowing and economic stimulation (in Japan, open market operations for a time did little but add to banks' excess reserves just as did the Fed's extensive and varied activities during the great credit crisis that led to rapid expansion of its balance sheet).

My diverse economic training presumably was of some help in understanding the differing thought processes of various policymakers and advisers at the Fed and elsewhere with whom I came in touch. Greenspan obviously came from the right side of the professional economic spectrum (probably a bit farther right than Arthur Burns, I would say). This position was clearest in what I would characterize, at the risk of stating it too baldly, as his laissez-faire attitude toward regulatory issues and his rather pronounced desire to keep taxes and government spending both as low as possible in order to maximize the economic space available for private-market incentives and thereby attain (I assume in his view) the most efficient and effective employment of the nation's resources.

Greenspan, of course, understood the countercyclical usefulness of fiscal policy under certain economic circumstances. Nonetheless, as a long-run matter, he seemed, so far as I could tell, to favor keeping the role of government in the economy to the minimum possible. Indeed, because his basic posture on the role of government seemed so strongly held, during his long tenure at the Fed he did not appear able to resist supporting a particular administration political position once in a while—on, for example, tax reduction, partly as a means of starving the budget over the long run and keeping governmental spending in check. Needless to say, many believed (as I did) it was unwise to drag the Fed into a political minefield. All Fed chairmen came out in favor of fiscal restraint, but it was not considered good form to express an opinion on the specifics of the tax or expenditure sides of the budget.

Be all that as it may, in his attitude toward macroeconomic conditions and monetary policy, Greenspan, like all of the preceding chairmen, seemed far from ideological. Like everyone else, he had to figure out, to put it in its simplest and most straightforward terms, whether economic activity was strengthening or weakening, whether inflationary pressures were waxing or waning, and what to do about these developments. The staff's elaborate analyses of current economic developments and projections of the near future were cornerstones for that understanding.

What a chairman or any other policymaker can also bring is his or her own judgment about the balance of risks in the staff's analysis and about the needed timing and degree of policy action. An ideological monetarist, for instance, might be influenced one way and thus place most emphasis on the money supply in assessing the economic outlook. A committed supply-sider might be affected in another way and thus judge that the economy's noninflationary growth potential is enhanced by certain structural changes, such as tax cuts. As noted in chapter 5, some policymakers at the Fed in the first part of the 1980s argued the latter view because they believed that the large tax cuts under Reagan, billed as supply-side cuts, would make people work harder and increase the nation's productivity. However, a sustained, enhanced rise in productivity occurred only much later during the latter part of Greenspan's term in response to the high-tech revolution of the time.

I would not have expected Greenspan to be anything but objective in making judgments about the state of the economy and the desirable stance of policy. He was open to the whole range of incoming economic information in all its detail and puzzling variability. It was not simply as if he were a student needing to understand the course material so as to make a good grade on a final exam and be done with it. Rather, he seemed engaged heart and soul. It was as if the material had its own fascination for him independent of the exam, as if he were compelled to keep looking for new economic relationships and their meaning, to solve them like puzzles for something like the joy of it.

At one point, his constant immersion in the sea of economic data—aided, I assume, by that most crucial attribute of a top policymaker, a good intuition—yielded a key insight about the timing and intensity of policy. Based on the public statements made by a number of his policy-making colleagues, Greenspan apparently understood before most anyone else that a high-tech productivity revolution was upon us as the 1990s wore on and that, as a result, the economy would be able to grow more rapidly than earlier suspected without setting off inflationary pressures in the average price of goods and services. He seems to have persuaded his colleagues at the Fed that, as a result, they need not be so quick to tighten or need to carry the tightening as far as they otherwise would have. Insightful as that may have been, unfortunately in the end, and for reasons discussed later in this chapter, it led to an inflationary bubble in asset prices that itself, once it burst, had recessionary repercussions on the economy.

Nonetheless, Greenspan's earlier reputation as a forecaster when he was a consultant to businesses in the private sector was not especially outstanding (forecasting is no more than a small part of such an economic consultant's stock in trade; door opening would probably be a more crucial skill). But it is almost impossible to find a consistently outstanding economic forecaster. It's just not possible to be right almost all or even most of the time. What's really important is who most quickly recognizes that their forecast is turning out wrong.

I had always thought Greenspan, objective as he was, might have had a slightly pessimistic bias as a forecaster, perhaps occasioned by his growing up during the Great Depression. Whether I am right or wrong, such a bias was not readily evident to the outside eye during his term at the Fed. It did not seem to be there when he understood that the economy would grow strongly in the late 1990s. However, some sense of pessimism might have surfaced during the early years of the new millennium. At that time, he took the view that monetary policy should be conducted on the risk-management principle of guarding against an economic outcome that had a very small probability (in this case, the probability that economic activity would be so weak that it would lead to actual price deflation, not merely disinflation) but which might be close to disastrous if it occurred.

These general thoughts about our diverse backgrounds and attitudes— some that I recognized at the time, some that subsequent events called to mind—of course were not really germane to our initial breakfast meeting or to a subsequent one before he took office. These discussions were, as I had expected, strictly about administrative matters.

At the first breakfast, we discussed the chairman's relationship to the board and the FOMC. At the second, he brought up the possibility of reorganizing the economics staff, particularly the domestic part of it. In those two areas, I was a natural source of background information for him because at the time I had been out of the Fed for no more than about a year, had served at the right hand of three preceding chairmen, and probably knew about as much as anyone else about how the Fed had over the years organized itself for monetary policy.

On the question of dealing with the board and the FOMC, he was obviously concerned with how best to get off on the right foot with his new colleagues. Although I do not have any detailed memory of the conversation, it remains in my mind that he must have heard that under Volcker, his immediate predecessor, the board and perhaps the FOMC had at times been restive. He seemed to be looking for a way to develop a more positive and less contentious relationship with his future colleagues. For instance, when we spoke, we were not far from the startling episode in the late winter of 1986 (described in the preceding chapter) when the board outvoted Volcker and came down in favor of a discount rate cut, then reconvened in the early afternoon to rescind that vote. Residual tensions among the concerned parties remained palpable over the balance of Volcker's tenure.

Another source of tension in those days—apart from some very obvious personality differences among the policymakers—might have been a feeling that the chairman did not include the board early enough in discussions of how to handle, for example, banking emergencies, such as Continental Illinois Bank's potential failure in 1984. So far as I could see, there was little reason for any such feeling. Perhaps some thought that Volcker did not delegate important responsibilities to other policymakers or did not include them in his early efforts to understand all angles of the problem.

Volcker tended to throw himself quickly and wholeheartedly into crucial issues and to examine the problem from all angles with relevant staff. One might say he had something of a love for crises; worst-case scenarios were like meat and drink to him; his eyes widened when he talked about the potential for them; and when they arrived and he could resolve them, well, it was almost heaven for him. But he was ever aware that board members would need to vote on solutions, and he kept them apprised, though not in exquisite detail, pretty much as he went along. Still, it is likely that some governors might have felt that they did not have an early enough input into the action and into the evolution of the best solution.

With regard to FOMC discussion, as I saw it, Volcker was quite inclusive and thoughtful, making sure that all viewpoints were given a fair hearing. In fact, I often thought he encouraged discussion beyond what was needed, imperiling at times the outcome he seemed to favor, at least from my perspective. So if there were tensions among policymakers because they believed the chairman was too domineering, those tensions did not seem to me to be rooted in the way Volcker conducted meetings. They were embedded more in personality differences and rivalries that were never far from the surface.

My response to Greenspan's queries at this first breakfast about how best to be off and running with his policy colleagues—influenced in part by these observations from the Volcker years, but also by my experience with other chairmen—was that he should try to make board and FOMC members feel that he was seeking their input into policy problems earlier rather than later. Relations would go more smoothly if they did not feel that they were being consulted only when their vote was required and when it might seem to them that options being presented for their consideration were too limited or biased in favor of the chairman's preference.

That advice is pretty obvious, of course, and would not seem to require three decades of experience to formulate.

Moreover, my response did not quite get at the heart of the issue. In my observation, chairmen have always been (reasonably) scrupulous in attempting to make sure policy deliberations take place on as level a playing field as possible, with all necessary information and background available to everyone. Contention and tension have evolved more from strong differences in political postures, economic philosophies, and working habits—with all compounded by personality issues. Whether Greenspan and I discussed that notion specifically, I rather doubt. In any event, I feel sure he must have understood something so basic.

I was surprised to get the next call from Greenspan two weeks or so later requesting another breakfast. Judging from subsequent events, he had come to know that the person who was then head of the Division of Research and Statistics at the board would be leaving rather shortly after his own official installation as chairman. However that may be, our second breakfast involved discussion of how or whether that division might be restructured to take account of existing talent if its current head left.

There is no need to review all of the boring ins and outs of how the Fed's research and policy staffs were adapted over the years to institutional needs and to the personalities and experience of the economists on hand. For instance, when I left the board, my then particular bureaucratic niche, Office of the Staff Director for Monetary and Financial Policy, was abolished, as was the accompanying title of staff director of the FOMC. The office's substantive domestic policy functions were placed under the authority of the head of the Division of Research and Statistics, and the few international finance issues (such as exchange-market operations) that for a while were part of my responsibilities, were again left solely to the head of the Division of International Finance.

Needless to say, no leadership vacuum was thereby created; everything that needed doing to support policy was done. Key staff members were well aware that cooperation, definitely not excessive competition, was the key to survival. This transition was facilitated because the board in Washington was not run as a rigid bureaucracy. The staff was essentially a meritocracy, and the institution was collegial in nature, at least in my day—and I tend to believe it has remained so subsequently. I certainly hope so.

With that as background, Greenspan and I discussed how to divide the Division of Research and Statistics to best take into account the skills of the two top officials who would remain. One of them was my former deputy, a relatively young Don Kohn, who, following my departure, had been shifted back to the Research Division as an associate director. His domestic responsibilities had not changed, and he was slotted more or less equally with another economist just below the departing director. The discussion focused on creating two divisions, one that would concentrate on the real economy and basic research, and another that would focus on monetary and financial policy issues, including directly connected basic research. I remember advocating that the newly created monetary division should include the area of capital markets and closely related institutions, as well as the obvious banking and government-securities market work.

In the event, the two divisions were created, but the monetary one did not include the capital-markets function and was entitled the Division of Monetary Affairs, without the dreaded word "policy," thus avoiding any possible doubt in the public's mind (if doubt there were, which strikes me as unlikely) that the staff might impinge upon board and FOMC's policy prerogatives.

Two sidelights to this administrative change are worth noting for what they might say about Fed attitudes, or at least some chairmen's attitudes, in relation to the policy process. The separation of capital markets from monetary affairs is quite consistent with the view taken by Greenspan (and by most central bankers so far as I can tell) that it is not the business of monetary policy to adjust its stance in order to stave off bubbles that might be emerging in particular markets—although it was, so he has noted, clearly policy's job to moderate adverse economic repercussions should bubbles burst.

However, in today's world of highly diversified and interconnected markets, banks and bank holding companies are inextricably linked to capital markets. Moreover, the funds once held for transactions and store of value functions in old-fashioned money supply (currency and deposits at banks and other depository institutions) have come to be increasingly mixed with other funds in a broader spectrum of credit and equity assets, some quite risky. In addition, the effective real tightness or ease the Fed's operating federal funds rate target cannot be evaluated apart from ongoing impacts more broadly on such changeable broad capital market conditions as the term and quality structures of interest rates that influence the cost and availability of credit to businesses and consumers.

There is no question that such subjects can be well analyzed within the Fed whether or not capital markets are part a monetary affairs division. But being more closely integrated with monetary analysis would, in my mind, better integrate capital market developments into ongoing assessment of monetary conditions and, thereby, the appropriateness of any particular funds rate target in terms of its implications for economic growth and inflation. Generally speaking, in today's world the judgment about the effectiveness of a particular funds rate for achieving policy objectives should be evaluated through its connection to evolving capital market conditions broadly, in the same sense as in earlier periods its significance was evaluated by reference to money supply and bank credit behavior.

Another, and unrelated, sidelight comes out of the evolution of Don Kohn's career. He subsequently became a Fed governor and shortly thereafter vice chairman, but before that, after something like fifteen years as director of the Division of Monetary Affairs, he was appointed as advisor to the Board. He was thus relieved of administrative headaches, but apparently retained much of his substantive function for giving policy advice. I called to congratulate him and told him a story to pass along to Greenspan, who, I thought, might be amused in light of his long acquaintance with Arthur Burns. Whether Don did, I do not know.

Before becoming staff director for monetary and financial policy, I too had the title of advisor to the board, indeed was the last person to hold that title before Don. At one point during Arthur Burns's tenure as chairman, I was asked to prepare a letter to be sent to the *New York Times* indicating why something that venerable institution had printed in connection with a financial issue indirectly related to monetary policy had in fact been wrong (I have long since forgotten the specifics).

The letter completed, Chuck Partee (then my boss on the staff and holding the title of managing director) and I met with Burns just before the letter was to be sent.

"Who should sign it?" asked Burns.

"Steve should," said Chuck. "He wrote it."

"I don't care," I interjected.

Looking at us in wonderment, Burns asked, "Don't either of you see the problem?" Innocents that we were, neither of us did; nor could we think of anything to say. Burns went on to enlighten us, "It's Steve's title as advisor. A board does not need advice; it needs research and statistical help" (something like that, anyway). Chuck stayed silent, not volunteering to sign with his less offensive title. Burns remained unyielding on my title.

This immense bureaucratic crisis was resolved by the suggestion—from Chuck, as I remember—that I sign the letter with the title "Economist (Domestic Finance)," which at that time happened to be my official title as an FOMC officer. Later, after Chuck was appointed a governor and I became staff director, the title "Advisor to the Board" disappeared, as did, if I recall correctly, the advisor-type titles that at the time also existed within the Research and International Finance divisions.

To this day I am not sure whether Burns was worried merely about public perceptions. I think not. He was also concerned, I would assume, about how the attitudes of staff holding the title of advisor might be affected. He seemed afraid that the staff might become a little less inclined to view themselves simply as people tasked with no more than aiding and abetting the policy decided by the board. They might come to think that they should actually tell him or the board, unbidden, what they thought about policy and collateral issues. Or, more subtle but more dangerous, they might let their own policy views influence their analysis.

Burns once let me know how irritated he was with another person holding an advisor title who took it upon himself to come to his office and tell him—tell, mind you—that he (Burns) should work to have a particular person rather than another appointed as head of a certain international institution. I also have a vague memory of being told that some kind of resignation threat by said advisor was at least implicit in the comment. Burns clearly thought that the advisor in this case had greatly overstepped his bounds. So did I, though I still wonder about the full credibility of the story as told to me.

I had one more conversation with Greenspan before he took office at the Fed. He called to ask who at the Fed could respond to an obscure (to me) technical question about nonlife insurance. My credibility as someone who knew the policy processes at the Fed unto their remotest underpinnings was clearly at stake. What indeed was the name of the person deep within the capital-markets section of the Research Division whom I knew to be the appropriate expert? Experts filled in almost every cranny of economics on the board staff. In a miracle of self-preservation, my brain cells somehow fired off the right combination; the person's name popped into mind and was duly relayed to Greenspan as if there were never any doubt as to its correctness.

I spoke very little with Greenspan after that. When I happened to be in Washington either for business or personal reasons, which was not frequent, I would sometimes make an effort to see him. If he were in town, he would usually make time for me, perhaps about fifteen minutes if I had not called in advance and not much more if I had. What I could bring to the table now was an outsider's assessment of economic conditions and how the market perceived Fed policy. Because of my extensive Fed background, I flattered myself with the thought that my comments might be a bit better focused on the current concerns of policy than others' comments would be, but I am far from sure that such self-flattery was warranted.

Be that as it may, chairmen always seem to value inputs from knowledgeable and active business and market leaders, so they can have some kind of (at least secondhand) foothold in or experiential sense of the so-called real world. Those inputs can then be set alongside and help them interpret the generally excellent staff reports and forecasts that are their main conduit into the economy and all its diverse cross-currents. In bringing an outside view to policymakers' attention, I never expected to hear anything back from Greenspan or from anyone else at the Fed that even remotely hinted at future policy beyond what had already been published. I was never disappointed in that expectation.

I do not have any idea, of course, how others spoke to policy officials or what their expectations were—nor, for that matter, how policy officials spoke to them. I did happen to be present at one session that turned out to be a perfect illustration of how not to speak with a chairman. Rather early in my tenure at Nikko Securities, its president and CEO in Tokyo and thus the head of Nikko worldwide asked if I could arrange a meeting between him and Greenspan. He planned to attend the annual meetings of the International Monetary Fund and the International Bank for Reconstruction and Development, which were being held in Washington that year. Greenspan, as a courtesy, agreed to fit a brief meeting into his schedule during what would obviously be an extremely busy period for him.

Not at all unusual for Nikko in those days, this particular president had a minimal command of English and little experience in the ways of conducting international official-type discussions. To help prepare him for the meeting, an upper midlevel Japanese executive at Nikko in New York had been asked to provide some questions and talking points for him. Ironically enough, but perfectly consistent with the company's peculiarly insular attitudes, I was not consulted in the development of the document even though I was the senior American in all of Nikko worldwide and obviously at that time also a person with very considerable direct knowledge of the Fed and its workings. I did have an opportunity to glance through the document once it was finalized. After all, what could a *gaijin* (Japanese for "foreigner," a word with somewhat pejorative connotations) know about how a very senior Japanese executive should behave?

As I recall, the president did ask me very late, and basically out of politeness given the need to make conversation while we were biding our time in the waiting room at the board's offices in Washington, how he might approach the discussion. My response was that he should open by offering his views on developments in the Japanese economy and stock market; because Nikko was perceived as a big player, Greenspan would probably be quite interested in these views. Later in the discussion, he could then ask Greenspan for his views on the U.S. economy. I am not absolutely sure whether I also said that he should definitely stay away from questions about U.S. monetary policy. Possibly not, because I probably assumed that everyone in the world would understand that the area was out of bounds.

After opening amenities, Greenspan turned to the Nikko president and in effect asked what questions or issues he would like to raise. Right out of the box, the president asked, "What will your future monetary policy be?" And there it was, just like that, the absolutely forbidden topic! Alan, no doubt surprised and incredulous, as I was, burst out laughing and said, "Ask Steve." I must have said something innocuous as my reflexive grimace turned into an idiotic smile.

As it turned out, the rest of the interview, though a bit stilted and self-conscious, went fairly well. Greenspan may have learned a bit more than he already knew about the Japanese market (and unfortunately also a bit more than he might have suspected about the astuteness of Japanese financial executives of that day), whereas the Nikko president learned nothing about the U.S. economy beyond the Fed's already published attitude. However, the president had achieved a primary goal; he could report on the conversation to his board. Also, as a Japanese friend informed me, he had gained months of name-dropping pleasure as he gossiped with his peers in the locker rooms of Japan's elite golf courses.

There was one other advantage for him in the meeting, and it was unexpected. As we were walking down the hall away from Greenspan's office, a personage no less than the governor of the Bank of Japan was approaching the office. The governor was visibly surprised, though he kept it very fleeting, to see the Nikko president. The president evidently could not have been more delighted. So all, finally, was well, indeed very well. And Alan was a very understanding man.

As the Greenspan years progressed, the Fed's attitude toward the amount of information that should be released to the public about the posture of current policy and indications of future policy changed radically. The early part of his tenure was still in the days when the Fed was not specific about current policy decisions. It provided no official background for those decisions—which were stipulated in qualitative terms (e.g., unchanged, tighter, easier)—until the abbreviated policy record released well after the FOMC meeting. It also generally did not provide any clear indications about future policy beyond the period between meetings. Later, as the 1990s progressed, the Fed began the process of providing the market with more and more information about the parameters of current and future policy.

In its first step toward making monetary policy more transparent, the Fed, by means of press releases issued at the end of FOMC meetings, began in 1994 to indicate the federal funds rate that it had adopted to guide operations until the next meeting.[3] This approach seemed very sensible to me. It had the advantage of eliminating the remote possibility that actions by the FOMC's manager for open market operations at the New York Fed could inadvertently mislead the market about the Committee's decision (I do clearly remember one instance in which this happened during my time). Such an incident could occur either because of a mistake in judgment by the manager or because of the effect of an unexpected change in the daily flow of figures he or she used to gauge pressures on the banking system's reserve position. As a result, the press release eliminated the unnecessary, though small, degree of uncertainty that formerly existed in markets about the ultimate cost of liquidity.

Thus, the market and the banking system could at least become quickly sure about the basic cost of liquidity underpinning the flow of funds throughout the economy for the next few weeks. The funds rate is certainly not the rate at which consumers, homeowners, and businesspersons can borrow, but it is the pivotal rate around which the whole interest-rate structure in financial markets tends to revolve.[4] Although the bulk of borrowing in the federal funds market is overnight, funds rates are also quoted for longer-term borrowing, such as three and six months ahead, providing market participants with an opportunity to bet on future Fed policy.

Announcement of the specific funds-rate objective for open market operations was merely the first step in a string of moves by the Fed through the balance of the 1990s and into the early 2000s leading to greater transparency of its policy intentions. The Fed began, one way or another, to hint at future policy by, for instance, including in the statements released directly after FOMC meetings some sentences and phrases that assessed the balance of risks it saw as between inflation and economic growth. For several years, it also took to giving much more specific hints about the degree and pace of the future direction of the funds rate.

As another aspect of the effort to increase policy transparency, the Fed also began to release the official minutes of the FOMC meeting two weeks after it took place. They had previously not been made available to the public until typically six or seven weeks after the meeting and thus following the next month's meeting. In my judgment, the earlier release was always technically possible, but it was avoided partly out of fear that the market would be either confused or misled. It is an interesting question whether or to what extent this increased openness has acted to inhibit discussions at FOMC meetings. (I suspect it has inhibited them a bit.) In any event, once released on the accelerated schedule, the early release provided the market with yet another opportunity to evaluate official policy intentions.

Not very much useful new information was made available to the market by accelerating the publication of the minutes. What can be gleaned about FOMC intentions depends, of course, on how the long discussions about the economy and policy issues are summarized in the minutes, and, in particular, about how differences of opinion are characterized. Public interpretation of the tenor of discussions would depend, for instance, on some knowledge or educated guesses about Fed usage of words.

In judging whether or to what extent opinion may be shifting within the FOMC, one needs to know whether an opinion attributed to "some" members has more weight than an opinion attributed to a "few" members, both of which would seem to have less heft than opinions attributed to a "number" or "many" members, not to mention the unredeemed explicitness of "most" members. Absence of such arcane knowledge may not be much of a loss in practice because the only genuinely valuable added information in the minutes would be a revelation of a forward-looking or slightly variant opinion by the chairman, at least once that personage has attained the stature of a Martin, Volcker, or Greenspan.

It is hard to judge what influenced the Fed's step-by-step implementation of a policy of increased transparency. It might have come after long deliberation about how to adapt monetary policy better to the modern world of instant communications and to the ever deeper and more quickly responsive, if not overly responsive, markets in the United States. Or it might have taken place more like a piecemeal evolution as one bit of transparency and its associated market reaction more or less inevitably led to another. I suppose a combination of both, but I would give somewhat more emphasis to the latter explanation.

From my narrow perspective, one rather accidental event seemed to be at least a partial contributor to the evolution, or at least the timing, under Greenspan of the probably inevitable trend toward increased transparency. I received a call one day while still at Nikko Securities from a *Washington Post* reporter named John Berry. He had been following the Fed for decades and was rumored to be a chosen source of "leaks" by chairmen who might wish to correct misinterpretations of one sort or another about policy issues or even, on quite rare occasions, to prepare the market, in a way that was obscure and without commitment, for action that just might be taken.

I knew Berry from years back. In my role as staff director at the Fed, a very small part of the job brought me in contact with a number of the principal reporters and writers of market letters who covered the Fed. I never discussed policy with them, but I had been assigned the task of trying to help ensure that they were up to speed on technical issues affecting markets and interest rates, such as whether corporate bond issuance was rising or falling, or on technical factors affecting monetary figures, such as institutional developments in the banking industry that might be occasioning changes in deposit flows and money supply. Such background information would presumably at least minimize the chances that the reporters would significantly misinterpret the role of policy in market developments.

By the time Berry called, that connection with the press was long in the past. What he asked surprised me. He wanted to know if the board still had verbatim transcripts of taped discussions at FOMC meetings going back into the Burns era. He must have heard about their existence from somewhere. At any rate, I affirmed that when I left, there still were such transcripts and that we had made and retained transcripts of discussions during the Miller and Volcker years. As he knew, the Fed in the 1970s had stopped publishing the very long so-called memorandum of discussion that was based on tapes and detailed notes taken at the meeting and that had been released five years after the relevant FOMC meeting. But following discontinuance of the memorandum, there were no inquiries, so far as I knew, about whether there were transcripts of tapes of subsequent meetings.

These earlier memoranda of discussion had represented an effort to turn the wide-ranging and rather free-form FOMC discussions into something akin to an orderly literary document, setting forth the detailed views expressed by specific members and staff without altering the content or significantly affecting the sequence of the discussion (with appropriate omissions connected with national-security concerns, international sensitivities, and maintenance of confidentiality with respect to information about individual institutions). The memorandum had been the official record (or minutes) of the committee's discussion and decision making.

However, in response to the call for greater openness (as typified by the Freedom of Information Act suit brought in 1975 by Merrill and the Government in the Sunshine Act passed in 1976), the FOMC had instead decided to publish a shorter summary of the discussion soon after the next meeting and to discontinue the memorandum of discussion. That decision struck me at the time as a great advance because in this way the essential elements of the discussion that went into the decision were made available to the public much more promptly. The transcripts were retained, however, in case there was a call for the more extended memorandum in the future through a change in law or public demand.

When the existence of unedited transcripts of meeting tapes came out (Berry's article seemed only to give added publicity to what had already been hinted at or leaked earlier), there was a mild uproar within the congressional oversight committees. The Fed, which had already in March 1993 turned the short summary of discussion into official minutes by adding organizational material, responded further. First, in November of that year, it agreed to publish lightly edited versions of the backlog of transcripts for the period since the memoranda of discussion had been discontinued; it later decided to keep publishing such transcripts on an ongoing basis with a five-year lag. Whether by coincidence or not, it was also around this time that the FOMC began the cautious process, earlier noted, of becoming more transparent about current policy.

Whatever the mix of intellectual conviction and public-relations need that influenced the Fed in its drive toward increased transparency, there are obvious limits in the degree to which the Fed can provide assurance to the market through openness. Like anyone else, the Fed is aware that economic conditions can change quickly and unexpectedly. Thus, for the most part it is forced to surround its indications about the direction of future policy with escape hatches, sometimes narrow and sometimes gaping. As a result, market participants are never relieved of the need to make their own judgments about future policy because the Fed at any meeting might well change how it expresses future intentions, and, even if it did not, the precise timing and degree of tightening or easing implied in a currently expressed attitude are not without uncertainties, sometimes considerable.

Whether the Fed is relatively open or closed about its intentions, market participants necessarily remain eager to find some unique insight into the pattern of thinking within the institution that might give them an edge relative to their competitors. Doing so is by no means easy, perhaps even impossible on average, but much time and energy are expended in the effort. Economists are hired. Fed officials in Washington and around the country are visited. Former officials are hired as consultants. Rumors of who might have said what to whom abound. Speeches by FOMC members are eagerly mined.

There is always the hope that hidden nuggets of precious information might be found somewhere somehow, the golden glow of a future foretold. Perhaps there is some benefit in the effort. However, I suspect the benefit may be less than the cost, particularly if allowance is made for the risks of misinterpretation inherent in the eagerness, given the immense potential market rewards, to find and believe in some little glimmer of something that is in reality simply not there. In any event, I came to think that it was an unwise market participant who paid any serious attention to speeches or commentary by anyone other than Greenspan—some attention, yes, but not the really serious kind of attention that might significantly influence one's market bets.

The upsurge in the urge to communicate by the Fed and its officials in the last part of the 1990s and the early 2000s has had mixed results. Greenspan's widely noted comment warning the stock market against "irrational exuberance" in December 1996 is an example of how a public pronouncement that was perceptive on the face of it can, as its significance mutates in the course of a largely unforeseeable series of events, tends to, of all things, encourage what it was originally designed to discourage. At the time of his comment, the Dow Jones Industrial Average, for instance, had already risen sharply in the course of that year, passing through the 6,000 level, and investors were coming to believe that much more was in store. And the stock market did keep rising. But there was no follow-up action by the Fed.

Moreover, not long after his expressed worry about irrational exuberance, Greenspan began to suggest that the economy was entering a new period of strong productivity growth. From a market perspective, investors were encouraged to believe that business profits would remain strong and sustain stock values. Whether rightly or wrongly, the market acted as if the chairman were backtracking, at least to an extent, from his original concerns about excessive exuberance.

As the stock market continued to rise late in the 1990s, a number of people, myself included, thought that it would be desirable for the Fed to raise margin requirements (essentially the down payment required when credit is employed for the purpose of purchasing or carrying stocks) in an effort to take some action that would at least serve as a concrete sign of the Fed's concern about irrational exuberance. My occasional efforts to persuade the powers that be at the Fed to do so were advanced quite diffidently because I was all too aware that margin requirements had long since fallen into disuse and that the Fed had virtually no desire to resurrect them. But even if others with more prestige and clout had forcefully advanced the arguments, as they may have for all I know, it would have made no difference. The Fed had no doubt considered the question on its merits and simply found the policy wanting.

The Fed has the authority by law to impose margin requirements on stock purchases.[5] But, in fact, the requirement has remained at 50 percent for a great many years as the Fed lost its appetite for attempting to influence the stock market in that fashion and in any event seemed to prefer that regulatory action affecting stocks be taken by the Securities and Exchange Commission and by the stock exchanges themselves.

Consistent with that general attitude, during the run-up of stock prices in the last half of the 1990s, the Fed apparently concluded that an increase in requirements would be futile because only a small share of total stock transactions would be affected, and, in any event, given the fungibility of credit and money, other sources of financing could easily be found. However that might be, I still felt that a rise in the margin requirement would have at least symbolized the Fed's concern and would have helped at the margin (pun intended) to restrain the stock market's ebullience; but perhaps this feeling was no more than a lingering residual of my practical inclination to employ whatever tangible instruments are at hand if they might even marginally smooth the way for basic monetary policy.

All that being said, I have no doubt that the principal restraining influence on stocks would have been a more aggressive monetary policy. One of my consultees around that time—a very well-known manager of billions for a prominent hedge fund—seemed quite sure of that. As he happily pocketed his bubbly earnings and hoped (but did not quite succeed, I think) to get out before the inevitable market implosion, he told me at one point in the course of our then usual very brief weekly telephone conversations that the profitable speculation on stocks was not going to stop until the Fed seriously tightened policy.

During the buildup of the bubble, however, the Fed seemed to ignore the dangers posed by an unduly excessive inflation in the stock market— that is, in the value of equities and thus in the underlying valuation of the nation's existing physical capital stock that produced the current flow of goods and services. Instead, policy was aimed, as usual, at maintaining satisfactory economic growth and keeping inflation in the price of goods and services under control, which was in fact the Fed's indicated price goal.

Although I had no fear of inflation in currently produced goods and services at the time, I was quite worried, based in part on my observations of Japanese behavior while working with Nikko, that the run-up in our stock market was undermining the potential for continued satisfactory economic performance. In some sense, it was in the stock market that one could see the inflationary effect of too much money chasing too few goods, in this case the goods in effect being the country's stock of capital.

It seemed clear that inflation of equity prices, especially if it was outrageous enough, could create growth-threatening imbalances in the economy similar to those created by sizeable inflation in currently produced goods and service prices, and thus leading to the similar risk of a very serious recession. That very thing had happened in Japan in the 1990s. Because it had become so cheap during their bubble period to finance capital spending with equities or convertible bonds, corporations found that once the bubble burst, they were saddled with a huge stock of greatly overvalued capital equipment that had been built up well beyond any reasonable estimate of businesses' ability over the next few years to sell profitably what that capital could produce. The necessary corporate pullback in spending, coupled with the very large overhang of bad debt afflicting the economy and the banking system, greatly prolonged the Japanese economy's weak performance thereafter.

That the United States was at such risk was hardly apparent at the time Greenspan made his seemingly prescient "irrational exuberance" comment or for some while afterwards. Stock prices had just begun to show signs of seriously outrunning their normal relationship to corporate earnings, whereas business investment spending was not yet showing especially unusual strength. The Fed apparently believed that attainment of its economic growth and price objectives did not require much change in monetary policy, and the funds rate actually changed little on balance from early 1996 (a slight rise occurred in early 1997) through the late summer of 1998 even as the stock market continued to rise substantially beyond its original "irrational exuberance" danger level.

An unfortunate series of events then occurred in the latter part of 1998 that further persuaded the market that the Fed and Greenspan in particular were at best half-hearted in any worry about irrational exuberance and that the Fed would go to some lengths to rescue markets from their own worst behavior. A kind of market-wide moral hazard was beginning to form and then seemed to spread more widely into credit markets early in the new millennium through the market's interpretation and practical use of the more explicit information then being given about the direction and pace of change in future monetary policies.

In any event, in the last few months of 1998 the Fed eased monetary policy by reducing the funds rate in three steps by a total of three-fourths of a percentage point in an apparent effort to help stabilize U.S. financial markets and by extension world markets. The basic purpose was to keep the U.S. economy on a steady growth course. Confidence had been greatly shaken in the aftermath of the Russian financial crisis in August of that year and the consequent well-publicized problems of a large U.S. hedge fund, Long Term Capital Management (LTCM).

The probability of an exaggerated loss of confidence in markets and a weakening of the economy must have seemed high to the Fed in part because these market shocks followed rather closely upon the unexpected onset of financial crises about a year or more earlier in a number of key emerging Asian countries of the time, such as Taiwan, Korea, and Malaysia, which remained fresh in the market's mind and no doubt heightened sensitivities. The U.S. stock market in fact dropped rather sharply throughout the summer of 1998.

In that period, there certainly was a feeling among many observers, at least for a while, that it would not take much for the bottom to fall out of the world economy. In that context, I for one had no problem with the degree of the Fed's monetary easing. Now, with the great benefit of hindsight, I believe the last quarter of a percentage point was a stage too far. That amount does not seem like much, but, as every comedian or tragedian knows, the effect is all in the timing.

Monetary policy did attempt to offset the excessively expansionary impact of its easing by reversing course. Unfortunately, what could not be so readily offset was the longer-term impact on market attitudes caused by the Fed's involvement in keeping LTCM itself from an immediate total implosion. It publicly entangled itself in a market effort to ensure that the hedge fund's financial problems would be worked out in an orderly fashion over a period of time.

True enough, the Fed apparently did little more in relation to LTCM than to take the initiative for a private-market solution and indicate a clear sense of urgency in this situation; to provide a meeting place for certain discussions among the key lenders and large investors who were involved, some of whom unfortunately were simultaneously both investors and lenders; and of course to gather information necessary to appraise the situation. No federal government money was advanced or apparently promised. Nevertheless, the Federal Reserve System as an institution was perceived to be the leader in these efforts, even if no public funds were involved.

In the eyes of many market participants, Greenspan, as the Fed's leader, was acting counter to his oft-stated views that private institutions left to themselves could be relied upon to resolve market problems in response to traditional price and profit incentives. As a result, he was close to falling into the conventional moral-hazard trap, encouraging financial institutions to take excessive risk on the thought that the Fed would bail them out at least to some degree. Moreover, such an interpretation was unfortunately encouraged and generalized to the market as a whole when the FOMC was observed to be in the process of easing monetary policy at the same time as the LTCM problem was being dealt with basically through market processes.

I do not believe at all that the monetary easing in any way represented an effort to lower interest rates as a means of benefiting the LTCM portfolio so as to make that specific situation more attractive as a workout. The Fed was in fact reacting to the very damaging possibility of broad systemic instability in the banking and financial system that would inevitably threaten economic stability here in the United States and abroad. However, I suspect such a suspicion could well have arisen in the minds of many active and sophisticated market participants, a group for whom survival seems to require, or at least comes to entail, a very high quotient of cynicism.

The idea of a "Greenspan put" came to be bruited about in markets (meaning, in effect, "Don't worry so much, fellows; we can always put off some of our losses on Greenspan"). It was something of a joke, but enough seriousness underlay it, I would contend, to contribute at least in some degree to the reemergence and continuation of excessively bullish attitudes in the stock market once the market and LTCM crises had passed and the Fed had begun to tighten its monetary policy.

My interest in LTCM and its significance was heightened when I was asked to testify before Congress about the episode and its regulatory implications. The reasons why I was asked are unclear, but were probably related to the status derived from my previous close association with Volcker. I was one of the last speakers among several others on a panel from private markets. By that time, it was quite late in the day, and there was practically no one left in the hearing room except the committee chairman, Congressman Jim Leach, who had been gallant enough to stay on. Other committee members' interest had dissipated once the committee heard from the Fed (represented by Greenspan and Bill McDonough, then president of the New York Fed) and from other relevant top government regulators.

In working on the testimony, I found that my rather strong residual loyalty to and confidence in the Fed as an institution was in some conflict with my view about what should have been done in the LTCM crisis. The conflict was not just a matter of loyalty. It also stemmed from knowledge that a nation's central bank has the ultimate and rather awesome responsibility for ensuring that a broad systemic financial crisis does not burst forth from the action(s) of one or a few market institutions. Indeed, as noted earlier, central banks were invented to be institutions that stood outside of ongoing market developments, whose viability was not threatened by those developments, and which therefore would have the capacity to step in as lender of last resort to banks or other similar institutions that were in deep system-threatening trouble.

The Fed had always used its immense lender-of-last-resort powers very cautiously in order to avoid moral-hazard issues associated with emergency-type lending to individual institutions. As already noted, it advanced no funds to LTCM or to banks lending to that institution, but it did make the judgment that it was worth taking a modest initiative in relation to LTCM by bringing private-market participants together and thereby imparting a sense of urgency to the situation in an effort to guard against the risk of a systemic crisis, even if the risk was small, because it apparently believed that the outcome could otherwise be disastrous.

My own view was that the Fed overreacted in this instance, though I held back from giving such a clear opinion. I did indicate that the failure of a hedge fund, even one so large as LTCM, was not likely to threaten public confidence in the core of the nation's financial system. It was not significant to the payments mechanism that assured a smooth flow of funds for business and other transactions around the country, nor would its failure affect the safety and soundness of the banking system and other institutions holding the great bulk of the nation's liquid savings. At the same time, though, I understood that the Fed had full knowledge of the company's condition, and, given overall market conditions at the time, the situation may have appeared very much more threatening to the Fed than it seemed to me from my distance. Nevertheless, all that being said, I thought I was waffling in the direction of criticism of the action taken by the Fed.[6]

I did wonder about Greenspan's personal views on the matter—how he reconciled his confidence in the ability of private markets to take care of their own problems sans government intervention with the action taken by the Fed in this instance. From my vantage point in the audience while the regulators were testifying in the congressional hearing, I had the impression that he wished to be almost anywhere but there.

Maybe I am overstating. Reading someone else's body language is obviously a perilous business, but Greenspan seemed to be shrinking as far back as he could in the room while aware that his prominent seat was a very distinct impediment to such an effort. His statement and responses were of course supportive of the Fed's action. But I was particularly struck by the paragraph in his statement where it was twice noted that the judgment of the New York Fed and its officials were instrumental in the Fed's involvement in this situation. And as if in emphasis of this view, McDonough offered his testimony first, and Greenspan spoke second, an unusual sequencing that seemed to leave Greenspan with a secondary supportive role.

Certainly, the chairman must have been informed very early in the evolution of the LTCM situation, as would be consistent with everything I had observed and participated in during my tenure on the board staff. Although reserve bank presidents are the point persons in resolving issues with banks or institutions in crisis in their districts, their actions are carefully overseen and, in particularly important episodes, even micromanaged by the chairman of the board in Washington with the help of board staff. So far as I can remember from my time at the Fed, no key decisions were taken by any reserve bank president without the specific approval of the chairman, who, in turn, kept the board apprised of events and consulted on decisions made along the way (whether or not direct lending by a reserve bank was to be involved).

Perhaps Greenspan was more prone to delegate than other chairmen. I cannot be sure. Whether or not, I took his demeanor, the wording of his testimony, and the sequencing of his appearance as indicative of some ambivalence toward the operation concerning LTCM.

Taking place within a comparatively short period of about two years, all these various actions—a monetary policy that in retrospect seemed a bit easier than needed to stabilize markets and keep the economy growing, the Fed's involvement with LTCM, and the loss of credibility in connection with the comment on the market's "irrational exuberance"—came home to roost in the outrageous further stock-market rise through 1999 and into 2000, when at long last the bubble burst. The market dropped very sharply, especially the high-tech sectors, and did not regain its footing until the latter part of 2002.

The Fed responded to the potential for economic weakness in such a crash and the actual evidence from incoming economic data by a vigorous easing of monetary policy. The economy recovered rather quickly (the recession lasted eight months, from March to November 2001, according to the National Bureau of Economic Research), but the Fed, in light of its risk-management approach to policy, maintained a very accommodative monetary policy for a sustained period and, as earlier noted, continuously told the market that it would do so.

In one sense, the U.S. economy's fairly quick recovery following the stock-market crash around the turn of the twenty-first century and in wake of the Fed's policy easing might seem to be solid evidence for Greenspan's fundamental view that the Fed cannot and should not adapt monetary policy specifically in response to possible emerging bubbles in individual sectors of the economy (which in any event are by their nature inherently difficult to gauge). Instead, it should do what it can to ensure that the economy suffers as little as possible from the aftereffects should bubbles materialize and burst.

But the great credit crisis later in the first decade of the new century, with its attendant widespread and far from easily remediable social and economic dislocations, belies any sanguine implications that one might be tempted to derive from Greenspan's view at the time. Moreover, I also believe Greenspan and the Fed were quite lucky in the economy's positive response after the economic crash at the turn of the century.

"Luck" is an odd word here. The result in this situation was not the kind of good luck to be wished on anyone. To me, the strength of the recovery seemed to be in substantial part a response not to monetary policy but to a sudden and unexpected turn to a very expansive fiscal policy. Such a fiscal shift of course reflected the large increase in U.S. government spending occasioned by the security, defense, and military needs following the disaster of September 11, 2001, and the subsequent invasion of Iraq in 2003, all in combination with the tax cuts of 2001 that followed Bush's arrival in the presidency. With the economy uncertain, the Fed chose to accommodate the sharply expansive swing in the federal budget with a sustained easy money policy.

It was not until the recovery was well along that the Fed began to tighten, but so gradual was the process that the real funds rate remained somewhat negative on average over the four-year period from 2002 to 2005[7]—shades of Arthur Burns, though accompanied by only a quite modest buildup of overall inflation pressures in the different economic environment of the time. Unfortunately, however, the policy did eventually help to generate yet another asset-type bubble, this time in the housing market.

I would argue that the bubble was also abetted to a degree by the virtual guarantee contained in official FOMC statements that the easy availability of cheap short-term debt would be long sustained—a guarantee that probably encouraged market participants to take on more risk, not only in housing but also in other market areas, than was good for them or the economy. At one point, I attempted to explain this point to a squash-playing friend active in equity markets on Wall Street—that it was not merely the excessively low level of rates that was harmful but in particular the virtual guarantee that they would be around for years, which tended to take away normal market risk worries. Suddenly, he looked straight at me and said, "Oh, you mean, they made it too easy for us." Yes, indeed, the Fed had unwisely encouraged excess leverage—since it seemed at the time to be giving assurance that refinancing costs of the short-term debt which funded longer-term positions would remain cheap for a good long time, even as lax regulation of the whole credit process also helped the crisis along.

Toward the end of initial period of sustained Fed ease after the 2000 stock market crash, when the funds rate had reached a low of 1 percent, the Fed began to include in its official statements such phrases as "policy accommodation can be maintained for a considerable period." Subsequently, as it shifted toward tightening in the summer of 2004 the FOMC started to announce that monetary accommodation can be removed "at a pace that is likely to be measured" as indeed it was.[8]

The Fed clearly found it difficult to interpret the behavior of rates in the market as it began to tighten—to know whether the failure of longer-term rates to rise at least a little was signaling expectations of less underlying economic strength than there seemed to be, or a growing conviction that inflation would remain low, or no more than a misperception of the Fed's own attitude toward longer-term rates (my vote is for the latter). In any event, given the persistence of relatively low long-term rates, officials began suggesting in speeches that the behavior of longer-term markets in face of the gradual tightening in short-term rates was a quandary. It would seem that they did not look long and hard in the mirror before speaking.

Whatever the most reasonable interpretation of rate behavior and Fed intentions might be (and there is always some ambiguity), the market seemed to have interpreted the "measured pace" phrase as a license for continuing to bet that they could keep making money by borrowing short and investing long. Ultimately, the ensuing speculative boon for market profits ended when the housing bubble finally burst and spread to other markets that were also highly overleveraged.

These efforts to hint about the future seem to have been undertaken in the belief that increased transparency about the FOMC's policy attitude would improve the implementation and presumably the effectiveness of policy by placing markets and the Fed on the same page as much as practically possible—that is, to increase the odds that the behavior of markets and of consumers and businesses in their spending decisions would be more in tune, rather than out of tune, with efforts by policy to contain inflation and maintain satisfactory economic growth. Not on the face of it a bad idea, but it does assume that the Fed's judgment about the likely course of the economy (much of which is far from under its control) is better than the market's. Also, it does increase the chances that the Fed will inadvertently entice the market into actions with unfortunate consequences—that is, create a market moral hazard of sorts, which indeed took place.

The measured pace phrase was eliminated shortly before Bernanke's tenure began, in effect leaving new leadership with something of a clean slate. It was probably dropped also because the Fed believed that the economy was by then sufficiently strong and the market need not be given any assurances about the rate's future.

Looking back at the Greenspan Fed from the perspective of his almost two decades in office, his management was obviously associated with a long period of prosperity with virtually no inflation; in that respect, he surely managed the bulk of his tenure well. But the last part of his tenure was strikingly damaged by a severe stock market crash, by a sharp recession rescued primarily by fiscal policy, and by easy money policies that persisted too long, were too predictable, and helped sow the seeds of the great credit crisis.

I take Greenspan's principal innovation in the policy-setting process to have been increased openness in clearly and promptly revealing the current Fed policy decision and the thinking behind it. However, and much less fortunately in my opinion, Greenspan also took the step of revealing the likely direction and, to a degree, dimensions of future policy decisions. Moreover, at times he (and his colleagues) seemed to employ jawboning in speeches in an effort to influence, in ways consistent with how the Fed saw the economy developing, the course of longer-term interest rates and yields (on stocks, for instance) not directly controlled by the Fed.

In general, I believe it is best all around for officials to avoid commentary about the future of rates they cannot directly control or are unwilling to control—that is, rates other than the funds rate. I also think it is best to avoid commenting on the probable future of rates and markets they do control. In either event, they taint the information being conveyed back to themselves and other market participants by the behavior of rates. Also, and more dangerously, because of misinterpretations and unintended consequences, they risk causing reactions in the spending and borrowing decisions by businesses and individuals that make the underlying economic and also financial situation worse rather than better for the economy and its future.

In short, the future is unknowable both to the Fed and to the markets. And little seems to be gained, and much can be lost in terms of the chairman's and the Fed's credibility and policy effectiveness, by getting into the mug's game of exposing policy intentions and wishes in ways that may be misinterpreted and, in the end, as market conditions change, misleading and ultimately damaging.

7

Bernanke and the Response to the Great Credit Crisis

The arrival of Ben Bernanke as chairman of the Board of Governors of the Federal Reserve System at the beginning of February 2006 marked a generational shift in leadership away from the cohort that had grown up during the Great Depression of the 1930s and the Second World War— a shift that also seemed to be typical, as one should naturally expect, of appointees in general throughout the Obama administration once it took office.

The economists now coming into leadership positions were trained differently from earlier generations, with more stress being placed on the application of increasingly sophisticated mathematical and statistical techniques to the understanding of economic issues. Whether the advantages of this more rigorous type of training have been at the expense of a diminution in the intuitive-type skills that help in understanding the ever-changing, and often puzzling and self-defeating, behavior of market participants is, to me, an open question. It is also an open question whether it has been at the expense of effective, empathetic public communication skills that might be needed to advance and smooth the way for policy shifts during turbulent times.

Highly intelligent and a distinguished academician well known for his monetary and financial research, Bernanke began his governmental service under President George W. Bush, who in the summer of 2002 nominated him first as a governor of the Fed, then after almost three years called upon him to become chairman of the Council of Economic Advisers, and subsequently nominated him to be chairman of the Fed Board. President Obama appointed him for a second term, beginning in February 2010.

Bernanke inherited a very difficult situation from his successor. Monetary policy had been too easy for some time. Inflationary expectations seemed poised to rise, given the ongoing strength of commodity prices and the continuation of some ebullience in consumer and business spending. At the same time, however, it was clear that the housing market was getting ahead of itself, both in the potential for a large buildup in excess housing inventory and for far too much mortgage debt—debt that was being taken on not only to finance homes that were in many cases barely, if at all, affordable but also to fund consumption more broadly. Indeed, in early 2006 residential spending had already begun what proved to be its long-sustained decline. Financial conditions in the mortgage market had become fragile at best and its viability, such as it might be, depended greatly on a continued rise in home prices and sustained low interest rates.

As noted in the preceding chapter, the "measured pace" phrase used essentially to guarantee no more than a very gradual removal of monetary accommodation by the FOMC had been finally deleted toward the very end of Greenspan's tenure, as the funds rate was moving into a positive real range. Under Bernanke, the funds rate rose further, peaking at 5¼ percent in the early summer of 2006, where it remained for about fifteen months. At that point, the Fed apparently believed the rate was about neutral, taking into account the many cross-currents in the economy at the time, which featured the gathering weakness in the housing sector and also the somewhat puzzling and, it would seem, speculatively fueled acceleration in commodity prices that actually continued into the summer of 2008.

From the perspective of the economy and inflation, judging over history, perhaps the rate was neutral or more likely the high side of neutral. However, from the perspective of profound instabilities latent in the mortgage market at the time and, as it turned out, credit markets more generally, it proved to be too high. Fed policymakers should have phased out the unfortunate measured pace phrase much earlier, and the funds rate should have risen more quickly (though not quite as high) to help stave off the potential housing bubble. But that is hindsight, which is always more accurate than foresight. All it really does is illustrate the huge dilemma faced by Bernanke, one certainly not to be wished upon him or indeed even one's proverbial worst enemy.

In the end, the fine balance the Fed thought it had achieved between its goal of keeping inflation expectations under control while also keeping the real economy in good shape was about to be undone by the great

2007–2009 crash in credit markets. As best as one can judge from rather sanguine early official comments, Fed officials were apparently surprised that a crisis in the relatively small subprime sector of the mortgage market morphed into the very major crisis of confidence in credit markets more broadly and in the viability of major financial institutions, including both major depository institutions and investment banks. They were hardly the only ones so surprised.

To contain the crisis and its potential for damaging economic consequences, the FOMC after a time sharply lowered its targeted federal funds rate in several steps back to the point where, by the early part of 2008, it was again around zero or in negative territory in real terms. At the same time, the Fed began to stretch its statutory authority and adapt its regulations in innovative and dramatic ways to ensure that day-to-day liquidity flowed where needed, that its role as lender of last resort could in effect reach beyond banks to other financial institutions, and, in short, that the functioning of modern interconnected markets and their diverse instruments could be sustained.

Most of these actions represented a more extensive use of the discount window or something like such a window. As the crisis was gathering momentum, the Fed, toward the end of 2007, permitted individual banks and depository institutions to bid for loans of somewhat longer-term funds from the window, the so-called Term Auction Facility (TAF). This represented a quite creative (though a rather belated) response to signs that trading in federal funds, the key market for meeting day-to-day financing needs of banks and the economy was becoming a less liquid and reliable source of liquidity, especially for loans that were longer than just overnight. As credit flows more broadly also tended to falter, the Fed took other actions in March 2008 that extended its reach beyond the banking system and into the investment banking community—a recognition of the breadth of the crisis, but one might also say a recognition of the way in which the institutional structure of finance had changed as markets had become more complex and interrelated.

For instance, the Federal Reserve Bank of New York was authorized around mid-March 2008 to establish an overnight lending facility for primary dealers (consisting of twenty securities firms at the time, including many major ones, authorized to be counterparties in the Fed's open market operations) to advance credit that could be collateralized not just by

U.S. government securities but also by a broad range of investment-grade securities. The interest rate to be charged would be the Fed's relatively low prime credit rate. In September, when the crisis took a major turn for the worse, the program was extended to include loans to a set of other dealers on very similar terms.[1]

But most importantly in the latter part of March 2008, the Fed engaged in a major bailout of a securities firm. It announced its approval of the acquisition of Bear Stearns, a sizeable investment firm, by JPMorgan Chase. In the process it agreed to provide $29 billion of guaranteed financing through term loans from the New York Fed against $30 billion of presumably dubious collateral—the loan to be made at the primary credit rate, not at some premium rate that might have been expected from what was clearly an emergency transaction to be backed by very risky collateral. The financial system's stability had come to be seen as depending on a lot more than the health of the banking system, though the latter was, to be sure, heavily involved in the crisis.

The resolution of the Bear Stearns situation, quickly arranged over a weekend, was designed to avoid very damaging psychological and contagious effects on highly sensitive and almost reeling markets from an otherwise inevitable bankruptcy of a major investment bank. In consequence of this action, much public print and market talk was devoted to the issue of whether the Fed had unduly increased moral hazard risks, by encouraging a broad range of institutions in the belief that the Fed can be relied on to rescue them from bad management decisions.

This is a genuinely troubling issue, but it needs to be recognized that being "rescued" by the Fed is no bed of roses, or certainly should not be. Reputations of the institution's top executives are generally badly damaged, their prestigious and profitable positions are lost or highly imperiled, and stockholders are faced with almost a total loss in value of their equity in the firm. In my view, bad and unduly risky management decisions by executives are mainly if not entirely the product of their personal temperament and competitive pressures, and are not influenced in any especially significant way by a questionable future prospect of being bailed out by the Fed (or any other government entity). However, one cannot rule out the possibility of a very subtle background influence.

The principal beneficiaries in a Fed rescue are the firm's creditors, such as uninsured depositors in the case of banks or, in this case, lenders who financed the mortgage-backed security holdings and other assets of a troubled investment bank and who will now be more assured of prompt payment than they would be in bankruptcy proceedings. By keeping creditors more or less whole, a Fed rescue works to avert the further spread of market harm and uncertainties from the consequent strain on creditors.

In a sense then, the real moral hazard innate in the process involves not only the possibility that institutions may be encouraged to take on excessive risk but also the chance that creditors may not feel the need to push their due diligence as far as they should before lending to the institutions (even while placing whatever faith they can bring themselves to think reasonable in the judgments of rating agencies). Indeed, the moral hazard that creditors will not perform adequate due diligence strikes me as the more likely psychological risk if the market comes to believe that there is some implicit assurance that the Fed or some other governmental institution will step in and help rescue a company.

The multiple moral hazard issues in connection with use of the Fed's lending facilities cannot and should not be played down, nor of course, as earlier stressed, should the actual market behavior that was encouraged by the moral hazards implicit in the conduct of open market operations and public communication in the latter part of Greenspan's tenure. However, by Bernanke's time as chairman, the challenging market situation that had evolved truly forced the Fed (moral hazard or no) to rescue individual institutions and also, as it turned out, market sectors more broadly (involving much more extensive use of its funds) in the interest of keeping markets and the economy from the threat of total collapse. Indeed, as will soon be argued, at one point the Fed, perhaps worried a bit too much about moral hazard in connection with institutional lending, disastrously failed in that very challenge.

The threat of systemic instability was particularly heightened by the ludicrously high degree of leverage (i.e., extensive use of borrowed funds) that had evolved across interconnected markets and institutions as they financed and dealt in numerous sophisticated and not especially transparent instruments—such as the by now well-publicized collateralized debt obligations (CDOs). Once prices of highly leveraged assets begin to drop, their value to holders would quickly threaten to fall under water (since in the circumstances even a relatively modest price decline might eliminate any positive equity). Calls for additional cash or acceptable collateral from lenders greatly quicken as their safety margins are more rapidly eroded. Pressures on borrowers intensify, and they can be forced to sell other assets in the course of meeting the margin calls. In the end, markets, here and also abroad in today's interconnected world, can come to resemble a tottering house of cards as the availability of adequate collateral becomes increasingly scarce and prices of other assets are in turn being squeezed as additional cash is sought, causing further and spreading problems throughout the system.

In addition to problems inherent in excess leverage, markets were afflicted by a general slackening in regulatory alertness as the governmental policy of deregulation—initiated about three decades earlier and needed at the time to help modernize the structure of banking and finance—had gone too far and was showing signs of wearing down into carelessness. For instance, the recent crisis brought out deficiencies in policing customer suitability in mortgage and other transactions—particularly evident in the subprime mortgage sector—as well as other well-publicized signs of laxity, such as apparent weaknesses in investigating the potential dangers in the financing and balance sheet treatment of CDO's or to follow up adequately on detecting financial scams that subsequently became widely known. Still, in my view, it was the uncontained spirit of leverage and high-stakes gambling that contributed most significantly to the intensity of the crisis, although the general slackening in regulatory and supervisory attitudes was permissive, quite damaging, and probably close to being a sine qua non.

Looked at more basically, the intensity of the crisis cannot be divorced from the overall social and economic atmosphere of the past decade or so. Perilous credit market behavior, weak or careless leadership within the regulatory community, and a permissive political and congressional context influenced by well-heeled financial interest groups all were fostered by a pervasive nationwide culture that increasingly valued risky investments and thriftless spending while devaluing even a reasonable degree of prudence.

All that being as it may, the Bernanke Fed's response to the crisis can be criticized as being too delayed. Apart from serious questions about the conduct of monetary policy noted earlier, the Fed, in its various regulatory roles as well as in discount window administration, could have put some programs to safeguard markets, consumers, and mortgage applicants in place earlier. That it did not helped to signal that the Fed was not particularly worried about the potential for catastrophe in the evolving situation.

In general, the psychology of fear among market participants (e.g., about the financial viability of counterparties) that so accelerated the crisis might have been better contained if the Fed early on had succeeded in demonstrating, in some way or another, that it was well aware of the potential for very serious damage in the complex, highly leveraged, and highly tenuous market activities that were rife at the time. Some leadership charisma was required. A feeling in the market, irrational as it might have been, that the Fed was not sufficiently interested in or adequately conscious of ongoing market processes likely added in some degree both to market uncertainties and fears and also, on the other hand, to some lack of restraint.

For a few months after the spring of 2008, the severe financial crisis that originated during the latter part of 2007 in the United States and also was noticeable, though perhaps less so at first, in key international markets seemed to stabilize. Unfortunately, however, that was not much more than a lull as disorderly and disruptive forces latent in the shaky structure of finance at the time became more obviously infectious both here and abroad. Neither U.S. nor key international markets could remain as relatively calm as the Fed (and presumably also the U.S. Treasury), and also foreign banking authorities and finance ministries, might have anticipated or at least hoped.

The next major crisis point arrived in mid-September 2008, when it became necessary for the Fed to decide whether or not it should help rescue another investment bank, Lehman Brothers, as many in the market expected that it would, given the Bear Stearns precedent. By that time the stock market, which had been in a declining trend since late 2007 and had recovered modestly over the first few months following the Bear Stearns rescue operation, had by early summer again begun to retreat further. In credit markets, quality spreads on interest rates had been widening somewhat further. Rumors had remained rife that other major institutions, and especially Lehman, were in trouble.

But these developments could be read as still consistent with a shaky though as yet systemically stable market responding to increased economic uncertainties as a recession appeared to be looming or perhaps was already in process. Since mid-March of '08 the Fed had found it necessary to take only very few additional special measures, such as further increasing swap lines with foreign central banks by a moderate amount and authorizing access to the Fed discount window at the basic lending rate to Fannie Mae and Freddie Mac (the federal housing lending agencies that operated with an implicit government guarantee). And it was not until December 2008 that the cautious and careful National Bureau of Economic Research designated December 2007 as the latest cyclical peak for the U.S. economy, following 73 months of expansion since the previous cyclical low. (In September 2010, the group designated June 2009 as the cyclical trough, following eighteen months of intense contraction.)

At its open market policy meeting on September 16, 2008, the Fed kept the nominal federal funds rate policy target at 2 percent, where it had been since the end of April, following a fairly substantial reduction at the time of Bear Stearns and a small further downward adjustment in April. That seemed to confirm official sentiment that while the overall credit situation remained perilous, markets were functioning well enough and the financial system had not moved significantly closer to a breakdown.

Very quickly, however, right around the time of the mid-September FOMC meeting, the market situation changed utterly. After the Fed would not make an emergency loan to Lehman Brothers, the firm filed for bankruptcy on Monday, September 15. Furthermore, on September 16 the Fed, with the support of the U.S. Treasury, was literally forced by the market situation to lend $85 billion on an emergency basis to the insurance giant AIG, partly so that it could make payments to major market creditors related, among other things, to such instruments as credit default swaps (CDS), for which it was liable (and presumably exposed without an adequate, if any, hedge).

The Fed, the Treasury, and the U.S. government as a whole were at that point face to face with an actual systemic financial crisis, perhaps not a complete breakdown of the system but one far too close for comfort. Not only was the stock market beginning to look more like it was in a free fall rather than an orderly retreat from unsustainable cyclical highs, but risk spreads in credit markets quickly widened further. Worse yet, in some ways, the market for short-term liquidity funds—the monies that pave the way for business and finance to work smoothly and meet their obligations on a timely basis—virtually dried up. London interbank borrowing rates (LIBOR) quoted in dollars, recognized as key rates in dollar markets around the world, rose sharply and rapidly to an unusually large premium over the Fed's targeted federal funds rate.

This threatening development in the world's basic market for dollar liquidity was not dissimilar, although more extreme in the short run, to difficulties faced in the latter part of 2007 in the domestic U.S. interbank federal funds market, as already noted. Gathering uncertainties about the viability of traditional banking counterparties were at the heart of the earlier problem—the big banks essentially being the counterparties whose repayment capacity was most subject to question, as they were mainly the borrowers in the interbank market and smaller banks chiefly the suppliers. This must have reflected underlying doubts about the value of assets held on or off bank balance sheets and, by extension, one could assume, doubts about similar assets at other institutions. The suspicions of that early period, whether or not fully recognized or internalized in thinking by the policy authorities, were by the fall of 2008 greatly magnified. And the credit needed to keep the economy going was becoming increasingly difficult for borrowers to obtain, almost at any price in some cases.

It is difficult to come to a sure judgment about the degree to which the failure of the Fed to use its emergency lending powers for Lehman Brothers and keep it in business for however long it took to find a buyer (apparently none was readily available at least on terms the Fed found acceptable) led to the extreme deepening of the financial crisis in the fall of 2008. I believe it contributed to a significant extent. But at the time there was also a whole complex of conditions influencing the confidence of investors, business executives, and consumers in the ability of markets to function. Not only was the creditworthiness of counterparties in all spheres of finance and the economy becoming more overtly suspect, but also, and just as important, the capacity and willingness of governments and other official institutions worldwide to respond constructively to the situation was coming more into doubt.

Several factors could have been behind the Fed's judgment about Lehman Brothers. Perhaps it believed that an emergency loan in this case (with no quick exit in sight) should not be undertaken, as a way of emphasizing the central bank's concern about moral hazard issues—that it did not wish to give any signals that would undermine the need for prudence at financial institutions, large or small, or by creditors. There could have also been questions about the adequacy of collateral and the availability of sufficient votes at the Board of Governors (under the law at the time, collateral for emergency loans had to be satisfactory to the reserve bank making the loan and a five person vote of approval by the Board was needed). Also, an apparent unwillingness by the U.S. Treasury to provide explicit support, as it had done for Bear Stearns (and also quite quickly for AIG), would have certainly discouraged the Fed.

I would guess that some combination of all the above was involved in the Fed's judgment. In any event, such an approach could have seemed the more plausible at the time if the Fed had not yet fully grasped how extremely weak and tenuous were actual underlying market sentiment and conditions—that is, had not expected the intensity of the destabilizing market reaction that was to come.

However that may have been, in the weeks immediately following, the Treasury's initiative to help stabilize the crisis—a proposal for the government to acquire troubled assets from financial institutions (that came to be known as TARP)—was initially so badly handled both by the Treasury and Congress itself that it became a major contributor to a further disastrous weakening in public and market confidence that the crisis could be readily smoothed over. There was no evidence in the sketchy proposal that the Treasury first put forth to the Congress of any sort of earlier contingency planning (as one might well have expected given the potential for a major financial crisis that had been so clear for many months); the Fed appeared to be no more than a passive participant in the public's eye; the Congress had a most difficult time in agreeing on a detailed plan once work was put into its development; and the looming presidential election and the behavior of the contenders did nothing but cloud the picture.

An unexpected rejection by the House of Representatives in its initial vote in late September on a very detailed, negotiated proposal appeared to catalyze public doubts about the government's ability to cope with the crisis. That was amply demonstrated by a further sharp drop in the stock market. The House then passed a revised plan a few days later; and, as an incidental matter, the Fed was also at the time given the power to pay interest on required and excess reserve balances held by depository institutions at their reserve banks.

Moreover, once the TARP was established, the Treasury waffled in its implementation. Rather than carrying through on its original intention of taking troubled assets off the market, in the end it resorted to injections of capital into needy large banks and financial institutions.

Perhaps price uncertainties in the market were so great and the variety of assets so diverse that neither an auction system nor a patterning of bids made by a governmental instrumentality could have quickly been put into practice, but I cannot help believing that a practical solution for acquiring bad assets might have been aided by some substantial contingency planning well in advance. Also, and rather revealing of attitudes, there did not seem to be much political will, either in the Congress or the administration at the time, to set up some sort of governmental refinancing-type agency either to bid for the securities at some price or to set up an auction process. In general, it looked as if the government felt that it was too complicated and cumbersome in the panicky situation quickly to devise a system that would permit it to discover a fair market price for the distressed mainly mortgage assets that were weighing on the value of institutional portfolios—a valuation problem faced by institutions themselves.

The whole market picture was indeed being clouded by the conventional mark to market procedures being followed by banks and other lenders at a time when markets were barely functional and when prices were obviously being affected as much by panic as by fundamental judgments. Such a mark to market process—which, as it was followed literally, tended to perpetuate irrationality—was itself certainly contributing to what has often been termed a perfect storm of a crisis. In the future, one would hope that the authorities would encourage a more rational basis for marking assets to market. For instance, such procedures could make allowances for the special conditions of a panic, perhaps by the use of models that help filter out unusual quite short-term price variations, at least until they last long enough to seem less influenced by transitory speculative fervor or disenchantment and more by an underlying economic condition, either cyclical or trend.

In the end, the injections of capital did help to stabilize the position of major financial institutions and restore a degree of confidence in equity and other markets, but at serious costs politically and from a societal perspective. The injections were not very clearly linked to the financial position of the institutions, as might have been more the case if the government had actually acquired distressed debt in a competitive process at what was seen to be, say, no more than a modest premium. Public suspicions that financial institutions were being unduly rewarded for a bad performance were further reinforced by later payouts of substantial bonuses to executives by a number of institutions. It looked as if they had been facilitated by funds directly provided by hard-pressed U.S. taxpayers. Even though much of the capital injection was subsequently repaid, quite possibly they were.

The highly adverse impact on public confidence from the inadequate performance of the government as a whole (including the Fed) in the late summer and early fall of 2008 showed itself not only in financial markets but also, and in an economic sense more devastatingly, in the deterioration in attitudes of businessmen and consumers. As confidence collapsed, the most postponable spending for both—that is, outlays on durable goods— declined immediately and spectacularly.

For example, over the fourth quarter of 2008 and the first of 2009, on average business spending on structures and equipment, as reported in the nation's gross domestic product accounts (as of September 30, 2010), fell by about 29 percent at an annual rate, almost six times more than it already had on average in the previous two quarters of a recessionary year. Consumer spending on durables also dropped sharply in the fourth quarter of 2008 but was better sustained on average the next year thanks in part to some fiscal help. Outlays for residential housing had already been falling for about two and a half years (first heralding and then contributing to the seemingly moderate recession that began to appear in 2008), but in late '08 and early '09 they worsened by somewhat more on average. The recession deepened by more than it need have because of the widespread societal crisis of confidence.

The economy subsequently stabilized and began to show signs of some recovery, aided to an extent by stimulative fiscal policy actions, although not particularly aggressive ones, by the Obama administration following the election. It was also helped along by additional actions subsequently taken by the Fed to repair the deeply troubled financial markets. The Fed of necessity became more like an integral part of the private market instead of being the deus ex machina apart from the market that could through occasional interventions help avert systemic crises.

While continuing and modifying as needed domestic programs set in place before the catastrophes of September, the Fed took a number of further steps to enhance market liquidity. It expanded the swap lines with foreign central banks sharply further, as the dollar crisis spread abroad. Drawings on the line rose from around $20 billion in the early spring of 2008 to a peak of around $585 billion in mid-December 2008 before fading away (merely as a way of illustrating the huge dimension of the Fed's international commitment, this peak was well above the International Monetary Fund's total useable resources, designed for broader programmatic purposes of course, at that time). The Fed also introduced new programs, including a commercial paper funding facility (peaking at around $350 billion in early 2009), a money market investor funding facility, and the TALF to provide loans backed by asset backed securities (a program that turned out to be vastly underused as compared with the huge potential indicated by Fed officials at the outset).

When a central bank makes credit available that would in more normal conditions be undertaken in the commercial market, its balance sheet necessarily expands because it in effect takes on to its books private-sector credit that is no longer functionally available. Indeed, the Fed's balance sheet expanded about two and a half times from something over $900 billion in early September of '08 to nearly $2.3 trillion by mid-December of that year.

The expansion in the balance sheet could take place so rapidly because the magic of central banking permits the Fed to provide cash for the assets it acquires simply by crediting reserve accounts held by commercial banks at the Fed with the funds to be placed in the customer deposit accounts held at those banks. In consequence, when all is said and done, there will have been a sharp expansion in liquidity nationwide, either through expansion in the banking system's excess reserves and/or the money supply held by the public—the distribution between the two depending on the extent to which the banking system acquires additional assets and creates even more deposits with the reserves initially provided. While the central bank could moderate any undesired excessive expansion in ordinary times through offsetting market transactions to mop up liquidity, in exceptional circumstance, as when markets have dried up during a major crisis, there are only limited opportunities to do so.

Accompanying so spectacular an expansion in the nation's monetary base, and virtually a necessary result of it, the FOMC lowered the funds rate target in three steps from 2 percent to effectively near 0 (expressed as a range of 0 to 1/4 percent), by mid-December 2008, where it remained as this book went to press toward the end of 2010. Moreover, the FOMC has consistently noted that economic conditions are "likely to warrant exceptionally low levels of the federal funds rate for an extended period" a phrase first introduced in the press release following the January 2009 FOMC meeting. Both the phrase and its sustained use to date are rather too reminiscent for my taste of language in policy directives during the latter part of the Greenspan era, when germs of the housing bubble were being sown.

As it happened, banks chose to hold the great bulk of the expanded monetary base in the form of excess reserves, thus limiting the multiple system-wide expansion in bank credit and money that would have taken place if the reserves had been loaned out. They rose very rapidly from the $2 billion or so level just prior to the September '08 market debacle to almost $800 billion by year-end, and continued an upward drift to where they remained at around $1 trillion through the summer of 2010. Uncertainties about the status of borrowers, even as the worst of the recession passed, and probably a lingering shell shock in internal management, kept banks' lending policies on the tight side for longer than one would have hoped. Moreover, banks at the time also earned a modicum interest from the Fed on excess reserve holdings—no more than a mere 25 basis points (i.e., a quarter of a percentage point) during the period of extreme monetary ease, though even that was a little better than ordinary people could earn in many money market funds and bank savings accounts during the same period.

The money supply also showed a spurt in growth following the Fed's massive liquidity injections to stem the crisis. In the first year, the narrowest definition of money (M1) expanded by just under 20 percent, representing seven years or so of additional money judged by average experience of the previous decade. Subsequently, money growth subsided considerably from its initial burst. But its level has remained more than ample. Thus, as of this writing, looking at excess reserves and the money supply together, there has been plenty of instant liquidity available in the economy for a more certain and satisfying recovery than has so far been achieved.

The Fed's total assets (representative of the nation's monetary base and the foundation for the liquidity provided to the public) generally have remained in a narrow range around their very advanced December 2008 peak through to the early fall of 2010 . The easing of market liquidity conditions as the crisis abated led, as was to be expected, to a more or less automatic phasing out the Fed's special liquidity programs, of which the swap agreements and the commercial paper lending facility were the largest, along with the term auction facility (TAF) that had been implemented earlier. The total of the various liquidity programs had reached a high of $1.5 trillion by December 2008 and was virtually nil (under $30 million) by the early fall of 2010. Such a natural process had originally seemed the easiest solution for reducing the nation's monetary base to more normal proportions as the crisis abated.

However, and contrarily, the size of the balance sheet remained exceptionally large because of programs initiated by the FOMC and implemented through the system's open market account to acquire sizeable amounts of mortgage-backed securities guaranteed by Federal agencies as well as Federal agency debt itself and longer-term Treasury issues. These programs, phased out by the early part of 2010, were designed to ease conditions in longer-term credit markets, and particularly the mortgage market, so as to help stimulate the economic recovery. They raised the level of the Fed's outright holdings of securities, which had fallen to a little less than $500 billion as the crisis evolved in 2008, to an enormous and unprecedented $2 trillion by the spring of 2010 and has remained around there thus far through early fall—the great bulk in the form of longer-term, not easily marketable instruments.[2]

The long-term securities program can be viewed as part of a countercyclical monetary policy as much as it can be viewed as an effort to repair markets damaged by the pervasive loss of confidence in the crisis. I would argue that at least a moderate amount of such purchases could have, and should have, been undertaken as early as the summer of 2008 in the hope of easing mortgage financing conditions at the time and perhaps taking some of the edge off the gathering crisis. That this was not done strikes me as also consistent with a view that the Fed was not fully aware of how widespread and damaging the crisis might well become.

While the Fed was shifting the composition of assets held in its expanded balance sheet to help the recovery along, the huge amount of excess reserves in the banking system remained more or less unchanged. This illustrates a fundamental problem in relying so much on monetary policy to spur economic recovery in a period when businesses and consumers are still somewhat shell shocked and are behaving very conservatively.

Sometimes the old adage, noted in the first chapter of the book in connection with the Fed and the Great Depression, that you can lead a horse to water but you cannot make him drink is not simply an excuse for inadequate monetary policy. Instead, as evident early in the recovery period from the great credit crisis, consumers, businesses, and banks in the face of great uncertainties do indeed vitiate the effectiveness of monetary policy—consumers and businesses by holding back on borrowing and spending while increasing their saving, and banks by greatly increasing their preference for excess reserves rather than investing and lending the funds provided by the central bank.

Fiscal policy is the more effective expansionary instrument of choice for public policy in such conditions, and if pursued actively enough has a much better chance than monetary policy of succeeding. Still, there are some things that monetary policy can do to provide more incentives for the liquidity available to be more encouraging of spending.

The shift in composition of the Fed's assets to longer-term securities that was belatedly undertaken is one, and more could be done in that respect should the need arise. I would also argue that the Fed should long since have paid nothing at all to banks as they accumulated huge excess reserves. In view of the weak economic conditions of the time and the reluctance of banks to lend even as extreme monetary ease was continuously sustained, a refusal to pay interest by the Fed would have at least been a tangible demonstration of concern (along with exhortations from the chairman) that banks' lending policies were not contributing sufficiently to encouraging the pace of economic recovery, as indeed they were not.

Still, there can be potentially serious negative after effects from efforts by the Fed to ensure that the size and composition of its balance sheet is best designed to promote economic recovery. For instance, the dominance of the Fed's balance sheet by long-term securities raises questions once again—as had been raised in the early crisis days when the monetary base rose sharply as the Fed buttressed market liquidity—about the institution's ability to restore its balance sheet to a more normalized condition when economic recovery picks up and conflicts should begin to arise between its two fundamental policy objectives of sustaining growth and containing inflation. While the changed composition of the balance sheet has added to the complexity of the problem, solutions are in sight, and the Fed has been at pains to point them out.

It will in fact take a fairly long time for the Fed to unwind its late developing long-term asset program—for example, by letting securities mature over time or selling whenever markets seem beckoning. That it will indeed take some time was given some practical emphasis in the summer of 2010. As the economic recovery appeared to be faltering at the time, the Fed indicated that it would be replacing maturing longer-term mortgage-related securities with new purchases of longer-term Treasury securities, thus keeping its balance sheet from shrinking in the uncertain economic circumstances.

Nonetheless, when the Fed wishes to contract its balance sheet, it can employ its longer-term securities as collateral for short-term reverse repurchase agreements (temporary sales of securities to the market that are paid for in effect by reducing the Fed's liability to the market for bank reserves). They can easily be more or less continuously rolled over and marketed, presumably beyond the dealer community to such institutions as money market funds. In addition, the Fed's ability to pay interest on excess reserves and a program it has been developing to pay interest on term deposits placed with reserve banks by commercial banks can also help immobilize the extent to which an expanded monetary base will be converted into undesired excess market and public liquidity. In general, there is reason to believe, given conditions as they have so far evolved, that the Fed will be able to attain just about whatever nominal and associated real federal funds rate objectives it seeks over the months and years ahead.

On balance, considering the crisis as a whole, I believe that the Fed came to acquit itself fairly well, especially in the later stages of the crisis. After lagging behind for too long early in the crisis period, failing to communicate an adequate grasp of the underlying dangers, and becoming enmeshed in political crosscurrents that seemed to limit its independence of action, the Fed, in close to the nick of time, began to catch up with fast-moving, chaotic market events. It imaginatively stretched its legal authority to the limit in order to stabilize a market that was threatening to self-destruct and lead to a very deep depression. Much of this must be owed to the leadership of the chairman.

As elaborated in earlier chapters, particularly those covering the Fed's response to the great inflation, the chairman necessarily has a more dominant and singular role at times of crisis and major changes in policy emphasis than in periods when small policy adjustments are made in the normal course. For interpreting Bernanke's leadership in the great credit crisis I would divide the Fed's policy responses into four stages.

In the first stage, beginning in the latter part of 2007 and lasting until September 2008, the Fed was playing the traditional role of attempting to avert a systemic market collapse through more active use of the discount window—first by making funds available as needed to regular borrowers through an innovative auction system and then, as conditions worsened, through an emergency loan to an individual institution (Bear Stearns), and certain other actions. Overall, its balance sheet remained near normal, as expanded use of the discount window was countered by an offsetting decline in government securities holdings.

While Bernanke at this point seemed in practice to be demonstrating a practical sense of market necessities, he still did not seem able to communicate effectively enough with the market to help keep spreading market worries in check. He communicated in what seemed to be clear, though sometimes academic sounding, phrases, but there remained a feeling, I believe, that the Fed simply did not "get it." I would interpret "it" to mean how extremely worrisome were underlying market conditions. Market participants were looking for some understanding of that, in the face of the potential for disaster, from the man they all believed might ease their and the market's difficulties, self-inflicted as they may have been. A more empathetic type of communication might have helped smooth adjustments by calming underlying fears and the self-defeating actions they often bring forth. But still, it probably would have had no more than a marginal effect, given the deep-seated fragilities already built into the market structure.

The second phase of the crisis began in September of 2008. At that point, the Fed was eventually forced to become a much more active participant within a private market system that had become systemically unstable, or at least frighteningly near enough. This phase of the crisis was in good part the result, not of ineluctable market and economic developments, but, as earlier argued, of official actions themselves—actions that created huge uncertainties in markets and a startling nation wide loss of confidence that made the recession deeper than it need have been.

To an outside observer, as the second phase of the crisis got under way, it also looked as if Bernanke's freedom of action was being dominated and limited by the administration's goals and wishes. As a result, the Fed's vaunted independence came to seem a chimera, and he and the institution lost stature and market confidence.

In the third stage of the crisis, however, some stature and credibility was gradually regained as the Fed was seen as having implemented the various policies that eventually stabilized the financial system and helped set the stage for an economic recovery. In addition, Bernanke made an effort to become more available throughout the country to explain the Fed's policies and to humanize his own persona, an approach that seems to have met with some success.

It is obviously hard to pin down a specific date when the crisis entered this third phase, in which reasonable confidence in the Fed's performance was re-established. I would place it somewhere in the spring of 2009, when the market's reliance on the Fed's liquidity facilities was in the process of steadily falling, when the Fed had begun its sustained campaign to ease conditions in mortgage markets by extensive acquisitions of longer-term securities, and when the Fed continued to show no sign at all that it would take any hasty action to remove the huge overhang of excess reserves from the banking system. Further helping the Fed's stature along, by the last two quarters of 2009 the nation's output of goods and services exhibited positive real growth.

I would place the beginning of the fourth phase of the crisis—its aftermath—in the spring of 2010. The Fed by then was faced mainly with managing its policy as markets and the economy were moving gingerly toward normalcy, though with lingering questions and doubts especially about the economy.

In the history of major crises here and abroad, aftermaths can be—and often are—long, arduous, and uncertain. One need point only to the financial crisis generated by the U.S. 1929 stock market crash and banking failures of the early 1930s, which were followed by a long, deep depression, high unemployment, and a halting recovery cut short by ill-advised Fed policies. Adequate economic recovery was not really in place until spurred by governmental spending to arm the country as the Second World War broke out. Indeed, as a general point, it is not at all historically uncommon in the aftermath of severe crises experienced around the world for fiscal policy to be a major element in restoring more normal growth conditions, since crises frequently are followed by lingering negative effects on propensities to lend and spend in private markets and sectors.

In that context, Bernanke clearly is well aware that the Fed's principal contribution to normalizing the growth process is to encourage, as much as it can, the recovery of positive attitudes in private credit and related spending markets. How strong and sustained the economic expansion ultimately will be is, of course, unknown as of this writing. How it will interact with the huge government deficits and rising national debt now facing the U.S. is uncertain. And whether an undue threat of inflation will be generated out of efforts to deal with a powerfully rising national debt burden and the social need to increase employment adequately—especially if competing claims on world resources from large newly developing countries also come to be reflected in resurgent pressures on world commodity prices—is a compelling problem in this day and age.

As the Fed manages policy in the crisis aftermath, it will look to return its balance sheet and the nation's monetary base to more normal levels over time if the vast excess reserves created in the banking system during the crisis and the sizeable growth in money held by the public are not to risk funding, as time goes on, either too much inflation in the average price level or damaging market bubbles of one sort or another. As previously noted, there appear to be no very significant technical difficulties in either reining in the monetary base or at least minimizing the extent to which some larger than normal monetary base can be transformed into excess public liquidity.

But, the Fed's ability to undertake effective monetary policies in so complicated and uncertain a transition requires more than technical capacity. It also requires from its chairman, the only credible public face of the institution, a public stature that enables him to perform effectively on the national stage (i.e., sell his message) if the difficult transition to normalcy is to be smoothly handled, given the heightened political, social, and economic sensitivities typical of a crisis aftermath—all of which inevitably influence the timing, communication, and balance of risks taken in Fed policy.

As of this writing, such a stature does not yet seem to be firmly within Bernanke's grasp: the lingering memories of the traumas of the crisis, its social resentments, and highly damaging impact on jobs all remain too fresh. The stature and credibility of the Fed and its chairman may also depend, I would judge at this time, on the degree to which the Fed can be seen as better managing the balance between its regulatory posture and its monetary policy actions, after a crisis period when it had become evident to the public eye that the two were fatefully and unhappily intertwined. Issues raised by the monetary/regulatory policy nexus at the Fed will be further discussed in the next chapter on the Fed's image and in the final one offering concluding remarks.

8

The Fed and Its Image

There must be almost as many images of the Fed as an institution and of the wellsprings of its actions as there are viewers. Mine, born of a particular experience, generally has been a benign one. By and large, I have seen the institution as unbiased, straightforward, and diligent in carrying out its congressionally given mandates. Obviously, not everyone sees the Fed that way. And my own image of the Fed has become less benign in the wake of the great credit crisis.

Traditionally, when the Fed has worried about its credibility and image (as it more or less continuously has in one way or another), it has been concerned mostly with whether the public and the market believe its monetary policy is being conducted well and objectively, so that policy for achieving the nation's price stability and economic growth objectives can be implemented more convincingly and smoothly. But as experience amply demonstrates, monetary policy credibility can often come into question—either because the Fed misjudges the economic situation or because the situation requires policies in the short run that the public resents.

To help buffer itself against the unavoidable swings in opinion of how it is carrying out its fundamental monetary policy role, and to make it better able to continue the independent exercise of its best policy judgments amid recurrent and sometimes intense political and social pressures, the Fed also requires what can be termed *institutional credibility*. Such broad institutional credibility depends on the Fed's reputation with the public and the Congress for honest, and highly expert administration of itself as whole—not only of its continuously publicized and avidly followed monetary policy operations but also of other diverse responsibilities delegated by law. Impossible as it may be to quantify, it represents something like the bedrock of public confidence that sustains the institution.

The Fed's responsibilities, in addition to its widely publicized monetary policy operations, have encompassed such areas as the regulation and supervision of banks and bank holding companies, the protection of consumers in certain financial transactions, community investment and development, and the payments and settlements operations that undergird the banking system. They encompass locally and regionally important activities, carried out around the country by reserve banks and their branches (under regulations promulgated by the Board of Governors), and present the Fed in more of a "grass roots" context that can be, and usually has been, socially and politically beneficial for pubic understanding and support of the institution.

I believe the Fed retained a basic institutional credibility for much of the postwar period (not without vocal dissenters from one perspective or another). It was hurt for a time by the great inflation and the loss of monetary policy credibility, and restored more fully when inflation was conquered. But institutional credibility was more powerfully threatened by the more recent great credit crisis. Public confidence in the Fed organization as a whole appeared to be shaken. Doubts, reflected in a considerable stirring of Congressional discontent, seemed to reach into the beating heart of the Fed as an institution, going beyond the usual credibility issues raised by difficult monetary policy judgments with which the national credit and equity markets have long been familiar.

The organization was perceived as remiss not only in failing to grasp the intense threat of the crisis early on but also in seeming to neglect many of the regulatory and rule-making areas that were, so it came to appear, involved with the growing credit problems. Questions were raised in the press and in the halls of Congress about the competence with which the Fed had dealt with, among others, emerging developments in the subprime mortgage market, the role played by off-balance sheet reporting and its implications for bank capital, and its responsibilities for certain consumer and mortgage credit protection functions.

Indeed, the fundamental question about how much regulatory responsibility should reside in the Fed was much debated during congressional deliberations of the proposed new financial legislation generated by the crisis. However, as earlier pointed out, regulatory lapses were hardly particular to the Fed. They were endemic in the regulatory system as a whole, including other bank regulators and various authorities responsible for securities and commodity markets. And it will be some time, if ever, before any consensus is reached about the extent to which regulatory decisions and negligence, and whose, did or did not contribute to the intensity of the crisis.

In general, I have long believed that the Fed should have a strong, indeed a leading, role in bank and related bank holding company regulation—a role that remains with it following passage of the Dodd-Frank Act. The Fed itself has long argued that its monetary policy effectiveness is enhanced by its presence and participatory knowledge in the regulatory area. Some others have disagreed, arguing that the Fed should be relieved of all regulatory responsibilities or, at a minimum, be left only with those—such as for large banks and holding companies—absolutely crucial to its role for ensuring the systemic stability of the financial system as a whole.

However, the credit crisis has amply demonstrated how closely regulatory issues and monetary policy can be intertwined. It is not that regulatory issues impinge on monetary policy continuously. Indeed, they impinge in a serious way rather infrequently. But the Fed needs the assurance and knowledge on a continuing basis that the banking system is being soundly governed, an assurance that can come only from active participation and leadership in regulation and supervision. Most important, so as to minimize the chances that monetary policy may be faced with unpalatable dilemmas, the Fed needs the ability and will to act constructively on a timely basis in the regulatory area when serious issues that threaten the stability of the financial system begin to surface—an opportunity rather obviously missed in the recent crisis.

This applies particularly to use of macro-prudential kinds of regulatory actions, such as adjustments in bank capital requirements, to help supplement and ease the path for monetary policy under certain cyclical conditions. Hitherto, regulatory rules and principals have been set to encourage sound banking on a long-run basis irrespective of the particular cyclical condition of the economy and markets. It is notable in that respect that the Dodd-Frank bill recommends consideration of countercyclical capital requirements to regulators. However, for such an approach to be implemented in practice is not simple. It raises many knotty, practical issues, including matters of timing, potential for market misinterpretation, undue complications in bank business planning, and difficulties in domestic and international coordination among a variety of regulatory authorities.

While, as already emphasized, institutional credibility is of considerable value because of the practical support it provides for the monetary policy independence long since authorized by the Congress, there are also more parochial advantages to the Fed. For instance, institutional credibility has greatly helped the Fed avoid overt executive and legislative control over its annual operating budget (which is displayed in the federal budget document and is annually presented to congressional oversight committees). It has also made it easier to fend off efforts in the Congress to extend the reach of the annual audits undertaken by the Government Accountability Office (GAO) directly into the monetary policy area.

These have been perennial anxieties because they are seen as not so subtle approaches to undermining the institution's monetary policy independence. The recent extension of GAO audits to use of the Fed's lending facilities during the credit crisis, well justified as it is in any event on general grounds, can nonetheless be seen as one among a number of manifestations of the recent decline in the Fed's institutional credibility. They are also found in questions about whether the Fed has been too much under the influence of Wall Street, and large financial institutions, as can be seen in certain new provisions in the 2010 financial reform bill that affect Fed governance. For instance, of the nine reserve bank board members, the three who directly represent member banks are no longer permitted to vote for the President of the bank. There are also two curious provisions that specifically limit the Fed Board's ability to delegate authority to reserve banks and their presidents (curious to me because my experience was of a Fed board and its chairmen who seemed determined to maintain their authority). I would imagine these provisions reflect a worry that the New York Fed was permitted to wield too much authority during the crisis and was too much under the influence of its board chairman.

Congressional control of the Fed's administrative budget, the gradual creep of GAO audits closer toward the monetary policy area, and, more generally, legislative action to limit the Fed's administrative independence can most easily be fended off only when the institution is considered to be as pure as Caesar's wife. It is quite difficult, of course, to convince the world of one's purity. Purity always coexists with some impurities.

In any event, some observers are naturally cynical, whereas others, because of their background and the nature of their particular institutional responsibilities, see the Fed through something akin to tunnel vision. For instance, some people (such as, on occasion, influential Congressmen in the banking area and congressional staffers) seem to have seen the Fed as an institution that in its practices helps the rich, harms the poor, and seeks to preserve the position of a banking system dominated by large banks that exploit small borrowers and probably anyone else they can. Perhaps I am exaggerating a bit, but the feeling tones are right, and I believe became very evident at times in congressional debates and resolutions in the long course of discussions leading up to the new reform legislation meant to ensure that a great credit crisis is not repeated—or at least ensure to the degree than one can in the face of experience that tells us the future is essentially unpredictable and no financial systems and structures have ever been foolproof.

In any event, during my years there, I did not perceive the Fed as biased toward the large and rich and against the small and poor. The system is not oriented in that direction. Its objectives and the reach of the power delegated to it by the Congress are quite different. Its monetary policies are aimed at the economy as a whole, attaining price stability and encouraging economic growth. They are not and cannot, in the nature of the case, be aimed at such big socioeconomic issues as income distribution, economic welfare, and social fairness, over which the Fed has no control or direct influence and for which it has no mandate.

On the regulatory side, its policies are mainly designed to maintain the competitiveness, safety, and integrity of the banking system (including bank holding companies) under the guidelines set in law. When given authority by Congress, the Fed has exerted an influence on such specific social-type issues as ensuring truth in lending and avoiding discrimination in lending, which represents some positive contribution toward social fairness, perhaps minor in the large scheme of things but recently brought to the fore as aspects of the great credit crisis that surely could have been better handled by the institution.

Over the years, the Fed, so far as I could see, has taken neither regulatory nor monetary policy actions for the specific purpose of favoring particular big bankers or other large financial institutions. Under emergency or highly threatening market conditions, the discount window has indeed been employed to aid large banks and also, latterly in the great credit crisis, large investment banks and other market institutions. Any actions that did, such as helping to bail out a large bank in Chicago (Continental

Illinois) in the mid-1980s and big investment firms such as Bear Stearns in early 2008 and the insurance group AIG in September of that year, were taken only because of a perceived threat to the stability of the financial system as a whole. The object was not so much to rescue an insolvent institution from bankruptcy but more to provide enough liquidity to that institution, whether technically insolvent or not, to protect its depositors and creditors (when it is in the interests of systemic stability) while providing time to find a willing buyer of the institution, or a part of it, at a reasonable price if that seemed necessary.

One can argue whether or not any bailout at all for individual institutions, no matter how tough on management and ownership, is a desirable policy in this and other similar instances, as is often done on the moral hazard grounds discussed earlier. But from a public-policy perspective, and absent any other alternatives aside from bankruptcy court (such as would be the orderly liquidation authority now included in the Dodd-Frank Act that permits the secretary of the Treasury to designate the Federal Deposit Insurance Corporation as receiver for certain threatened financial institutions mainly at a time of financial panic), it remains the case that some institutions at some particular times simply are too big for the nation to take the risk of letting them fail right away.

But which particular potential failure represents such a huge risk is obviously a very difficult judgment call. The Fed did not see the need to put up any of its money to help save LTCM in the latter part of the 1990s, but did involve itself and its own credit very directly in the rescue of Bear Stearns and AIG in the first decade of the new century. On the other hand, its decision to let Lehman Brothers go into bankruptcy turned out to help turn a very bad crisis into a truly great one.

I would also note, in passing, that there are conditions in which smaller banks in relatively isolated regions may also need to be provided discount window funds to avert immediate bankruptcy and resulting undue problems for local depositors and creditors while a buyer is being found. This would be relevant only in such very exceptional circumstances as when a smallish region or community is highly dependent on the continuing services of a single institution that may be facing, say, a run on its deposits.

In general, if a bank run continues long enough on the suspicion of actual or imminent insolvency, even an institution that was solvent to begin with can hardly avoid becoming insolvent. Liquidity crises have a way of turning into solvency crises, whether institutions are large or small. For depository institutions, the Fed can through the discount window provide liquidity to stay in business for the time it takes to find another institution to absorb its basic business and accounts. The general point is that the size of the institution, per se, is not at issue in rescue operations. Rather, whether or not to provide temporary liquidity (it could be temporary for some while of course) to a depository institution while a buyer is being sought depends on a difficult judgment to be made about implications for the stability of the system in which it is a part—the danger to country's social and economic stability obviously being much the greater to the degree that that the nation's whole financial fabric is at risk.

At the time of the great credit crisis, the Fed could lend to potential borrowers that were not depository institutions, such as investment banks like Bear Stearns and Lehman Brothers, only by invoking its rarely employed emergency loan authority. The Dodd-Frank Act has now substantially altered the Fed's emergency lending authority. It no longer applies to any particular individual, partnership, or corporation as was previously the case but rather to a so-called program or facility with broad-based eligibility. Among other things, it specifically excludes loans to individual institutions that are insolvent or to the establishment of a program for assisting a particular company avoid bankruptcy. Indeed, any lending program or facility must be for the purpose of providing liquidity to the financial system and not to aid a failing company, and the collateral behind the loans is required to be sufficiently good to protect taxpayers against loss. Moreover, no program can be established without prior approval of the Secretary of the Treasury, which simply makes explicit what appears to have been practice during the crisis.

The law, so far as I interpret it, places some further distance between Fed lending activities in a financial panic and the public opprobrium that almost inevitably arises once it becomes necessary to lend governmental funds (whether indirectly by the Fed or directly from a governmental source on the budget) to keep the situation from getting more out of hand. The government in political power at a time of financial crisis—through its enhanced authority over the Fed's emergency loan programs, its orderly liquidation authority for individual institutions, and the responsibilities of the financial stability oversight council—would be more clearly in the front line, as politically and socially it should be at such a critical time.

How this approach works in a future emergency situation will be unknown for, let us hope, a considerable time. With regard to the new emergency loan provisions for the Fed, the clear indication that loans to insolvent individual institutions are to be avoided will have to be interpreted in future crises in light of the liquidity that needs to be provided through whatever programs or facilities are set up to keep the financial system functional. One certainly cannot tell how future administrations will interpret their mandate and to what limits they believe it can be legally and politically stretched.

As emphasized long ago by Walter Bagehot, the famous English thinker on central banking, when a central bank perceives a significant threat to the nation's financial fabric and to public confidence, its job is to step in as lender of last resort as needed, though presumably at a penalty rate, to shore up the system. Of course, he was writing at a time when banks were clearly at the heart of the financial system. By now, that heart is a much less simple an organ and encompasses a vast web of interconnected institutions and markets.

But in following Bagehot's mandate to keep the now more complex modern organ ticking, there still remain two important caveats in practice. First, those responsible for the debacle should suffer personally, by considerably more than they could have expected, as a way of minimizing moral hazard. Second, rescues by the central bank should be relatively rare, for if the central bank's balance sheet becomes loaded over time with what are perceived to be bad loans to financial institutions, the public will come to doubt the integrity and liquidity of the whole financial system, including also that of the central bank itself.

The potential for systemic crises will become even greater if the central bank comes to be viewed more as part of the problem than as a sound institution capable of safeguarding the financial system. The Fed sidestepped this problem during the great credit crisis as its enlarged portfolio was first filled mostly with shorter-term well collateralized credits to the private sector that would naturally run off as the crisis was resolved and later with relatively quite safe longer-term government or government-guaranteed securities

However, as a useful counter-example (though rather remote from the Fed's particular circumstances), such a problematic situation did become very evident in Indonesia in the course of its financial crisis of the late

1990s—one of the places where I did some consulting after my departure from Nikko. There, the central bank ended up with a balance sheet dominated by bad, nonpaying loans. As a result, its net worth and solvency disappearing, the bank had to be rescued by the government, with resulting enormous political contention and recriminations that held back economic recovery and public confidence in the integrity of both the central bank and the financial system as a whole.

Any such fate was averted in our recent credit crisis because of the underlying strength of the U.S. economy and financial markets and because of the continued basic credibility of Fed's own balance sheet (and reputation) in the course of the crisis. The Fed's expanded balance sheet during the crisis in fact turned out to generate huge profits that were almost entirely, as is normal, turned over to the Treasury ($47 billion in 2009 as reported by the Fed, a 50 percent increase over the year before as the composition of the expanded balance sheet came increasingly to include a large percentage of relatively high yielding longer-term debt).

From my perspective, the Fed has never found it easy to balance its responsibility to maintain the fundamental stability of the financial system in times of crisis against its obligations to be impartial in dealing with all institutions, whether large or small. At some point in the first half of the 1980s, I received a phone call at home one weekend from the Fed board's general counsel to inform me that the Fed and other bank regulators had decided to rescue what I remember as a medium-size regional bank that was in great difficulty because of bad loans; that is, the regulators had decided to keep the bank alive until a merger partner could be found, rather than letting it go into immediate bankruptcy. (I am no longer sure about the source of its problem, but I think it had something to do with oil loans in the Southwest.) In any event, what I most vividly recall is audibly gasping in surprise when told of the action, mainly because—so I must have thought—the situation, on the face of it, did not seem to pose any serious risk to the financial system as a whole or probably even to the more local market in which the bank participated. Because of my market responsibilities at the Fed, I was being called, I assumed, to be alerted to the potential for problems on Monday morning as the market attempted to assess the significance of the action that was about to be announced.

No sooner had the general counsel and I finished our brief conversation than the phone again rang. This time it was the chairman himself,

Volcker, to provide some background on the situation. Such a call was and remained unprecedented in my experience. There was no practical need to give me an explanation. I had no doubt that Volcker was well aware of the danger that the action might give the wrong signal to other institutions and encourage a dangerous, more generalized moral hazard, especially because this bank was not large enough to present an obvious risk of broad systemic failure (though perhaps it was involved in loans that had also found their way onto the books of large banks so that there was the possibility of more risk-provoking knock-on effects). His call to me was, in my interpretation, an indirect way of venting his own ambivalence.

However the interaction between policy—including not just monetary policy but also the obligation to keep the financial system from imploding—and institutional credibility works out in coming years, the Fed's stature as an institution is and probably will to an important degree continue to be buttressed by straightforward and essentially unbiased staff work. While the performance in the regulatory and supervisory area has been subject to question in the aftermath of the great credit crisis, it remains a very open question in my mind about the degree to which the issues involve supervisory staff quality and attention to duty, or rather leadership attitudes and the cultural and political environment of the time.

I like to think that the quality and diligence of the institution's large economics staff, with well-developed expertise in just about every sector of economic activity, domestic and international, are integral to the Fed's credibility as an institution in its key monetary policy role. Maybe there was some doubt among the more monetarist-oriented observers back in the 1960s and 1970s. Whether that group simply laid the responsibility for what they considered to be misguided policies on wrong-headed Fed policymakers or also believed the Fed's economics staff and staff leadership were not up to the task, I cannot be certain.

To me, the quality of the Fed's economics staff seemed rather high in the immediate postwar years before it appeared to decline a bit, though remaining more than competent, as numerous academic opportunities opened up with the expansion of university economics departments. The staff's stature seemed to rise later in academic eyes when the Fed began to hire people whose principal assignment was to engage in fundamental research and to have it published in learned journals.

At times, as the years wore on, a colleague of mine would remark, as we struggled to settle some economic issue in which we were entangled, that we had at least come "close enough for government work." When using that phrase, my colleague was not talking about the Fed's credibility, but was instead downplaying the Fed's capacity and its economists' ability for statistical and economic analysis as compared with academics. He was being facetious, I suppose, but his facetiousness reflected an undercurrent of self-disparagement on his part, not to say insecurity, about whether our work could fully measure up to the highest professional standards or even needed to do so.

Academic economic studies are generally rigorous and well presented, although, on occasion, the effort to distinguish oneself in the academic world by discovering something different might lead to less than exquisite care in the use of statistics or the power of reasoning. In my time at the Fed, we were at least as rigorous as academics in our analysis and use of statistics, but the institution, as such, was less hospitable to intellectual risk takers than were those universities where top academics gathered—in part, I think, because it feared the public consequences of being wrong or of being viewed as taking too much risk with its awesome responsibilities. It feared that its credibility could thereby suffer, that the public might lose faith in its fundamental soundness. Its prevailing philosophy emphasized that it was better to be dull, accurate, and within a very defensible position rather than brilliant, adventurous, and possibly reckless. That great marble building, reified, probably would not express itself in that way, but its practical situation and traditions spoke for themselves.

As a result, analysis and action within and by the Fed were constrained by a kind of institutional conservatism that inhibited but, to the Fed's credit, did not entirely forestall original thinking in research and policy. Most inhibited were those analyses and policies that the nation was meant to take as "official." Nevertheless, although they might not have been "original" in an academic sense, they were well thought through, in my opinion (obviously so, from my perspective as the person mainly responsible for them for much of the time), and benefited from widespread and honest review within the organization. At the same time, individual research and analyses by economists hired by the Fed were becoming increasingly published in refereed academic journals.

Nonetheless, truly creative minds of the very first rank were not to be found at the Fed. Nor, by the way and almost by definition, were they especially numerous in the academic field. Nonetheless, to the extent that the field of economics I know most about, macroeconomics and monetary economics in particular, was sufficiently challenging for adventurous and creative thinkers—that is, had not already been mined for its basic truths and their major variants—such individuals were more likely to be found in the very different atmosphere of universities, which were their much more natural habitat.

The academic world was home to winners of the prestigious award for economists issued through the Nobel Prize Committee. I was fortunate to have known, in a professional way, a number of the early honorees, who by and large were about a half-generation or more older and who, I still believe, made and perhaps came close to exhausting seminal contributions to the field. Their attitudes and temperament illustrate, in a heightened way, differences between patterns of economic thinking aimed at being more creative and the often more mundane casts of mind found in, and indeed effective in, bureaucratic contexts.

A few examples might help clarify the contrast. At one point, several years after having left the Fed, I was invited to speak on inflation control in the United States at a conference initiated by the Chinese government. The attendees were mostly Chinese bureaucrats involved in the economic policy process. This particular conference, held in 1994, appeared to be sponsored by the Communist Party faction that was in favor of controlling inflation (it was always important to know which faction was sponsoring a conference there if you were to understand fully the proceedings), which at the time meant bringing it down from something like 20 percent per year to the order of 8 to 10 percent.

The keynote speaker was a famous American economist, Franco Modigliani, a recipient of the Nobel award and, it so happened, a former tennis partner of mine when he was a postdoctoral fellow at the University of Chicago and I was a beginning graduate student. My role at the conference was to give a talk on how the United States had conquered inflation in the early 1980s. Other foreigners were there to show how such countries as Japan, Chile, and Singapore had contained inflation.

As anticipated by the organizers, we foreign experts who had been central bankers duly and rather dully explained why it was good to control inflation and how we did it. Franco, our academic representative and principal speaker, set forth, with his usual panache, the results of some research he had been doing on the relationship between inflation and economic growth—specifically on whether the degree of inflation negatively or positively affected the pace of economic growth. His results, convincingly and coherently explicated, seemed to show that the pace of inflation was largely unrelated to economic growth. He summarized the relationship as "orthogonal," sending me to the dictionary when I got home. Anyhow, his finding was clear: you could have growth at or near a country's potential both with and without inflation.

He thereupon concluded, as I remember, that because you can have growth with or without inflation, you might as well restrain inflation. Not the strongest conclusion to place before a group who had invited all of us to buttress their position that the Chinese government should set about more actively to control inflation. (I believe subsequent research in the field tended to show that high inflation was indeed less favorable to growth than low inflation, though it remained quite unclear whether very low or no inflation was more favorable than merely low inflation.) Yet Modigliani's presentation was exciting and intellectually stimulating. He was a dynamic thinker who had been set and slightly misplaced among the bureaucrats.

Others Nobel winners I came to know (sometimes as a student) included Milton Friedman, Jim Tobin, and Paul Samuelson. They all were obviously very intelligent men, though that trait, to me, was not the principal, or at least not the only important, distinguishing characteristic for earning their Nobel. The prize could not be won without also an intense obsession with the subject of economics, dreary as that might seem to 99.9 percent of the human race.

So far as I could see, these men were indeed obsessed, but it was the productive kind of obsession, not the kind that was an outgrowth of and appeared to be inseparable from painful neurotic compulsions. Instead, it reflected a creative interest in their professional field that was so deep and so strong that they could not let up; that compelled them to keep seeking for a truth, an innovation, a breakthrough; and that seemed to be a necessary condition to great achievement, though obviously far from a sufficient condition. The obsessive search, the continuous thinking, the chase—all of it was in the main, I would guess, a joy to them, but whether their only joy, I know not.

Milton once invited me to be a guest speaker at one of his seminars at the University of Chicago. At one point, before the session, he virtually pulled me into his office to reveal, with great enthusiasm and a gleam in his eye, some work he had been reviewing that very morning on the positive relationship between growth in the money supply and rising prices in various remote countries of the world. "See," urged he, "see what I keep finding as I keep looking." It was the fact that he would always be looking, could not stop looking, that impressed me.

In another incident, much earlier than our time together in China, Franco Modigliani rushed into my office at the Fed in Washington; he was there for some meeting or other.

"Steve," said he, "you have made a great mistake."

"How so, Franco?" I asked.

"Your new definition of the money supply is wrong," he replied.[1]

"Why is that?" asked I.

"Because my equations no longer work," he quickly responded. I laughed. His comments seemed so disproportionate to the relatively minor change at the time. He did not quite laugh, but his enthusiasm for work was so much part of an ebullient, likable personality that he could see some of the humor. In the end, I am sure his equations, or some variant of them, survived the enormity. In any event, I think I offered to send the missing data to him if he wished.

The temperament and personality that drove these Nobel winners and others into making discoveries that would make economics more interesting and fruitful as a field of work did not necessarily also make them better able than others to give policy advice. They were not absorbed in the policy process; they were not as sensitive to the issues and as immersed in the current flow of economic data and information.

The Federal Reserve Board of Governors in Washington at one point decided to organize a panel of academic consultants to come in twice a year to give advice on policy—a good idea, politically useful, and perhaps helpful in enhancing its image in the academic community. Many on the Fed staff became worried, though, that these well-known names would show us up. My view was quite different. I thought hearing them would be good for us. They would sound intelligent, but no more so than we were in the area of monetary policy and current economic conditions. It was our field, and, by dint of daily attention, we knew more about it. Moreover, great originality and creativity—pretty rare among academics in any event, as earlier noted—are not as important as insightful common sense when policy recommendations are to be made. They might even be an impediment. The appearance of academic experts would not diminish the board's respect for its own staff and might just increase it.

Because of the Fed's traditional stolidity and intellectual conservatism, the three-year period in the early 1980s when its approach to monetary policy dramatically shifted to an anti-inflationary posture was all the more exhilarating. It demonstrated the possibility that when the audience was ripe and a leader was willing to take risks on the public stage, long-held traditions did not preclude a vigorous and unique production.

In an environment like the Fed's, this short period was a rare instance when one's work felt innovative and useful in a way that was out of the ordinary. Even the research produced by the economics staff in that period struck me as taking a significant step beyond at least our norm. The problems became more interesting and the intellectual and political need to engage with the criticism and views of academic and other economists more pressing. All those economists we had been hiring to do fundamental research demonstrated their practical value. Since then, so far as I can tell, research undertaken in the Federal Reserve System—both the board and the individual reserve banks—has remained relatively sophisticated and more directly comparable to the monetary research of top academics. That three-year period, in retrospect, also seemed to be one of the rare instances when a shift in the approach to monetary policy not only greatly reinforced policy credibility, but also buttressed institutional credibility and enhanced the Fed's overall image.

Also, the Fed's image has probably been enhanced to an extent, I would suppose (despite my carping in preceding chapters), by its efforts over the past fifteen years or so to communicate more openly, clearly, and promptly about monetary policy. In many ways, the more frequent and clearer the communication, the better. Still, there are no easy or lasting answers to the numerous practical difficulties and risks in employing communication as an arm of monetary policy. As described in the Greenspan chapter, the Fed has not always avoided the potential negative effects of an increased openness that at times took the form of employing verbal suasion and continuing assurances about the future of policy ease as an additional instrument of policy to influence market behavior. In monetary policy, however, performance always and obviously trumps communication.

From that perspective, I would argue that communication about conventional open market policy operations should be limited to a clear statement of the Fed's policy target for the period between FOMC meetings. It should avoid indications of the likely future changes in its operational objectives. The Fed may think it knows more about its own intentions than the market does. It may, but it cannot be absolutely certain. The economy and unanticipated financial and political events can surprise the Fed—witness the credit market crisis of 2007–2009—as much as they surprise the public and the market.

What the Fed can and should do about the future is provide the public with knowledge about the economic context for its policy deliberations. For some time, it had done so by twice a year providing its projections a year or two ahead for economic growth, the behavior of prices, and related variables to the Congress in February and July, consistent with the Full Employment and Balanced Growth Act of 1978. This practice continued even after the act formally expired in the late 1990s. The Bernanke Fed in October 2007 decided to update the forecasts quarterly in a more comprehensive format and also added a third year to them.

The market has subsequently been more amply provided with knowledge of the economic conditions the Fed foresees in setting current policy. Market participants have more information for making their own decisions, which obviously may assume an economic outcome that is the same as or different from the one the Fed assumes. And the Fed has multiple opportunities to change its mind—for the good or ill of its public image; it is hard to tell which. There seem to be two theories about making predictions: one being that if you must predict, you should predict often, on the idea, I suppose, that your track record will become sufficiently obfuscated in the process; the other being that you should predict very rarely so that no track record can be established, given the public's short memory.

The addition of a third year to these projections by the Bernanke Fed in effect finessed the vexed question about whether the institution should or should not announce a specific target for inflation. The third year is far enough ahead so that the inflation projection for that year can be taken as something of a target, thus saving the institution from the political and practical dilemma of announcing a specific target for inflation (as many countries around the world have done and as Bernanke had often advocated in one forum or another) when by law the Fed has a clear dual mandate to maintain both price stability and maximum employment.

I very much doubt that announcement of an explicit inflation target would help enhance the Fed's image or, for that matter, more surely anchor inflation expectations, which would be the ostensible economic gain from such an approach. In the end, and to risk again introducing an over-worked refrain, practice counts more than words. At the same time, words can indeed unduly, and impractically, fence in practice.

When the eminent British nineteenth-century politician Benjamin Disraeli was asked to give his opinion about whether man should be viewed as descending from apes or angels, a characterization of issues raised by the Darwinian controversies of the period, he saw no need to waffle, responding in effect, "I, my lord, am on the side of the angels." He could afford clarity; markets would not carefully mark and test his every word (though he no doubt had elections, a different matter, on his mind). The Fed has found an ambiguous way to be on the side of the angels—that is, to indicate how low it would like inflation to be in future without quite clearly specifying a target. That's a wise approach, I would say, since it is far from solely in the Fed's hands to determine how everything works out, as the institution must well know. Fate—in this case, unforeseen changes in economic structure and events—will always play a role, and often an unexpected one.

During the great credit crisis, when conventional monetary policy was swamped by the need instead for innovative and unusual actions to stabilize a deteriorating financial system, the Fed, and its chairman, initially did not appear to communicate as effectively as one might have hoped to help reassure markets. Once the full depth of the crisis was clearly revealed in the fall of 2008, that tended to change, and the chairman seemed to become more accessible and sensitive to market issues and to public and of course congressional concerns.

Moreover, as time went on, the flow of information from the Fed became particularly detailed and useful, program-by-program, for understanding who was receiving Fed credit, the lending terms and nature of the collateral, and the credit risks borne by the Fed (and thus ultimately the U.S. tax payer). However, the gathering cascade of information, resulted, so it seemed, not simply from unbidden Fed initiatives but also from prodding by the Congress and the exigencies of a political and social environment often suspicious of the interactions between the Fed and major financial institutions.

In that connection, the interactions between leadership at the Fed and the financial chief executives represented on reserve bank boards around the country, and notably in New York during the crisis period, tended to become of more interest to the press and the public. No doubt these executives generally have played a constructive and objective role in deliberations about governance at reserve banks. Nonetheless, and especially in such an intense period of press and congressional scrutiny as was aroused by the sheer magnitude of the crisis and its threat to the nation's welfare, questions can, and should, arise about whether any advice they may be asked for or give is totally without a taint of self-interest and institutional protection. It does not seem unreasonable to consider whether a CEO's opinions may be excessively influenced by natural loyalty to and confidence in his own institution as well as by the potential dangers faced by his or similar institutions stemming from their own positions and behavior in the run-up to the crisis. Moreover, questions also arise about whether the Fed tends to be overly influenced because of the closeness in relationships over time between its high officials and financial executives and their companies.

The amendment to the Federal Reserve Act noted earlier that keeps reserve bank directors who represent member banks from voting to select a reserve bank president (a much milder version of earlier proposed amendments to maintain distance between member institutions and the Fed that supervises them) is really little but a warning shot across the Fed's bow. It by no means limits the possibilities of informal contact between Fed officials and leading financial institution and market executives—which can be very useful for gauging and understanding emerging market and banking developments.

To sum up my view of the Fed's image and its institutional credibility—the basic pillar for its effectiveness in monetary policy and for the practical application of its independent stature granted by the Congress—I would judge that it became badly frayed in the run-up to and in the course of the great credit crisis. Its organizational reputation for unremitting diligence and objectivity was damaged, though mitigated as time went on by the obvious, intense efforts put in by all parts of the system that helped resolve the crisis. Nonetheless, the Fed's institutional credibility requires careful nurturing in the years ahead.

9

Concluding Remarks

I have tried to depict how the Fed managed monetary policy over the past almost six decades and, in particular, how the various chairmen of this period attempted to exert their own influence on policy, sometimes effectively and sometimes not. Such a perspective can have the unfortunate side effect of seeming to diminish unduly the role of other FOMC voting members, not to mention also the reserve bank presidents who participated in meetings in years when it was not their turn to vote. But it is not meant to. They, too, have been critical to the policy process. Governors on the Fed Board in Washington and presidents of regional reserve banks have been well aware of their prerogatives and clearly have had their full say, as a reading of the copious policy records, memoranda of discussion, and transcripts of FOMC meetings will reveal.

Nonetheless, it was mainly up to the individual in the chairman's seat to take the lead in policy formulation, whether it was to introduce significant structural changes in the process of policy implementation or to provide guidance in the regular policy discussions at each meeting when the intermeeting target for open market operations was set. I came to believe that significant structural changes could not be introduced without the chairman's leadership.

However, when the FOMC is in its normal mode of deciding whether or not to tighten or ease money markets, the chairman's influence appears more limited. The FOMC always seemed willing, up to a point, to give the chairman the benefit of the doubt because he will have to defend the policies put in place. That benefit, however, was often surprisingly limited. It had to be earned by the chairman through his leadership qualities, the perceived sense of his capacity for judgment, and his public stature.

The FOMC (as well as the Board of Governors, of course) will work better if the chairman is a well-respected leader, though there is no guarantee that the policy implemented will, in retrospect, look like the best one. But regardless, if there is no leadership, if the chairman spends his time effectively doing no more than searching around for a consensus, the committee will almost certainly flounder, not to mention lose respect for the chairman.

It is always difficult to evaluate and compare leadership qualities of Fed chairmen (or any other group of leaders for that matter). Apart from the subjectivity inherent in making such judgments, each chairman holds office under different, sometimes radically different, economic, social, and political conditions. One is hard pressed to judge how much a leader's track record (looking only at those in office long enough to establish one) is due to his individual dynamism and how much to being placed in circumstances that permit, even require, a heightened performance. And to come to a judgment about whether one chairman would have performed as well or better than another if places had been changed is little better than a guessing game.

Volcker and Bernanke surely faced the most difficult external circumstances of the postwar period. Volcker confronted a great inflation that had persisted for a decade or more by the time he took office and had seriously shaken the Fed's monetary policy credibility. Its persistence was clearly weighing heavily on the domestic and international credibility of the dollar, affecting the international competitiveness of major U.S. industries, and dragging down real incomes and job opportunities in the country. Bernanke found himself in the middle of a great credit crisis that so damaged confidence in markets (and also in the governmental institutions that were supposed to safeguard them, including the Fed) that credit availability was drying up and a major economic recession was looming and a deep depression was not out of the question.

Both Volcker and Bernanke exhibited leadership qualities that in varying degrees helped restore confidence in the economy and markets—at the cost of relatively severe recessions in both cases, but one tempered under Volcker by an overall performance that was associated with considerably less financial and economic havoc. While the economic contraction related to the credit market crisis under Bernanke lasted only two months longer than the recession following the Volcker anti-inflation initiative (after abstracting from the ups and downs related to the Carter credit control vagaries of those days), it did proceed at a somewhat more rapid pace and was deeper. But much more tellingly, the subsequent early stage of cyclical recovery was very much weaker under Bernanke—with the economy's real output (measured by real GDP) expanding at only an average annual growth rate of about 3 percent over the first four quarters of recovery following the credit crisis recession as compared with about 7¾ percent for the comparable stage of recovery in the Volcker period.

The blow to economic and societal confidence from the great credit crisis and its resolution had a lingering effect that significantly restrained the recovery of business and personal spending in the crisis aftermath, while the repression of the great inflation was greeted mainly with a sense of relief and the release of strong pent-up demands for goods and housing from businesses and consumers. Much of this relatively better outcome in the Volcker era reflects the widely differing underlying economic and financial circumstances of the times (including, for instance, a stock market that had been in the doldrums during the preceding great inflation and was poised for a sustained, confidence-enhancing rise once inflation was convincingly subdued). Nonetheless, at least some of the difference also resulted from the damaging effects of recognition lags by the Bernanke Fed (and also the administration and other market regulators) about the severity of the evolving credit crisis that not only worsened it but also involved considerable public and political contention in the process of finally bringing it under control, thus heightening cautionary attitudes in financial markets and among businesses and consumers that lasted well into the recovery period.

In introducing his paradigmatic shift in monetary policy, Volcker "artfully" exhibited an intuitive grasp of timing in policy action, a sensitive feel for underlying market trends and sentiment, and an ability to enhance policy through convincing and empathetic communication with markets. Moreover, his effort was deliberate and individual. It did not arise from any clear groundswell of support for his particular approach that I could detect in the FOMC, though there did seem to be something like a groundswell of concern by FOMC members about the failure of previous policies to reduce the domestic rate of inflation and to avert the periodic collapses of the dollar on exchange markets—which must have made them more amenable to the chairman's initiative. The success of Volcker's policy of "practical monetarism" permitted committee members to bask in a kind of reflected glory for a while.

Success in controlling inflation greatly burnished Volcker's image with the public and also the stature of the Federal Reserve. He was not associated with the inflation during the Burns era, though he was in fact vice chairman of the FOMC during the latter part of Burns's term and through Miller's brief tenure. But he assumed that position after the institution's anti-inflation credibility had already been clearly tarnished, and in any event chairmen always and rightfully bear the brunt of blame or praise. However, late in his second term as chairman, Volcker's leadership influence within the institution waned in the wake of discordant relationships with the new Reagan appointees on the board, as typified by the discount-rate controversy described in chapter 5.

In contrast to Volcker, Bernanke was faced with a crisis situation for which the public held him at least partly responsible, and with some reason. The crisis occurred and deepened in apparent response to Fed policy approaches on his watch. However, he did in the end turn the tide of the crisis by various innovative actions earlier described in chapter 7. He stabilized a very bad situation by galvanizing the full legal, regulatory, operational, and economic resources throughout the Fed system, and by arduous, full-scale, and sometimes hit-or-miss efforts to provide whatever amount of liquidity was necessary. His performance may not have been like an inspiriting and timely intuitiveness about the markets and policy that could have earlier spared us much of the trauma. Nonetheless, in the end, his policies worked and averted a systemic breakdown and a major economic depression.

He had clearly grasped that, contrary to usual central banking shibboleths, the Fed's balance sheet and the nation's monetary base should be permitted to expand as much as necessary to contain the ominous deterioration in market and economic attitudes that was rapidly developing. It was his reputation in history that was clearly on the line. And it was the Fed's overall institutional credibility that was in peril and needed to be reinforced. How that will finally evolve remains uncertain as of this writing, partly because we are still early in the traditionally very difficult aftermath phase of such a severe crisis and the pace and quality of economic recovery remains uncertain.

Other chairmen in the postwar period did not demonstrate innovative leadership qualities on anything like the scale of Volcker or, in a more workman-like way, of Bernanke (once he realized the fix he and the country were in), either because the opportunity did not present itself or because they failed to recognize it. In confronting the great inflation, Burns was inhibited by an excessively cautious personality. He was also faced with a difficult set of historically embedded market conditions that were out of phase with the imperatives of a vigorous anti-inflationary policy. Moreover, there was an apparent lack of public support for such a policy. From his perspective, the time was simply not ripe.

Unfortunately, his approach to policy caused the Fed to lose all anti-inflation credibility. Even so, he continued to maintain his influence on the FOMC because of his intellectual capacities, strong personality, and the absence of any countervailing policy model in which the committee as a whole had any belief. I cannot be sure that any of the other chairmen I observed in action would have had a lot more success than he in taming inflation in the 1970s. It was a tough period. However, Burns's particular problem was that he pretended to implement a vaguely monetarist policy—in part forced into this posture by pressures from the Congress and in particular the House Banking Committee—but did not really mean it.

I would not particularly fault him for being far from a monetarist at heart. Nonetheless, if, for whatever reason, you do make money-supply measures more important to policy operations and seem to publicize them as targets, you cannot also be seen as ignoring them, unless you can give a convincing explanation for this stance—not too easy while inflation pressures remain untamed.

Martin and Greenspan had by far the longest tenures of the postwar chairmen, between 18 and 19 years in both cases, or more than twice as long as each of Volcker's and Burns's two terms. Neither had powerful, dramatic crises to deal with. But each had troubles in the latter part of their tenures that foreshadowed major issues confronting their successors and raised questions about their leadership qualities, much more so in my opinion for Greenspan than Martin.

Inflation picked up noticeably in the last four years of the 1960s, which were at the end of Martin's otherwise low-inflation tenure. He attempted to stem the tide, but not aggressively enough. For instance, the real federal funds rate in those years remained little changed on average from the preceding six price-stable years, even as inflation accelerated. From that perspective, and especially taking account of future developments under Burns—and also, more recently, Greenspan—when the real funds rate turned negative, one would have a hard time contradicting the opinion held by a number of economists that the Fed in those years was not very well focused, if at all, on the significance of real interest rates and the distinction between real and nominal interest rates for gauging the effectiveness of the Fed's policies. Still, and to his credit, Martin did manage a policy that kept the real funds rate in positive territory in an effort to contain inflation.

For much of Greenspan's tenure, he presided over a period of low inflation and reasonably well-sustained growth. He took office when the hard work of reducing inflation and inflation expectations in the United States had largely been accomplished under Volcker (which Greenspan freely and generously admitted), when market structures and institutions had become more modernized and adaptable, and when a prolonged non-inflationary environment was enveloping much of the world. On the innovative side, he was responsible, about midway through his tenure, for a significant shift toward more open communication by the Fed that was long overdue.

Greenspan's troubles in the latter part of his long tenure arose at the same time as policy communications and associated efforts at verbal suasion began to be actively employed by the Fed to condition market attitudes in directions the Fed believed would be consistent with policy needs and the economic outlook. But, as interpreted by markets these efforts seemed to encourage a counterproductive market-wide moral hazard that had especially damaging consequences (e.g., the buildup to the credit crisis) when conjoined with the very easy monetary policy stance in the early years following the 2000 stock market crash. At the time, the easy money policy was justified in part on risk management policy grounds to avert the small threat of price deflation. Ironically, however, in the process the market itself was encouraged to take on excessive risk. In the end, speculative bubbles had replaced inflation as the bane of Fed policy.

In the FOMC's consideration of major structural shifts in its approach to policy management, members other than the chairman will on occasion make suggestions for change, but if the chairman strongly opposes these suggestions, they will not take place. For instance, in the inflationary 1970s when other FOMC members advanced ideas for more marked structural changes in policy implementation, Burns employed the time-honored method of averting these ideas by setting up a subcommittee to consider them. When the Maisel subcommittee proposed an offbeat reserve aggregate (reserves against private deposits) as a guide for day-to-day policy operations, the proposal was in effect sidetracked. After discussion by the FOMC, Burns suggested that the staff, as an experiment, attempt to keep track for a time of what might happen to money supply and interest rates if the proposal were followed and to report the results in the blue book. In the process the proposal died of its own weight.

In more recent times, Bernanke seems to have used the subcommittee approach not so much to avert proposals, but to find, in this case, a way to implement an approach to inflation targeting in some form acceptable to the FOMC as a whole at a time when opposition to setting clear explicit inflation targets was too widespread. Something like Bernanke's purposes was accomplished in a report, from a subcommittee headed by then vice chairman Don Kohn to consider the much broader subject of how best to communicate key elements in the Fed's economic outlook, the results of which were noted in the preceding chapter.

The Fed as an institution and its chairmen will in the future undoubtedly have to adapt to new and unpredictable circumstances. Over the past six decades, the Fed first moved toward paying more attention to money supply as inflation surged, then began to move away from money as inflation came under control, and finally came to ignore money altogether as it became more and more difficult to measure in any way that was useful to policy, given the radical changes that had taken place in the structure of banking and securities markets.

So the potential for inflation came to be seen as more of a problem detectable from real variables, such as the gap between actual output and productive capacity and by whether the level of real interest rates is above or below "neutral" (which I take to mean the level that will neither inhibit the economy from growing at its potential nor encourage excessive inflation—a neat trick if both objectives are to be accomplished more or less simultaneously). And, crucially, it is also seen in market and public attitudes toward inflation, as indicated by measures of inflation expectations—as has been strongly stressed by the Bernanke Fed.

But whether focusing on real or expectation indicators, very pragmatic issues of interpretation remain that continue to place a high premium on policymakers' judgment, and particularly that of the chairman in fulfilling his leadership role. For instance, how does one know when, in practice, policy has attained the nirvana of a neutral real federal funds rate and thus in theory need not worry about raising or lowering the existing funds rate? That is something of a guess. Many of the economic factors that one imagines should inform one's view of the neutral rate are highly uncertain. Among them: the real return on capital tends to fluctuate with productivity changes and with the perhaps even more uncertain ongoing demand for the goods relative to existing productive capacity; businessmen, consumers, investors and institutional attitudes toward risk shift about, as very amply illustrated by the broad and sharp deterioration in attitudes during the recent great credit crisis and in more normal times by evolving changes in the structure of interest rates; and the valuation of the stock market relative to the underlying capital stock is subject to change cyclically, secularly, and speculatively.

Thus, judgments about the appropriate so-called neutral funds rate and about whether the real funds rate appropriate to current policy operations should be below or above it, and by how much, make a careful evaluation of incoming data for policy formulation as necessary as it ever was or even perhaps more so. Friedman-type monetarist rules, as in the old days, and a Taylor-type rule in today's world may be of some help, but only as background music. To adapt an old saw, the more things change, the more the underlying dilemmas in policy formulation remain the same. Uncertainties abound, and the judgmental aspects of policy remain at the fore. What counts are the current flows of data and judgments about them.

Fed spokesmen have on occasion continued to note that inflation is a monetary phenomenon. Maybe they mean no more than that it is a monetary policy phenomenon. Of course it is, but that statement sheds no light on the basic sources of inflation. The Fed can with some success guide its policies by evaluating real developments and inflation expectations. Nevertheless, it remains difficult to shake the sense that once inflation arises, it still may be well characterized, in the old-fashioned sense, as too much money chasing too few goods.

If so, where can the Fed or we as the public detect the monetary part of the phenomenon now? Some of it may still be seen in old-fashioned money and in the very closely related highly liquid assets. But money's behavior, as endlessly reiterated in this book and by policymakers and analysts in recent decades, has not for some time exhibited any convincing predictable relationship to the economy and prices. This raises the question of whether inflationary money might also be held, to some degree, in home equity and stocks? Does it also reside in the huge rise of holdings of U.S. government securities abroad that may eventually be spent here or elsewhere? What about the myriad of other eminently tradable assets available here and abroad in our now highly globalized financial markets? And how are the credit and price risks of such a variety of assets taken into account by holders in assessing the extent to which they might influence the use of "money" held in such assets for spending? These are hardly new questions but they seem more pointed in today's complicated, and rather amorphous, financial world.

I doubt that financial markets will become any less complicated in future years, though maybe they will, at least for a while, become better regulated in response to the public furor and legislative changes following the great credit crisis. Also, again at least for a while, consumers and businesses could become more conservative in managing their spending and finances, and markets may become more mindful of the perils of excess leverage. But if history is any guide, over time there will be little letup in the conundrums raised by fluid and inventive modern markets for the Fed.

The institution will always be faced with questions about whether evolving changes within the financial structure, some actually as a countervailing response to Fed policies, are or are not dangerously stimulating inflation-type pressures in either goods markets or markets for capital assets—both of which, as the experience of past decades demonstrate, can lead to economic recessions. In the longer run, it seems obvious that the Fed should focus on price stability in the market for currently produced goods and services. But there is also a good argument to be made for adjusting policy, to an extent, in an effort to avert excessive inflation pressures in capital-asset markets, difficult as such a judgment may be.

Moreover, as a further complication, I suspect that future Fed chairmen will also need to take more direct account of international markets in making judgments about policy and its management. The Fed in the past for the most part has had the luxury of more or less ignoring the rest of the world in formulating policy, but at times it may have overindulged.

For instance, in the latter part of Greenspan's tenure, and persisting into the early years of Bernanke's, the nation's international deficit on current account with the rest of the world (measured relative to the size of our economy) expanded considerably further, reflecting, and contributing to, growing imbalances in the world payments system as a whole. The Fed at the time did not appear to take sufficient account of the longer-run dangers in such a development. Instead, it seemed more or less passive in face of the large inflow of saving from abroad and the accompanying imports of cheap foreign goods that were a feature of the worldwide imbalances.

In the short-run, these flows had certain distinct advantages for our economy. They provided credit from abroad to compensate for domestic saving deficiencies and permitted excess spending here with less upward pressure on prices and interest rates. But from a longer-run perspective, unsustainable as they were, they encouraged distortions in asset prices and debt burdens that imperiled the development of our, and the world, economy.

In practice, there was probably little the Fed alone could have done in face of global imbalances, recognizing the uncertain crosscurrents in our own economy at the time. Moreover, key foreign countries, China being an obvious example, appeared unwilling to do their part to smooth the transition to a better and more sustainable international balance. For China—whose current account surplus surged dramatically during the first decade of the new century—that would have required more quickly taking effective actions that would have enhanced its domestic spending and significantly raised the real value of its exchange rate. Nonetheless, in retrospect, perhaps some recognition of the potential dangers by the Fed was in order, especially since it is arguable that the credit crisis was facilitated to some extent by the ready availability of credit from abroad to compensate for deficient domestic saving.

In any event, the luxury of ignoring the rest of the world has gradually been eroding. It will be not easy to admit because Congress tends to blanch at any idea that U.S. monetary policy will have to be formulated, at least to a degree, in response to developments abroad, or in light of exchange-market developments, or, hardest of all to swallow, in cooperation with other countries' policies.

In my day at the Fed (ending far back in 1986), the blue book's policy alternatives barely mentioned international conditions or assumed they had any significance for domestic policy formulation. A short paragraph about events abroad or in the exchange market was duly inserted, but it really did not matter what that paragraph said. Policy decisions always zeroed in on the domestic economy, an approach that I generally favored at the time. Of course, the staff responsible for economic projections had to take into account (in the green book) events in foreign countries because of their effect on the domestic economy and prices—considered quite minor then but of more significance now as large, newly emerging countries have become increasingly important in the world economy, and the U.S. share of world output has been tending to diminish.

While the Fed's independence to make policy on purely domestic grounds is becoming more hedged in by the great world, it will probably be some time before the Fed's capacity to implement an independent policy becomes as significantly dented as, for example, was the case for small countries in Europe in face of the deutschmark's power in the days before the euro. And also as it is now for the much larger number of countries in Europe, including Germany, who are members the European Central Bank and whose monetary polices are no longer independent but tied to the euro as a currency. The United States at this point simply still is too large an economy and an independent currency area.

It would probably take an all-encompassing world currency to nullify the Fed's capacity to play a reasonably independent effective role in influencing the U.S. economy and inflation. Such a currency lurks, if it lurks at all, only in the far distant future.

But monetary independence for the U.S. is not likely to be total as the world economy unfolds in the not too distant future. The U.S. could come to face competition on roughly equal terms from, and may have to consider its policies in relation to, a number of equally sizeable mastodons. While the sovereign debt crisis in 2010 in the euro zone cast doubt on the continued cohesion of the zone and the value of its currency, the euro zone as it now exists has also become a very large economy with a market potential comparable to ours. The emergence of China and other major countries, such as Brazil and India, may eventually lead to other sizeable currency areas on or close to a par with the dollar in worldwide acceptability—though that is not likely to occur for quite a while until they show persistent, reliable signs of continuing market stability and economic growth, coupled with a welcoming and reasonably predictable political and social environment.

All in all, changing international conditions, the increasing linkages among banking and other financial markets (both here and abroad) and the complexity and interconnections of financial instruments involved suggest to me that future Fed chairmen not only will need a keen intuitive sense about market behavior, but also should be prepared to implement policy operations rather more flexibly than in recent decades. For instance, I believe that the Fed, in its day-to-day open market operations, should interpret its target for the federal funds rate with less rigidity—that is, the target might best have a little give to it (it should have at least an implicit range around it) in the name of overall market stability.

Such an operational approach—with some flexibility delegated by the FOMC to the chairman's good judgment in the period between meetings—may give the Fed an opportunity either to help smooth out disturbances in particular markets that might otherwise adversely impact market and business psychology or to get a leg up that might help keep longer-lasting disturbances from reaching crisis proportions. For instance, the funds rate might be permitted to drop below target for a time as the Fed supplies more liquidity needed to moderate threatening market pressures or to rise as signal for restraint in overly exuberant markets. Whether such movements did or did not lead to a follow-up basic change in policy at the next meeting (or the need to call a special meeting earlier) would depend on market and economic conditions that developed, including judgments to be made about how markets responded to the Fed's own intra-meeting actions.

As markets become even more quickly and widely internationally connected, I also think there is a role for foreign-exchange-market operations as a (minor and occasional) complement to domestic government-security-market transactions. Such operations may help moderate sudden volatility in exchange markets that has the potential for upsetting domestic psychology. They may even provide a useful countervailing signal, not only to private market participants but also to relevant policy officials in other significant countries, at a time when the ebb and flow of international flows of funds are unduly influencing exchange-market values and even actual domestic market conditions.

I have no intention of claiming too much for such action. They would be of minor significance, given the huge size of international markets and the very limited amount of foreign currency the Fed as a practical matter is likely to buy or sell. It is more a matter of showing the flag, so to speak, when it might be marginally useful and generally consistent with underlying domestic policy objectives.

Apart from the value of increased flexibility in day-to-day monetary policy operations, there is also a strong argument, in light of the great credit crisis, that monetary policy authorities should have the capacity to take action, or at a minimum strongly encourage actions by others, that might forestall the potential for market destabilization stemming from undue prudential imbalances within the financial system. This is much easier said than done.

It is difficult to identify clear signs of a looming danger of systemic instability. Nor, for that matter, even if one could, is it simple to organize actions on a timely basis that might work to contain the chances of a market eruption. A drawn out process of coordination among the wide variety of regulators in this country might well be required, depending on the nature of the potential imbalance. While the process here might be expedited by the reforms enacted in the Dodd-Frank Act, it remains to be seen how the practical relationships among the Fed, other regulators, and the newly established financial stability oversight council chaired by the Secretary of the Treasury work out over time

In addition, coordination with authorities abroad would probably be needed in most cases because the same transactions that have become problematic (either because they have become cumulatively too large and widespread to be sustainable or are too highly leveraged or both) can be conducted in dollars directly in foreign markets or in foreign currencies hedged with forward dollar transactions.

If the potential for an eruption in credit markets seems to be evolving, or a speculative rise in equity prices appears under way, monetary policy can be faced with an unpalatable dilemma. To avert the threat of a systemic crisis, it might have to consider open market operations that would raise interest rates sooner or by more than they wish even though overall economic conditions at the moment do not suggest the need to do so. But such an action risks weakening the economy unduly. On the other hand, if the policy approach remains unchanged, the financial imbalances may continue to worsen, and the eventual, inevitable financial collapse may turn out to be even worse for the economy.

Of the two unsatisfactory choices, the monetary policy authorities have generally avoided the first so far as I can see. In the Greenspan and Bernanke years, this seems to have been partly on the grounds that bubbles embodying extreme danger for the economy as a whole cannot be pin-pointed with any reasonable degree of certainty, especially in their earlier stages, and partly because of what turns out to be a misguided faith that markets themselves will in any event figure out how to cope in an orderly way as the bubbles are inevitably recognized and begin to lose momentum. Unfortunately, as a result the authorities have ended up having to confront the second and, I would say, worse alternative.

The Fed as an institution does have a number of macro-prudential instruments that might be readily brought into play in those relatively rare instances when it is confronted with such a policy dilemma and speed of action is required. Changes in margin requirements on stocks are one when excesses in stock speculation threaten market stability, but, as noted in the Greenspan chapter, they have long remained at the 50 percent level and fallen into disuse as an instrument for financial stabilization.

When a threatening financial bubble seems to be emerging from credit sectors of the economy, it is possible for the Fed to employ its regulatory authority over bank holding companies, rather lightly exercised to date, and depository institutions to tighten up by, for example, adjusting capital ratios (or liquidity requirements) in light of changing risk evaluations at the institutions. Indeed, as earlier noted, the new regulatory framework in the 2010 legislation states that countercyclical capital requirement should be given consideration. More crucially, perhaps, the legislation gives the Fed a special role in regulating, in coordination with the Financial Stability Oversight Council, large bank holding companies and other large nonbank financial companies deemed systemically important—including some flexibility to adjust certain prudential standards in light of an evolving potentially difficult situation.

However, prudential actions alone, even if they could be implemented on a timely basis under the new very complex regulatory framework in the 2010 legislation and in face of concerns about equity in treatment among differing institutions, may not have intended restraining effects in practice because of the essential fungibility of money and credit in domestic markets and around the world. Still, I would argue that they could alter market attitudes in a more stabilizing direction because they would be an early signal of policy concern. For instance, it seems likely that the intensity of the recent credit crisis would have been moderated if the Fed had early reflected in careful regulatory and prudential actions its concerns about mortgage market developments and the evolving exposure of banks and bank holding companies to excessive risk.

While the need for unusual prudential actions in coordination with monetary policy would probably be infrequent, the Fed's views on the current state of systemic stability and the implications, if any, for monetary policy could also be usefully addressed in the Fed's semi-annual monetary policy report to Congress and in the chairman's accompanying regular testimony to the banking committees. Most of the time that will not prove to raise issues of any particular significance for monetary policy. However, there is always the risk that the issue may be downplayed for bureaucratic reasons; in the interest of interagency cooperation and political and administrative peace, the Fed's views could turn out to be no more than benign and pro forma. Still, an established custom for the Fed and its chairman to include some commentary about overall market stability in relation to monetary policy, with the occasional nuanced difference here and there, would reinforce the importance of timely supportive regulatory actions should the need become more apparent in the actual course of policy implementation.

In any event, in an effort to keep the Fed on its regulatory toes in the wake of perceived deficiencies in the institution's supervisory posture in connection with the great credit crisis, the Dodd-Frank law requires the new Fed vice chairman for supervision to appear twice a year before the relevant congressional committees to report on the Fed board's activities and plans for supervision and regulation of depository institutions and other financial firms supervised by the Board.

The role of regulatory issues in connection with monetary policy also raises questions about the whether the current institutional structure of the Federal Reserve System is well adapted to today's technologically advanced and sophisticated world of highly interconnected markets. In that context, one might recall that the proponents of the Federal Reserve Act of 1913—failing to recognize that the United States was no longer a collection of regionally differentiated markets, but a single economic and financial entity—originally contemplated the possibility of varying discount rates among district banks to reflect particularized regional economic and financial conditions. That approach was an anachronism virtually at the time of the law's enactment as markets in this country quickly became national in scope.

Modern technology has for some time now been in the process of making the payments system (the plumbing, so to speak, that keeps finance flowing) truly national and of greatly reducing the technical need for individual reserve banks, or at least so many of them in that respect. Moreover, with the development of bank holding companies and interstate branching, regional banking has retreated further to the margins.

Is there a role left for reserve banks other than as regional offices for carrying out certain administrative functions, such as administering the discount window or examining bank or bank holding companies in their area? In short, should there be elaborate buildings, boards of directors with the power to recommend discount rates (a power now practically irrelevant given the Fed board's decision to amend its regulation so that the discount rate is to be set at a fixed percentage point relative to the FOMC's targeted federal funds rate), and a large staff for economic research and community relations? Most delicate of all questions, should reserve bank presidents, who are not appointed by the president of the United States and approved by the Senate, be given a vote on national policy?

Nonetheless, rather outdated as the structure of the Federal Reserve System now seems to be, I would still argue against radical changes (though economies certainly may be in order). It has worked well over time. Reserve bank presidents, in my experience, have generally made effective contributions to monetary policy. The independent research staffs at the banks, although something of a luxury in their total size, have added spice to the economic basis for policy discussions and have usefully interacted with the economics profession and the regional community in discussing, debating, and explaining policy.

All that being said, I believe the Fed, as a system, would work better if reserve bank presidents were chosen principally for their insights into and close connection with the supervisory and other operational aspects of the Fed's responsibilities. Unlike the staff and policymakers at the Board in Washington, they are not as removed from practical issues and changing practices within the banking system and among other financial institutions, and should be better able to sense, and make known, banking and market developments of potential concern in their early stages. That important regional and local function, along with their perspective on monetary policy from the field so to speak, is important to the Fed's institutional credibility.

Economists have come to play an increasingly important role in the leadership structure during recent decades, whether as presidents of reserve banks or as members of the Board of Governors. In point of fact, this seems to be a worldwide trend as central banks are given independence of a sort and considered more as technical-type institutions in business mainly to keep inflation under control—and thus, in that sense, allegedly removed from the need to make choices among competing objectives that have social and political implications.

But of course, and as recent events make eminently clear, there is more to central banking than monetary policy, and even monetary policy in practice is anything but merely a technical focus on inflation control. In the U.S. the Fed is required by law to wrestle with two principal macroeconomic objectives of both low inflation and maximum employment, along with the need to help assure financial stability and to be the primary source of liquidity as may be needed to avert impending threats to such stability. The Fed's institutional credibility and stature depend on somehow finding the judgment to implement all of its principal functions with a minimum of social and economic distress—a very tall order indeed.

Technical expertise is needed area by area throughout the Fed system, but given the institution's key role within the financial system and our society, individuals with a broad capacity for judgment are also required, especially for top leadership. Particularly for monetary policy, but also in some degree elsewhere, judgments inevitably have to be made about such matters as timing of actions, the psychology and underlying condition of market participants and counterparties, and how far the boundaries of conventional thinking influenced by the prevailing economic, social, and political norms can, and in practice, should be stretched in light of changing circumstances.

Such a characterization suggests what I suppose should be obvious in any event: the usefulness within the Fed's top leadership structure of a mix of skills and backgrounds embodied in high-quality individuals so as to increase the odds of effective and convincing policy judgments in all areas of its work. Doubtless, such ideal-type people are difficult to find given the waywardness of the political process in the Congress, the potential for insular attitudes within reserve banks and their boards, and the undoubted fact that the Fed chairman's job tends to put all others in the shade. Still, a somewhat more diverse leadership corps, if it can be well chosen, would usefully add practical weight and something like "street cred" to economists' useful skills and insights—derived in part from their familiarity with, and sometimes unfortunately misplaced faith in, the latest economic models and theoretical thinking affecting the role of the central bank in a modern economy.

That much being said, there is in the end no avoiding the weight of responsibility that has to be placed on the chairman. Obviously, the person filling such a position, in addition to having intellectual curiosity and capacity across all areas of the Fed's responsibilities, needs, for success, to have a genuine interest in the ins and outs of central banking from both market and macro-economic viewpoints. In the wake of the great credit crisis, I would especially stress the need for a keen grasp of the importance of the Fed's regulatory and supervisory responsibilities and for seeing that those involved are somehow accorded the same stature within the Fed system as are participants in the monetary policy area, which has traditionally been seen to be more prestigious.

With regard to general character traits that might distinguish a chairman with the best odds for success in a variety of circumstances, the following seem particularly important: as much leadership charisma as is practical in the traditional low voltage atmosphere of central banking; a feel for the potential in the nation's political and social environment for action "outside the box" and the courage to act if needed; an aptitude for empathetic and effective communication with the public; and—perhaps most crucial to the mix like the yeast required for bread to rise—native good judgment and plain old common sense. It's hard to find all, or even most, of that in any one of us, much less in an intelligent, self-possessed person with an abiding interest in central banking and, I must add, an intuitive feel for markets. It's a wonder that it sometimes is.

Appendix A: Chronology of Federal Reserve System Chairmen and U.S. Presidents

Chairmen of the Board of Governors of the Federal Reserve System, 1951 to the Present

William McChesney Martin	April 2, 1951, to January 31, 1970
Arthur F. Burns	February 1, 1970, to January 31, 1978
G. William Miller	March 8, 1978, to August 6, 1979
Paul A. Volcker	August 6, 1979, to August 11, 1987
Alan Greenspan	August 11, 1987, to January 31, 2006
Ben S. Bernanke	February 1, 2006, to the present

Presidents of the United States, 1945 to the Present

Harry S. Truman	April 12, 1945, to January 20, 1953
Dwight D. Eisenhower	January 20, 1953, to January 20, 1961
John F. Kennedy	January 20, 1961, to November 22, 1963
Lyndon B. Johnson	November 22, 1963, to January 20, 1969
Richard Nixon	January 20, 1969, to August 9, 1974
Gerald Ford	August 9, 1974, to January 20 1977
Jimmy Carter	January 20, 1977, to January 20, 1981
Ronald Reagan	January 20, 1981, to January 20, 1989
George H. W. Bush	January 20, 1989, to January 20, 1993
Bill Clinton	January 20, 1993, to January 20, 2001
George W. Bush	January 20, 2001, to January 20, 2009
Barack Obama	January 29, 2009, to the present

Appendix B: Key Economic Objectives and Monetary Policy Indicators

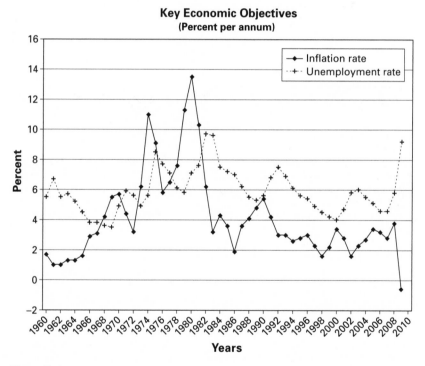

Figure B.1
Key Economic Objectives (Percent per Annum)

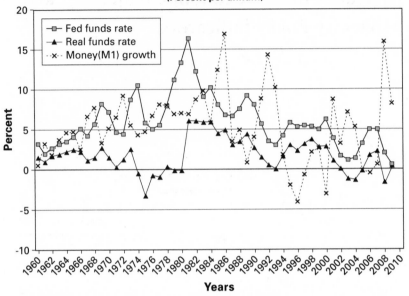

Figure B.2
Key Monetary Policy Indicators (Percent per Annum) *Source: Economic Report of the President, 2010,* appendix B. Figures in charts B.1 and B.2 are for year over year through 2009, except for money supply, which is from December to December. Money growth figures before 1966 are from earlier versions of the *Economic Report.* The real funds rate is its market rate less the annual percent change in the consumer price index for the same year.

Notes

Introduction

1. Over the course of time, I rose from the lowest to the topmost end of the professional staff, and during the latter part of my tenure came to hold the titles of staff director for monetary and financial policy at the Fed Board of Governors, as well as staff director and, for much of the time, secretary of the Federal Open Market Committee, the Fed's central authority for monetary policy.

Chapter 1

1. To be eligible for appointment as chairman, the candidate must also be appointed as a governor (member of the Fed Board of Governors), whose full term is fourteen years. A chairman's term lasts only four years, but he can be reappointed so long as time remains within his term as governor. Governors cannot be reappointed if they have served a full term, but they can be reappointed into a full term if they have previously served only part of a full term.

2. Each reserve bank president is by law nominated by the Board of Directors of that bank and approved by the Fed Board of Governors. That the presidents do not go through a presidential appointment process has on rare occasions been raised as a political issue because through their membership on the FOMC they have a vote in determining national monetary policy.

3. The chairman generally has regular contact with the administration through the secretary of the Treasury. In my day, weekly Monday breakfast meetings usually took place between the secretary and the chairman in the secretary's dining room at the Treasury, though of course other meetings took place on occasion by phone or in person as the need arose (for instance, in connection with foreign-currency operations). In addition, the chairman hosted regular Wednesday luncheons at the Fed building that were attended by a Treasury deputy or undersecretary and assorted senior officials and staff. I had no idea what the secretary and the chairman said to each in their tête-à-têtes, but at the Wednesday luncheons, which I attended for a bit more than two decades, there were, to my memory, no discussions of

monetary policy. Treasury debt management was the main topic, though it eventually became too routine to be very interesting, and discussion focused more on regulatory issues or economic conditions in general.

4. One reader of a draft thought the originator of this maxim was Marriner Eccles, chairman of the Board of Governors from 1934 to 1948; another suggested that it was Alan Sproul, a well-known former president of the Federal Reserve Bank of New York from 1941 to 1956.

Chapter 2

1. Since the Fed pays over to the Treasury almost all of the interest it earns on its holdings of U.S. government securities, the Fed's holdings are for all practical purposes retired debt; the interest on the debt no longer absorbs tax revenues, in contrast to interest on government securities held by commercial banks, businesses, individual savers, and others outside the Fed.

2. See K. Brunner and A. Meltzer, *The Federal Reserve's Attachment to the Free Reserve Concept,* House Committee on Banking and Currency, 88th Cong., 2d sess. (Washington, D.C.: U.S. Government Printing Office, 1964), pp. 1–64. The weak, if any, relationship between free reserves and money supply, and thus the relationship's deficiency as a guide for a monetary policy that actively sought money-supply control, had been pointed out earlier by Jim Meigs, a student of Milton Friedman, in his book *Free Reserves and the Money Supply* (Chicago: University of Chicago Press, 1962).

3. W. Riefler, *Money Rates and Money Markets in the United States* (New York: Harper, 1930).

4. This would happen because, given the amount of total reserves already provided in the reserve period, revisions in required reserves would necessarily entail offsetting adjustments in excess reserves and thus in free reserves.

Chapter 3

1. Various adjustments to deposit ceiling rates were made in the course of the inflationary period to alleviate the competitive pressures on banks and thrifts. For most of the time, it was thought that banks had a greater capacity to pay higher deposit rates than thrifts did, mainly because fixed-rate long-term loans did not bulk so large in their portfolios. Adjustments to ceiling rates could be made only at the pace consistent with the slowest boat in the convoy—that is, the thrifts, which also had considerable political clout in large part because of their then crucial role in the mortgage market. The Monetary Control Act of 1980 eventually provided for, among other things, the phasing out of ceiling rates entirely over a six-year period and established an interagency committee to oversee the process.

2. As part of the controls apparatus, the administration created the Committee on Interest and Dividends. Burns became its chairman, creating the potential for an obvious conflict of interest with his duties as Fed chairman. I suppose he must

have believed there was less risk of contention that might upset the markets if he took the job than if it were given to someone else. I am almost tempted to believe that his taking this position was also some sort of unavoidable price for apparently helping to persuade the U.S. president of the efficacy of price controls in the circumstances of the time. In any event, I saw nothing to make me think that his role in their implementation through the Committee on Interest and Dividends influenced his monetary policy attitudes. I was chief economist to that committee (or so I vaguely remember), but the only task I can recall is overseeing the draft of the committee's final report (written by another economist on the board staff who did whatever real economics work was required for implementing the committee's business). On reading the draft, Burns's reaction to me was that it would do neither him nor me proud. I revised it to claim that the guidelines established for dividend increases (around 3 percent, as I recall) were an important contribution to the credibility of price and wage guidelines, or some such line of thinking. Clearly, the work was not to be seen as all in vain.

3. A. F. Burns, "The Anguish of Central Banking," 1979 Per Jacobsson Lecture, Belgrade Yugoslavia, September 30, 1979.

4. A somewhat similar proviso had also been included in the policy directive during the last four years of the 1960s as inflation picked up. It was related not to behavior of money supply, but to a so-called bank credit proxy. In any event, it had very little practical effect, given the continuing very conservative attitudes toward money market conditions by the FOMC. See S. H. Axilrod, "The FOMC Directive as Structured in the Late 1960s: Theory and Appraisal," in *Open Market Policies and Operating Procedures—Staff Studies* (Washington, D.C.: Board of Governors of the Federal Reserve System, 1971), pp. 1–36, especially pp. 6–7.

5. See S. Goldfield, "The Case of the Missing Money," *Brookings Papers on Economic Activity* 3 (1976): 683–740

6. See R. D. Porter, T. D. Simpson, and E. Mauskopf, "Financial Innovation and the Monetary Aggregates," *Brookings Papers on Economic Activity* 1 (1979): 213–229.

Chapter 4

1. The legal foundation never seemed quite clear to me; in any event, whatever may be the uncertainties and areas of contention, they are in practice irrelevant.

2. The G-11 countries are ten leading industrial nations belonging to the International Monetary Fund, plus Switzerland. They met regularly at the Bank for International Settlements in Basle, Switzerland, to discuss common financial issues such as monetary policy and structural banking issues such as clearing, payments, and regulatory policies.

3. We developed, as I remember, a rather elaborate formula that set differing reserve requirements that would serve to equalize the reserve burden and the competitive position for banks country by country, taking account of relative interest rates among countries involved and the costs of forward exchange transactions.

Chapter 5

1. For example, if a monopolist producer such as a state attempts to control the quantity of a good produced as well as its price, it will generally fail; for instance, if there is more demand for the good, either black-market prices will rise, or long waiting periods for buyers will effectively represent a price rise.

2. See D. Lindsey, A. Orphanides, and R. Rasche, "The Reform of October 1979: How It Happened and Why," in *Reflections on Monetary Policy 25 Years after October 1979, Federal Reserve Bank of St. Louis Review* 86, no. 2, part 2 (March–April 2005): 187–235. Also in the same issue, see S. Axilrod, "Commentary" (pp. 237–242).

3. The 15 percent was probably based on a current inflation rate of about 12 percent, plus three percentage points to represent restraint. Looking back, I should obviously have added more because restraint had to be especially powerful to overcome the market's strong built-in inflation expectations. In any event, a real interest rate of 3 percent was not much, if any, more than the potential real return on capital in those days, so it was not a strongly restrictive addition, even taking account of current feelings that the real economy was on the weak side.

4. My explanation was based on the following set of relationships, though it was certainly shorter and not algebraic. It is a truism that the total of reserves held by the banking system (T) is equal to banks' excess reserves (E) plus the reserves they are required to hold behind deposits (R). So $T = R + E$. The banking system can obtain some of these reserves through reserves loaned to individual banks from the discount window, the so-called borrowed reserves (B) obtainable at banks' initiative. Nonborrowed reserves (N), whose amount is controlled at the Fed's initiative and made available through open market operations, are the only other source of total reserves. Subtracting borrowed reserves from both sides of the preceding equation, it is clear that $(T - B = R + (E - B)$. $(T - B)$ is of course equal to N, and $(E - B)$ is our old friend free reserves, F. Thus, the equation reduces to $N = R + F$. Under the new policy, the Fed chose to control N, so that F (and associated money-market rates) would fluctuate in response to the behavior of required reserves (R) demanded by the banks to support deposits in the money supply. Under older polices, the Fed in effect chose to control F, with the result that free reserves and associated money-market conditions would not vary in response to money-supply behavior. They would be unchanged because open market operations would have to provide sufficient nonborrowed reserves (N) to supply the banking system's demand for required reserves without forcing banks as a group to change their liquidity position (F), either through borrowing from the Fed or through altering excess reserves. This explanation is simplified and leaves out complications from lagged reserve requirements, changes in banks' demand for liquidity (free reserves), and other much more technical matters, such as banks' need for clearing balances and unexpected changes in the deposit mix and in the public's demand for currency relative to deposits. The essential point is that in the old days the Fed controlled F in aiming at very close control of money-market rates, but in the new policy approach the Fed controlled N (as the

operational proxy for money) and let interest rates fluctuate within a much wider tolerance range.

5. In the end, all of the contending parties did their econometric research, the result being, as I remember, that money growth over the intermediate-term period, given the institutional environment of the time, was shown to be at least no less controllable using the Fed's chosen reserve-operating technique, as compared with others.

6. At that time, with the aggregate amount of bank reserves provided through open market operations (the so-called nonborrowed reserves) being deliberately limited, a rise in the discount rate would automatically raise short-term rates further (because it raised the cost to banks of borrowing the additional reserves they needed at the Federal Reserve Banks' discount windows) without any action by the FOMC. This rise gave the Board of Governors a little more leverage than it usually had for affecting market interest rates. When the FOMC took a level of money-market rates as its operating target, a change in the discount rate would not necessarily affect money-market rates unless the FOMC also voted to change its money-market-rate target.

7. The chart show (including both the staff presentation and the accompanying charts) is available on the Fed's Web site as an appendix to the November 4–5, 1985, FOMC meeting. The FOMC's discussion of it is not included, presumably because it may have contained discussion about the attitudes of individual foreign countries.

Chapter 6

1. John Maynard Keynes's seminal book *The General Theory of Employment, Interest, and Money* was first published in 1936 in the middle of the Great Depression.

2. I received my undergraduate degree magna cum laude in economics at Harvard and was elected to Phi Beta Kappa. At Chicago, I passed the comprehensive exams in economics at the doctoral level, but never wrote my thesis for the PhD, apparently being content with rapid promotions at the Fed. My graduate degree at Chicago was a master's obtained from the Program for Education in Research and Planning, a program that the university has long since abandoned.

3. The funds rate was initially indicated through a transparent qualitative statement when policy changed, then at the beginning of 1996 the specific rate was announced whenever policy shifted, and finally in the spring of 1999 the rate was indicated after every meeting—central-bank caution in action.

4. In effect, the funds market has the same influence on market interest rates as would the central bank's lending facility if there were no funds market and no open market operations. Under those circumstances, if depository institutions could borrow at will from the central bank (assuming away the important issue of adequate collateral), the posted lending rate at that facility (commonly called the discount rate in the United States) would then represent the ultimate liquidity rate

in the market. As of this writing, the Fed's basic discount rate (officially termed the *primary credit rate* since the discount-window program change approved by the Board of Governors on October 31, 2002, and effectuated on January 9, 2003) is by regulation set one-half of a percentage point above the targeted funds rate. It was set at one percentage point above the targeted funds rate from January 2003 to August 2007, when it was lowered to a one-half-point premium in the Fed's initial effort at dealing with the severe subprime mortgage crisis at the time. On March 16, 2008, the spread was further lowered to one-quarter of a percentage point. In mid-February 2010 it was then raised back to a one-half point premium, as a very early sign that the credit crisis was easing. There are few restrictions on borrowing primary credit, and that rate therefore comes close to representing an upper limit for the overnight federal funds rate. A rate for secondary credit at the discount window applicable to institutions that do not qualify for primary credit is set at an additional one-half-point premium to the primary credit rate. Emergency credit could also be extended to individuals, partnerships, and corporations that are not depository institutions in "unusual and exigent circumstances" at a rate above the highest rate available to depository institutions. The emergency provision was altered by the Dodd-Frank Act, as explained later in the text.

5. Technically, margin requirements may be adjusted not in reaction to changes in stock prices, but in response to excessive use of credit for purchasing or carrying stocks.

6. The prepared text of my remarks, "Comments on Public Policy Issues Raised by Rescue of a Large Hedge Fund, Long-Term Capital Management," can be found in *Hedge Fund Operations, Hearing before the Committee on Banking and Financial Services, U.S. House of Representatives, October 1, 1998* (Washington, D.C.: U.S. Government Printing Office, 1998), pp. 288–293.

7. As measured by the average nominal funds rate in each of the years less the average percentage increase in the consumer price index (CPI) for each year. I have used the total CPI. The Fed focuses on a CPI measure less its volatile food and energy components, though it seems to prefer and stress a similar price index derived from the nation's GDP accounts—to wit, average prices for personal consumption expenditures less food and energy (the core PCE). The total index for CPI or PCE seems more relevant to me in gauging inflation pressures over time, even though on a month-to-month basis they can be distorted by large, transitory fluctuations in energy and food costs. Nonetheless, I believe their trend indicates much better the cost pressures on the consumer that would lead to stronger wage demands and the potential for greater inflationary pressures through rising labor costs. More recently, the Fed has been giving more weight to overall inflation as an indicator.

8. See, as examples, the official statements in the press release of October 28, 2003, when the funds rate was 1 percent, of the use of the phrase "policy accommodation can be maintained for a considerable period," and in the press release of June 30, 2004, when the funds rate rose to 1¼ percent, of the initial use of the phrase that accommodation can be removed "at a pace that is likely to be measured."

The latter language was probably intended to avert an excessively strong rise of longer-term interest rates or perhaps an adverse stock-market reaction in the tightening process—both of which would imperil the continuing economic expansion, or so it may have been thought. However, longer-term rates did not rise at all on balance, and indeed tended to decline as short-rates rose.

Chapter 7

1. Also, several days earlier, the Fed had initiated a program of twenty-eight-day term repurchase agreements for dealers against delivery of any collateral eligible for purchase in regular open market operations (i.e., U.S. government securities and federally guaranteed agency debt or agency mortgage-backed securities). Only a few days later, the Fed also announced an expansion of its securities lending program. Formerly, this was a small program to lend government securities to primary dealers in the rare instance when satisfactory collateral could not be borrowed in the market for delivery against a primary dealer's short position in a particular government security. The Fed expanded the program in size (up to $200 billion) and permitted government securities to be loaned for up to twenty-eight days (rather than overnight) and also and surprisingly added nonagency highly rated private label residential MBS to the eligible collateral—the latter not being eligible for purchase in open market operations. This facility was called the Term Securities Lending Facility (TSLF). One of its apparent functions in alleviating the crisis would be to provide government securities to the market that could be employed to meet margin calls on institutions that did not have an adequate amount of collateral satisfactory to the lender. This did not work out in practice, however, when just a few days later the Fed was forced to step in and lend money directly to facilitate the sale of Bear Stearns, an institution that had been long rumored as potentially unable to meet collateral calls.

2. For the Fed's balance sheet trends, see the Board of Governors Web site (at www .federalreserve.gov/monetarypolicy/bst_recenttrends.htm), especially the chart and supporting tables for Selected Assets of the Federal Reserve that show total assets, securities held outright, all liquidity facilities, and support for specific institutions.

Chapter 8

1. The Fed, on my recommendation, had just removed checking accounts held by foreign banks in U.S. banks from our measure of the narrowest definition of money in the hands of the public, so-called M1, on the grounds that they should be treated in the same way as interbank deposits among U.S. banks, which also were excluded from this definition of the money supply.

Index